Search

Hea

o

Ea

HOW TO FIND WHAT REALLY MATTERS IN LIFE

Searching for
Heaven
on
Earth

DAVID
JEREMIAH

INTEGRITY®
PUBLISHERS
Nashville

Library of Congress Cataloging-in-Publication Data

Jeremiah, David.
    Searching for heaven on Earth : how to find what really matters in life / by David
    Jeremiah
        p. cm.

    ISBN 1-59145-066-7

    1. Bible. O. T. Ecclesiastes—Criticism, interpretation, etc. I. Title.
    BS1475.52.J47 2004
    223'.807—dc22   2004015126

Printed in the United States of America
04 05 06 07 08 BVG 9 8 7 6 5 4 3 2 1

Dedicated

to

the faculty, staff, and students

of

Christian Heritage College

in

El Cajon, California

Contents

Acknowledgments ix

Preface xi

Introduction xv

1. Will the Circle Be Unbroken? 1

2. Bored to Death 11

3. Trivial Pursuits 21

4. Careening Careers 33

5. Impressions About Life 45

6. Insights About God 55

7. Read the Instructions 65

8. When Justice Isn't Just 73

9. From Oppression to Obsession 81

10. When 1 + 1 > 2 91

11. A God Who Can't Be Used 105

12. Governments Never Change 115

13. Dollars and Sense 123

14. Money Without Meaning 133

15. Employment Without Enjoyment 143

16. Solomon Answers Your Questions 153

17. The Joy of Misery 161

18. The Pleasure of Rebuke 169

19. The Hard Way Made Easy 177

20. Time to Move On 185

21. The Perspective of Wisdom 193

22. The Power of Wisdom 203

23. Hard to Be Humble 213

24. Dropping the "D" Word 225

25. Life Cheats! 237

26. Foolishness in Little Things 247

27. Foolishness in Leadership 257

28. Labor, Language, and Lunacy 267

29. Life Is Uncertain: Embrace It! 279

30. Life Is Short: Enjoy It! 289

31. Life Is Mysterious: Examine It! 301

Conclusion: Life Is Obedience: Express It! 309

Notes 315

Acknowledgments

WHENEVER I SEE THE WORD "acknowledgment," it seems so proper and so cold. I do not want to acknowledge the following people. I want to express my profound gratitude to each of them. I want to say "thank you."

To William Kruidenier and Rob Morgan for their research and their many helpful suggestions.

To Rob Suggs, my favorite editor, who always makes me sound better than I deserve. Rob, what a gift God has given you!

To Dianne Stark and Lois Spain, who have read and reread this manuscript with the purpose of making it grammatically correct.

To Diane Sutherland, my administrative assistant, who protects my time and makes it possible for me to have the hours needed for such a challenging assignment.

To Helen Barnhart! Helen, where would we all be without you? You managed this project from the beginning to the end, coordinating our efforts with the publisher, tracking down references, reading and rereading each draft, and so much more.

To my wonderful friends at Integrity Publishers, Byron Williamson and Joey Paul. You have made this book everything that I dreamed it could be.

To Sealy Yates and the entire Yates and Yates literary team! Sealy, without you, I might have given up writing years ago! Thank you for your constant encouragement and motivation.

To my son, David Michael, who manages the expanding ministry of Turning Point so that I can have time to study and think and write.

To Paul Joiner, the most creative person I have ever known, for your ideas and suggestions.

To Barbara Boucher, who faithfully administers my office at Shadow Mountain Community Church.

To the senior leadership team of Shadow Mountain Community Church. You manage the day-to-day ministry of this congregation so that I might have the time to put these life-changing principles into written form.

To my wonderful wife, Donna, who allows me the late nights and long days that inevitably become part of a book project! Her belief in me keeps me excited about the wonderful opportunities God has given us to touch the lives of people through writing.

Most of all, to my Wonderful Lord and Savior, Jesus Christ. This book is ultimately about You, for You are the End of the search for heaven on earth!

—David Jeremiah
Oceanside, California

Preface

Let me come right at you with a tough question: Is happiness still within our reach? Can there be a full life in an empty generation?

To put the question another way, is there some isolated corner, some hidden alcove, some distant hill where one can find a genuine touch of heaven on earth?

No trite answers will do. This particular question is too urgently important to most of us. Where is that elusive doorway, or perhaps just a keyhole, where we can catch a fleeting glimpse of the Eden we know in our hearts this earth should be?

Maybe perfect joy is just another myth—an empty reverie composed of wishes and what-ifs. Maybe we just haven't found the treasure map that would show us where to find what really matters in life.

Or maybe we've simply been looking in the wrong places. Could it be that a dusty old composition tucked into a book, found in your own home, has a message you and I have missed for too long?

Consider Ecclesiastes: thousands of years old, obscure, deep in the middle of your Bible, rarely disturbed by formal preacher or casual reader in these loud and crowded days. Oh, and one more thing about this book—it was penned by the wisest man on earth: Solomon. Remember him? Sure, we're comfortable among his pithy aphorisms found in the book just preceding this one—the one we know as Proverbs.

But Ecclesiastes . . . Apart from a few "greatest hits" pulled from its pages, you might well make it all the way through life without a single visit to Ecclesiastes.

You're likely to be startled, though, by this book's starkly modern insights into the human condition. Its message is as contemporary as a postmodern university textbook, a celebrity interview, or even a teenage suicide note. It's like an urgent "E-mail" (E for Ecclesiastes) written an hour ago.

It's not the "proverbial" Solomon, but a weary and despairing one who cries out into the emptiness his questions of passion and pathos: Why do I feel so empty? Why do the good guys so often lose? Why do the shadows of death block out the light of life?

From the loneliness of a crowded palace, he gives voice to his own afflictions—echoed by Courtney Love, who from the palaces of pop culture has sung: "It's the emptiness that follows you down. It's the ache inside when it all burns out."[1]

Solomon hits this year's nerve. He isolates the very places where you and I have ached lately with the probing finger of a skilled doctor who says, "Does it hurt . . . *right here?*"

Solomon explores the questions: What was it that pushed you and me into the wrong pursuits? The unwise relationships? The destructive habits? How can we climb out of it now, or is it too late?

His eyes fall upon the shadows that blanket our hearts, and he describes the problems and regrets that travel uncomfortably with us, like shackles upon feet that long to run free.

Listen to the hard-wrought titles of Solomon: anointed monarch, visionary architect, cherished son of David. Yes, he is all of these things. But in the final analysis, he is one more wounded human specimen in the Great Physician's waiting room, where the rest of us sit for months or years or decades.

Yet we need to know this Solomon, for by the grace and wonder of

God his wounds are mingled with wisdom. His pain is colored by perception. And not in *spite* of, but *because* of his suffering—supplemented at the outset by a special gift from God—Solomon becomes known as *the wisest man on the face of the earth.* We could do much worse for faculty in the school of life.

Listen, then, to the voice of wisdom and experience; the voice that, if you are willing to listen, will speak directly into the flesh and bones and blood cells of your life. Prepare for age-old secrets to renew and re-create you in heart, mind, body, and spirit, that you might recover the joy you have lost.

This is not only Solomon's voice; a deeper, quieter, yet more powerful voice breaks through his weariness and desperation. This One longs to bless your life with wisdom and to bring you to the crest of a hill where you can catch a glimpse of what seems impossible: heaven on earth.

Introduction

ECCLESIASTES 1:1–3

⌒───────⌒

IN THE WIDE WORLD OF POETRY, the name of John Berryman soared among the elite of his century. He seemed to have made every conquest a poet might crave. He was a beloved university professor. A Pulitzer Prize sat upon his shelf, given for *77 Dream Songs*, his boldly innovative collection of 1965. Widespread acclaim brought him fame, friends, and followers. He had seemingly found the pot of gold at the end of the rainbow.

But one frozen January day in 1972, he came to the final stanza. The poet walked across a bridge in Minnesota, waved to a stranger, and leaped to his death in the icy Mississippi River.

Why?

"At fifty-five, half famous and effective," he had written, "I still feel rotten about myself." And in one of his poems, Berryman wrote: "After all has been said, and all *has* been said, man is a huddle of need."[1]

Do you ever feel that way? Rotten about yourself? A *huddle of need?*

A recent survey asked 7,948 students at forty-eight colleges what they considered "very important" to them. The study, conducted by scientists from Johns Hopkins University, reported that 16 percent of the students answered "making a lot of money." We can't be too surprised. Even so, a whopping 75 percent said that their first goal was "finding a purpose and meaning to my life."

Psychologist Carl Jung, in his book *Modern Man in Search of a Soul,* wrote, "About a third of my cases are suffering from no clinically definable neurosis, but from the senselessness and emptiness of their lives. This can be described as the general neurosis of our time."[2] Jung wrote those words in the early part of the twentieth century, but with every passing year and decade their truth has become even more glaring.

Holocaust survivor Viktor Frankl produced an influential volume called *Man's Search for Meaning,* in which he wrote, "The existential vacuum is a widespread phenomenon of the twentieth century."[3]

That sense of a humanity-wide vacuum has followed us into the twenty-first century. Rick Warren's book *The Purpose-Driven Life* has been a *New York Times* bestseller because it isolates this need so well. Within every single one of us lies an intense desire to understand the *why* of our existence.

In his introduction, Warren describes a survey conducted by Dr. Hugh Moorhead, philosophy professor at Northeastern Illinois University. Moorhead wrote to 250 famous philosophers, scientists, writers, and intellectuals, asking a simple question: "What is the meaning of life?" Some offered their best guesses; others admitted they just made up a response; still others honestly admitted they were clueless. Several of the intellectuals even asked Moorhead to write back and tell them if *he* had discovered the purpose of life![4]

The conclusion is unsettling: in our time, the wise men are running low on wisdom.

Maybe this is why we look around at too many of our young people, expecting to see joy and humor and infectious energy, only to find instead substance abuse, promiscuity, and suicide.

Someone recently gave me a copy of an anonymous suicide note from a college student that said:

> To anyone in the world who cares: Who am I? Why am I living? Life has become stupid and purposeless. Nothing makes sense anymore. The questions I had when I came to college are still

unanswered and now I am convinced there are no answers. There can only be pain and guilt and despair here in this world. My fear of death and the unknown is far less terrifying than the prospect of the unbearable frustration, futility, and hopelessness of continued existence.

Wisest of the Wise

None of this is new. The times may be changing, but human nature is not. We can't feel a single shred of emotion that hasn't already been felt a million times over. The wisest of the wise have shared fully in our plaintive cry to the cosmos, including the wisest of them all—King Solomon. Successful though he was, luxuriously wealthy though he was, surrounded by great men and beautiful wives and concubines though he was, and exceedingly blessed by God though he was—Solomon still felt all that you and I feel today.

The book of Ecclesiastes is an inner road map of his quest—a testament to his search for meaning. It stands unique within the Bible as a classic of real-world, everyday philosophy, seen through the eyes of the most powerful, influential, and educated man in the world at the time.

Solomon was the king of Israel. We find his story, both private and political, within eleven remarkable chapters in the book we call 1 Kings. At the time of his birth to David and Bathsheba, the Lord gave him a special name: *Jedidiah,* meaning "Beloved of the Lord." So it was from the very beginning that an air of greatness and destiny hung about this prince.

Imagine the incredible day of Solomon's ascension to Israel's throne, in the reflected glory of his father's wild popularity and unprecedented achievements. God asked the newly crowned Solomon to make a request (1 Kings 3:5).

Can you imagine being granted such a privilege? What would you have chosen, once you caught your breath and reflected upon the staggering possibilities? Solomon had the choice of a thousand lifetimes . . . and he chose the gift of wisdom.

The Lord was pleased. Most of His children, He observed, would have opted for lengthy years or unlimited riches. It took wisdom to ask for wisdom; Solomon understood that this one precious gift is the key that opens the door to every other rightful desire.

That wisdom was granted, and Solomon enjoyed a gilded life for many years. Every decision seemed to be a sound and perceptive one. His people loved him. And the greatest legacy of all, his crowning achievement, was building the Jerusalem temple—a wonderful dwelling place for God and His people. In seeing this project through, he fulfilled the dream of his earthly and heavenly fathers.

During his reign, the nation of Israel reached its golden age. It became the empire that had always been within its capability—a light unto the ancient world. Rulers from many countries, including the queen of Sheba, made pilgrimages to Jerusalem to pay homage to Solomon.

How wonderful if we could pronounce a "happily ever after" ending on Solomon's life and the golden age of Israel. It wasn't to be, for man or for nation. Solomon's vast wealth, his fame, and especially his sensual appetites tainted his special standing before God. Wealth, power, and pleasure can be dangerous even in the hands of the wisest; these things long not to be mastered, but to master. Solomon compromised himself before the Lord who had given him enough foresight to know better. The drifting came slowly, deceptively, but the further he moved from Lord and Creator, the greater became his emptiness, frustration, and confusion.

The course of Solomon's life—and perhaps something recognizably yours—can be traced in the three biblical books that were his legacy.

In the morning of his life came the Song of Solomon, a prose rhapsody of passionate romance.

In the noontime of his life came Proverbs, a book of heavenly rules for earthly living on the Main Streets of the world.

Finally, in the evening of his life came Ecclesiastes, a regretful retrospective. In the disillusioned autumn of his years, Solomon revisited the wreckage of a wasted life. The proverbial pithiness purged, he made one final stab at redemption: an attempt to block others from his own perilous downhill road to destruction.

"It's what we learn *after* we know it all that really counts," someone once said. If Ecclesiastes were a movie, the posters might read, "Solomon is back—*and this time it's personal.*"

Ecclesiastes is indeed a personal book. Solomon personally presided over a forty-year season of peace. Free of the consuming rigors of military command, he had time to think and write.

He had personally accumulated the wealth of an empire. The riches of the world were at his disposal, as well as the counsel of kings across the Mediterranean world.

Above all, Solomon had navigated life as the most intelligent and well-educated man of his time. He writes: "I communed with my heart, saying, 'Look, I have attained greatness, and have gained more wisdom than all who were before me in Jerusalem. My heart has understood great wisdom and knowledge.' And I set my heart to know wisdom" (Ecclesiastes 1:16–17).

The traditional name of this book, *Ecclesiastes,* and the author's title in verse 1, "Preacher," both come from the same Hebrew term: *qohelet.* This term described one who convened an assembly of wise men and served as its principal spokesman. Solomon chose this as his pen name for Ecclesiastes. Perhaps instead of the "Preacher," we might call Solomon the "Searcher" or the "Quester."

EMPTY AT THE TOP

The words of the Preacher, the son of David, king in Jerusalem.
"Vanity of vanities," says the Preacher;
"Vanity of vanities, all is vanity."
What profit has a man from all his labor
In which he toils under the sun?

—ECCLESIASTES 1:1–3

Solomon begins his book with his conclusion: "The words of the Preacher, the son of David, king in Jerusalem. 'Vanity of vanities,' says the Preacher; 'Vanity of vanities, all is vanity'" (Ecclesiastes 1:1–2).

Immediately we stumble across that word *vanity*. Let's make a closer acquaintance of this word, for it will cross our path more than thirty times in this book. Today we connect vanity with egotism—with that man or woman who is overly self-involved. Vanity is always based on an illusion. A woman once told her pastor, "When I confess my sins, I confess the sin of vanity most of all. Every morning, I admire myself in the mirror for half an hour."

To this the pastor replied, "My dear, that isn't the sin of vanity. You're suffering from the sin of imagination."

As Solomon uses the word in his ancient Hebrew text, he refers to emptiness, to that which is transitory and has little meaning. In this case, vanity is akin to a vapor that lasts only a moment before quickly vanishing, leaving nothing behind. *The Message* paraphrases verse 2 this way: "Smoke, nothing but smoke. [That's what the Quester says.] There's nothing to anything—it's all smoke."

Talk about getting smoke in your eyes! Imagine getting to the top only to find that it's all smoke, illusion, vapor, nothingness, emptiness.

Jack Higgins, famous author of such bestsellers as *The Eagle Has Landed,* says the one thing he knows now that he wishes he'd known as a small boy is this: "When you get to the top, there's nothing there."

Solomon climbed the same ladder and made the same discovery. *There's nothing here; all is vanity.* His repetition of the word *vanity* was a Hebrew poetic device that intensified meaning. He was saying, "Life is utterly, absolutely, totally meaningless."

Jewish statesman Abba Eban tells of meeting Sir Edmund Hillary, the first man to climb Mount Everest. Eban asked Hillary precisely what he felt when he reached the peak. Hillary replied that there was an immediate rush of triumphal ecstasy—for a fleeting moment. It was quickly replaced by a sense of desolation. Where could he go from here? What mountains remained to climb?[5]

Interestingly, another Everest climber expressed a similar sentiment. In May 1996, journalist Jon Krakauer was part of an expedition that reached the top of Everest. Twelve of his companions were killed in the highly publicized descent, a story that Krakauer records in his chilling book *Into Thin Air.* But he begins his account by describing his feelings on May 10, 1996, as he reached the highest spot on earth:

> Straddling the top of the world, one foot in China and the other in Nepal, I cleared the ice from my oxygen mask, hunched a shoulder against the wind and stared absently down at the vastness of Tibet. . . . I'd been fantasizing about this moment, and the release of emotion that would accompany it, for many months. But now that I was finally here, actually standing on the summit of Everest, I just couldn't summon the energy to care. . . . I snapped four quick photos . . . then turned and headed down. My watch read 1:17 p.m. All told, I'd spent less than five minutes on the roof of the world.[6]

Solomon spent forty years on the roof of history, only to feel the same bland puzzle of anticlimax. Not only is it empty at the top, but it's empty at the bottom—and everywhere in-between. Life, in and of itself, is a cluster of electrons silently coursing through their appointed atomic revolutions; cells dividing and redividing; nature recycling its rituals ad infinitum. *Emptiness. Vanity.* As Peggy Lee used to sing, "Is that all there is?"

I think you know exactly what I'm talking about. What did you find at the Everest of your own life? Perhaps you received the promotion, won the lottery, made the dream vacation, got the book published—all for the thorny crown of unexpected despondency. It is that horrifying emptiness, not the first gray hair nor the unwelcomed birthday that is the real culprit in draining our youthful adrenaline. It is the vacuum of success, not the fullness of failure, that deflates in the end.

Dreams come true, not free, and part of that price is realizing that alas, one more time, that elusive joy has escaped our clutches. And deep within the quiet of the soul, something suggests that one more time we have looked in the wrong place. If heaven is to be found on earth, no mountain could be high enough, no ocean could provide the necessary depth. The search must continue somewhere else.

Come, then, and join the search. Climb with Solomon to the roof of the world and take in the panoramic view. Then climb down again and walk with him down the boulevards of life.

Our journey of discovery together is designed to require one brief month. Take one chapter at a time, one short reading per day. This is, after all, not a quick stroll but a crucial pilgrimage. You may never set out on a journey of greater import. You'll want to stop and smell a rose or two, take in a deeper truth, sit and reflect before moving on to the next short chapter and tall truth. Get to know Solomon—king, philosopher, philanderer, elder sage—as you've never known him.

Then, one month hence, we will rest like children, free and unbur-dened, with the weight of the world off our shoulders—for we will have found at last the object of every quest, the true North Star of every journey, the never-dimming light of our fondest hopes: heaven on earth.

1

Will the Circle Be Unbroken?

ECCLESIASTES 1:4–7

T HE SOBIBOR NAZI CONCENTRATION CAMP was set in the scenic woods near the Bug River, which separates Poland and Russia. The natural beauty of the setting stood in stark contrast to the stench and horror of the camp, where torture and death awaited every man, woman, and child who arrived there.

On October 14, 1943, Jewish slave laborers in Sobibor surprised their captors by using their shovels and pickaxes as weapons in a well-planned attack. Some of the Jewish prisoners cut the electricity to the fence and used captured pistols and rifles to shoot their way past German guards. Hundreds of others stormed through the barbed wire and mine fields to the potential safety of the nearby forest.

Of the seven hundred prisoners who took part in the escape, three hundred made it to the forest. Of those, less than one hundred are known to have survived. The remainder were hunted down by the Germans and executed.

One of the survivors was a man named Thomas Blatt—or Toivi, as he was known in his native Poland. Toivi was fifteen years old when his family was herded into Sobibor. His parents were executed in the gas chamber, but Toivi, young and healthy, was a prime candidate for slave labor. In the confusion of the escape, Toivi attempted to crawl through a hole in the barbed wire fence but was trampled by prisoners who stormed the fence. As a result, he was one of the last to make it out of the camp.

Toivi and two companions set off on a nightmare journey through the dense woods. By day they rested beneath the camouflage of brush and branch; by night they fought their way through a black expanse of tree and foliage. They were driven both by youthful vigor and fear; by determination and desperation. Most significantly, they were propelled by that elusive thing they had now reclaimed: *hope.*

What they needed and craved was a guide—someone who could read the stars, who knew north from south and east from west. These were city boys lacking in outdoor skills.

After four nights of stumbling through the cold forest, the three boys saw a building silhouetted against the dark sky in the distance. Could it mean sanctuary? Perhaps a woodsman to help them toward safety? With hope and growing gratitude, they hurried forward.

As they got closer, they noticed that the building they had seen was a tower—a familiar tower. It was part of the Sobibor concentration camp! The three boys had made one giant circle through the woods and ended up exactly where they started.

Terrified, horrified, they backed into the waiting arms of the forest once more. But only Toivi lived to recount their awful experience.[1]

Have you ever felt like Toivi and his friends? We spin our wheels. We throw ourselves forward, pushing toward some goal that seems like the meaning of life itself. Then we discover we might as well have run the marathon on a treadmill—we've gone nowhere. We're right back where we started.

Solomon understood the bleak despair that follows that realization. He begins his journal with the ultimate conclusion of his search for meaning: "What profit has a man from all his labor in which he toils under the sun?" (Ecclesiastes 1:3).

Notice the phrase *under the sun.* This is another of those characteristic phrases to be encountered nearly everywhere in this book—twenty-nine times, in this case. *Under the sun* implies an earthbound view of things. Solomon wasn't speaking from any pious eternal perspective. Remember, he had drifted away from his Lord over the years—day by day, inch by inch, worldly entanglement by worldly entanglement.

In this chilly season of Solomon's life, he comprehended the folly of a personal journey that lasted decades and went nowhere. There wasn't a great deal of self-righteous zeal to be found within him anymore. And with all the wealth, all the wives, and all the world before him— including an awe-inspiring temple on his personal résumé—there was nothing left in the world to bring him satisfaction. Oh, there were the fleeting pleasures of everyday life, the little things. But he well knew that none of those could deliver peace to his embattled soul.

To illustrate his conclusion, the Searcher presents several arguments about life "under the sun." In verses 4–7, his thoughts journey to four things:

1. The course of life (v. 4)

2. The circle of the sun (v. 5)

3. The circuit of the winds (v. 6)

4. The cycle of the water (v. 7)

By the way, notice that Solomon was a man for all seasons—part philosopher, part astronomer, part meteorologist, and part hydrologist. We're not embroidering the truth by declaring him the wisest and best educated man of his time.

THE COURSE OF LIFE

One generation passes away, and
another generation comes;
But the earth abides forever.

—ECCLESIASTES 1:4

Solomon's view is gloomy. "Generations come and go, but nothing really changes" (1:4 NLT). We could well imagine Solomon sitting at his breakfast table with the newspaper open, reading the birth announcements on one page and the obituaries on the next. Generations pass in parade. There is a deathbed in one room, a crib next-door. History is a running drama of millennial length; the earth abides, but the actors play their parts and move on.

Solomon returns often to the subject of death. Remember, he's in the twilight of life and his spirits have withered. No wonder! When life is built without a spiritual foundation, death is a killer on the prowl, peering in the window.

Bertrand Russell shares this same sense of despair when he writes in his autobiography, "We stand on the shore of an ocean, crying to the night and the emptiness; sometimes a voice answers out of the darkness. But it is the voice of one drowning, and in a moment the silence returns."[2]

Rabbi Harold Kushner tells of a man who came to him for counseling. After the usual chatter that precedes such appointments, the man told Kushner why he had come.

> "Two weeks ago," said the man, "for the first time in my life I went to the funeral of a man my own age. I didn't know him well, we worked together, talked to each other from time to time, had kids about the same age. He died suddenly over the weekend. . . . It could just as easily have been me. That was two weeks ago. They have already replaced him at the office. I hear his wife is moving out of state to live with her parents. Two weeks ago he was working fifty feet away from me, and now it's as if he never existed. It's like a rock falling into a pool of water, and then the water is the same as it was before, but the rock isn't there anymore. Rabbi, I've hardly slept at all since then. I can't

4

stop thinking that it could happen to me, and a few days later I will be forgotten as if I had never lived. Shouldn't a man's life be more than that?" [3]

In the midst of his own search, that could have been Solomon speaking—and it could be any number of moderns who have failed to find meaning in the day-to-day repetitions of their own lives. We get up, go to work, come home, watch TV, go to bed—only to repeat until retirement. Then we die. Or at least that's how a lot of people view life.

Solomon is saying, "On the surface, life looks like a gerbil running on a wheel. What's the point?" At least, that's how it can look if you don't have eyes to see beneath the surface.

THE CIRCLE OF THE SUN

The sun also rises, and the sun goes down,
And hastens to the place where it arose.

—ECCLESIASTES 1:5

We can excuse Solomon for not knowing that the sun doesn't revolve around the earth. Had he known, he would have just said the same thing in a different way: "This planet of ours circles the sun. Fall, winter, spring, summer—then we take it from the top and start again. One more birthday party for everyone, and *so what?* What's the big deal?" The science is irrelevant; the philosophy is a deadly killer.

Solomon's phrase, *the sun also rises,* speaks of the silent, uncaring machine that life and nature can appear to be. He seems bewildered by comparing the unblinking consistency of the cosmic machine to the inconsistency of the human machine. For him, every golden sunset represents another short day gone from his ephemeral life. The sun doesn't slow down; time cannot be stopped, and death marches toward us relentlessly like a conquering army. We can run, but we cannot hide.

It's intriguing that Ernest Hemingway chose these words, *The Sun Also Rises,* as the title of his first best-selling novel. He wrote of "lost generation" Americans and Brits after the First World War, and his book conveys the despair that characterized his life and writings. Years later, shortly before his suicide, the great writer confessed, "I live in a vacuum that is as lonely as a radio tube when the batteries are dead and there is no current to plug into." Douglas Caffey recently posted this poem on the Web site of the International War Veteran's Poetry Archives:

> The morning wears
> A fresh white rose,
> Gleaming white on white
> From head to toes!
>
> Noonday, the rose
> Begins to wilt,
> And splotches show
> Like a patch-work quilt!
>
> At eventide
> The rose is dead!
> Its fragrance lies
> In silent bed![4]

To be sure, not an encouraging outlook. But remember, Solomon's pessimism comes from his disconnect with God. When we see only what is under the sun and never what is behind it, we are left with that empty, churning cosmic machine, a great production line running to eternity and producing exactly nothing.

THE CIRCUIT OF THE WINDS

The wind goes toward the south,
And turns around to the north;
The wind whirls about continually,
And comes again on its circuit.

—ECCLESIASTES 1:6

Solomon the meteorologist is as impressive as Solomon the poet. He antic-ipates what is now known about the world's great wind circuits and the global circulation of the atmosphere. There's no evidence that ancient "scientists" understood anything about wind, clouds, and the great cyclical jet streams of the earth. But Solomon, with his special, God-given wisdom, knew some of these things and expressed them in words that are poetically poignant while being scientifically accurate.

Solomon seems fascinated by the wind. We can picture him pondering life, huddled on the roof of his palace, watching the clouds driven by strong eastern currents while his robe blows in the dust. He refers to the wind once in Song of Solomon six times in Proverbs and fourteen times in Ecclesiastes, where the references deeply move us because the wind becomes a symbol of his despair.

There's something about the wind that speaks to the soul. Jesus spoke of it as blowing "where it wishes, and you hear the sound of it, but cannot tell where it comes from and where it goes" (John 3:8). In that case, Jesus was speaking about the mystery and marvel of the Christian life.

But for Solomon, the wind represented the invisible brevity of life. As Margaret Mitchell would later express in the title of her great novel, *Gone with the Wind,* sooner or later everything in life—even our most cherished relationships and possessions—vanishes with the wind.

Remember this haunting pop song of some years ago? This is exactly what Solomon was saying:

Dust in the wind, all they are is dust in the wind.

Same old song, just a drop of water in an endless sea.

All we do, crumbles to the ground, though we refuse to see.

Don't hang on, nothing lasts forever but the earth and sky.

It slips away, and all your money won't another minute buy.

Dust in the wind, all we are is dust in the wind;

Dust in the wind, everything is dust in the wind.[5]

THE CYCLE OF WATER

All the rivers run into the sea,
Yet the sea is not full;
To the place from which the rivers come,
There they return again.

—ECCLESIASTES 1:7

As vivid as are his word-paintings, Solomon isn't satisfied with the canvas. He proceeds to give us another illustration: the cycle of water: "All the rivers run into the sea, yet the sea is not full; to the place from which the rivers come, there they return again" (Ecclesiastes 1:7).

Again, how did he know that? This is an example of what some Bible scholars call "prescience"—scientific statements in Scripture that far exceed the general knowledge of the time. Solomon describes the earth's amazing hydrologic cycle. Experts tell us that at any given time, 97 percent of all the water on earth is in the oceans; only .0001 percent is in the atmosphere, available for rain. The cooperation of the sun and the wind makes possible the evaporation and movement of moisture, and this keeps the water circulating. But the sea never changes. The rivers and waters pour into the seas, but the seas remain the same. Amazed at this, Solomon uses it as a picture of the remarkable, endless monotony of life without God.

8

A psychologist named William Moulton Marston asked three thousand individuals, "What have you to live for?" The answers shocked him. He found that 94 percent were not living at all; they were simply enduring the present while waiting for something in the future. They were waiting for *something* to happen—waiting for children to grow up and leave home, waiting for next year when things would be better, or at least different, waiting for the chance to take a trip, waiting for tomorrow. *Waiting . . . waiting.* For them, life had deteriorated to a cycle with little meaning in and of itself.[6]

We all feel it. We all have an enduring sense that the universe got it wrong, that things are exactly the reverse of what they should be. Shouldn't the ignorant machine of nature be temporary, and *we* be permanent? We just know this somehow; as Solomon will soon tell us, we have eternity set in our hearts (3:11). We refuse to see ourselves as temporal creatures. We're made for everlasting life, and the clock we live on should run down while we go on forever.

But under-the-sun thinking keeps us from making the leap—from finding out that our intuition is exactly correct. The truth can't be found under the sun, but in the One who set it in motion and presides over it.

On the other hand, over-the-rainbow thinking is equally deceptive. Baseless optimism is one more dead-end street. We are to live not *under* or *over*—but *above*. The Bible says, "If then you were raised with Christ, seek those things which are above, where Christ is, sitting at the right hand of God. Set your mind on things above, not on things on the earth. For you died, and your life is hidden with Christ in God" (Colossians 3:1–3).

We live under the sun, but our destiny is beyond its rising and setting. In 1890, Anna Price wrote a beautiful hymn that provides a fine tonic for the gloominess of Solomon in these first seven verses of Ecclesiastes.

> Above the trembling elements,
> Above life's restless sea,

Dear Savior, lift my spirit up,
O lift me up to Thee!

Great calmness there, sweet patience, too,
Upon Thy face I see;
I would be calm and patient, Lord,
O lift me up to Thee!

And when my eyes close for the last,
Still this my prayer shall be
Dear Savior, lift my spirit up,
And lift me up to Thee!

2

Bored to Death

ECCLESIASTES 1:8–11

P OPULAR NOVELIST KATHE KOJA has claimed to spin her tales from threads of bleak nothingness. She speaks of "a black hole [that] is at the heart of every novel . . . the emptiness we each carry close to our hearts, the emptiness of being alive in a world that doesn't care. And the way we fill that Freudian hole, well, that's the novel."

When asked about her statement in a recent interview, Koja replied:

> Everyone is cored by that existential void, the deep hole in the heart that cries for radiance; our entire consumer culture is predicated on the belief that, if you stuff enough things down that hole, you can finally satisfy it into silence. That has never been the case. Nor does creativity, sex, art, or even love fill that hole.[1]

Solomon would have agreed. In Ecclesiastes1:1–7 he tells us that life is *futile;* now in verses 8–11, he's going to tell us that it's also *frustrating.* Who hasn't heard stories about the old days of military training when recruits were told to dig a hole the first half of the day, then refill it in the second half? The point of such an exercise was to find the recruits' frustration threshold. How much futility could they endure before becoming frustrated enough to blow their top at the drill sergeant?

The natural outgrowth of futility is frustration—or worse. All around us in our world we see frustrated people—road rage on the freeways, shooting sprees in corporate offices, hopelessness in the hearts of individuals. In his observations, Solomon moves from the evidence of futility to the evidence of frustration when God is removed from the picture.

NOTHING IS FULFILLING

All things are full of labor;
Man cannot express it.
The eye is not satisfied with seeing.
Nor the ear filled with hearing.

—ECCLESIASTES 1:8

Life is frustrating, Solomon tells us, because nothing satisfies. "Everything's boring, utterly boring—no one can find any meaning in it. Boring to the eye, boring to the ear" (1:8 MSG).

"Boring!"—usually pronounced *"Boooooo-rring!"*—is the ultimate put-down in today's society, yet everyone and everything seems afflicted by it. This verse explains why. Nothing new "under the sun" satisfies. We can never see enough or hear enough to bring satisfaction. Everything ultimately brings weariness and boredom, forcing us to constantly seek diversion.

Our entire entertainment industry rests on this premise. Billions of dollars are spent annually around the world on producing and purchasing entertainment. Some people track their year, not on the basis of the months or seasons, but on sports: baseball in the summer, football in the fall, basketball and hockey in the winter, NASCAR in the spring. Where do you go when you conclude there is nothing truly meaningful in life? Back to the stadium, where at least there are games with consistent rules, rewards, and penalties.

Michael Crichton's thriller, *Timeline,* has an interesting take on this subject. A character named Robert Doniger is the CEO of an enormous and highly secretive technology company. Near the end of the book, Doniger addresses a group of people in his company's auditorium:

> In other centuries, human beings wanted to be saved, or improved, or freed, or educated. But in our century, they want to be entertained. The great fear is not of disease or death, but of boredom. A sense of time on our hands, a sense of nothing to do. A sense that we are not amused. But where will this mania for entertainment end?[2]

Where indeed? The implications are rather unsettling.

In his profound book, *Man's Search for Meaning,* Viktor Frankl wrote that phenomenally large numbers of modern men and women suffer from an existential vacuum that manifests itself mainly in a state of boredom.

> Now we can understand Schopenhauer when he said that mankind was apparently doomed to vacillate eternally between the two extremes of distress and boredom. In actual fact, boredom is now causing, and certainly bringing psychiatrists, more problems to solve than distress. And these problems are growing increasingly crucial.[3]

In 1958, American writer Barnaby Conrad was badly gored in a bullfight in Spain. Eva Gabor and Noel Coward were overheard talking about the incident in a New York restaurant. "Noel, dahling," said Eva, "have you heard the news about poor Bahnaby? He vas terribly gored in Spain."

"He was *what?*" asked Coward in alarm.

"He vas gored!"

"Thank heavens. I thought you said he was bored."[4]

There's a bit of wisdom there. Ultimate boredom—the fate of those who can look only under the sun for meaning—may be the worst fate of all.

Nothing Is Fresh

That which has been is what will be,
That which is done is what will be done,
And there is nothing new under the sun.
Is there anything of which it may be said,
"See, this is new"?
It has already been in ancient times before us.
There is no remembrance of former things,
Nor will there be any remembrance of things that are
to come
By those who will come after.

—ECCLESIASTES 1:9–11

Solomon gives us another reason for today's widespread frustration: nothing is fresh.

> What was will be again, what happened will happen again. There's nothing new on this earth. Year after year it's the same old thing. Does someone call out, "Hey this is new"? Don't get excited—it's the same old story. Nobody remembers what happened yesterday. And the things that will happen tomorrow? Nobody'll remember them either. Don't count on being remembered (Ecclesiastes 1:9–11 MSG)

We look at the world that is around us—what we can see and feel and hear under the sun—and we realize there is nothing new. It is as it ever was. The deist school of theology sets up the visual image this way:

14

God is the great watchmaker who built a beautiful watch (the universe), and then just walked away, abandoning it to run forever. Nothing is new, just the same old tick-tick-ticking.

Rudyard Kipling expressed the sentiments of Solomon when he wrote these lines:

> The craft that we call modern,
> The crimes that we call new;
> John Bunyan had 'em typed and filed
> In 1682.[5]

Recently a reporter named Chris Ross filed his last column for the *Jacksonville Daily Progress.* This is part of what he had to say:

> If I've learned anything in my days at the *Progress,* it's there really isn't anything new under the sun. One of the first things people said when I'd tell them what I did, was usually, "Wow, I bet that's interesting. Something new every day." And I'd smile and say, "Yeah, it beats getting a real job," or something. But the longer I worked as a reporter, the more I realized I'm doing the same stories over and over. Some of the names and places and even motives would change, but essentially it was the same old thing.[6]

So, as Solomon files the first chapter of his investigative study, his conclusion is that life under the sun, with its mechanical repetition, is all vanity. Nothing is satisfying and nothing is new and nothing is remembered. There is no profit under the sun.

Solomon had lost the sense of meaning—his reason to get out of his plush palace bed in the morning. He had the wealth and fame and power to do whatever he wanted, yet he could find nothing that was worth wanting.

We could compare him to a spider in an old European fable. It descended one day on a single thread from a barn's lofty rafters and alighted near the corner of a window. From there it wove its web. This corner of the barn was very busy and soon the spider waxed fat and prospered. One day as he surveyed his web, he noticed the strand that reached up into the unseen. He had forgotten its significance and, thinking it a stray thread, he snapped it. Instantly, his whole world collapsed around him.

Solomon had lost the silken thread that held his whole world aloft. He had forsaken the God of his youth. So far afield had the web led him that he had forgotten his godly dependence entirely.

Solomon would later summarize the central question of his book this way: "For who knows what is good for man in life, all the days of his vain life which he passes like a shadow? Who can tell a man what will happen after him under the sun?" (6:12).

There is only one Person who knows. Remember Solomon's powerful insight that still lies ahead of us: "He has put eternity in their hearts" (3:11). That E for eternity is engraved permanently within you, and it will not let you be content as an earthbound creature. As one hymnist wrote, "I want to live above the world . . . Lord, lead me onto higher ground."[7]

God has made us in such a way that until we return home to the arms of our Father, we will be like the prodigal son, a miserable and misplaced heir to a lost kingdom.

Howard Mumma was a Methodist pastor who, during several summers in the 1950s, served as a guest minister at the American Church in Paris. One Sunday after the service, he noticed a small crowd of admirers gathered around a man in a dark suit. The man was Albert Camus, a famous existentialist author whose books centered on the theme of the absurdity of the human condition. Camus had begun attending the church's services to listen to the organist, and he had continued attending to listen to Mumma's sermons.

Camus's novels, *The Plague* and *The Stranger,* and essays such as "The Myth of Sisyphus," were the talk of the intellectual community; and he won the 1957 Nobel Prize for literature.

Mumma and Camus became friends in spite of the gulf that separated their beliefs and their notoriety. For the most part, their discussions centered around Camus's questions of religious belief. Mumma kept the content of their conversations private for forty years. But Camus passed away in 1960, and Mumma, at the age of ninety-two, finally went on the record about his discourses with the nihilist philosopher. In one conversation, Camus told Mumma:

> The reason I have been coming to church is because I am seeking. I'm almost on a pilgrimage—seeking something to fill the void that I am experiencing—and no one else knows. Certainly the public and the readers of my novels, while they see that void, are not finding the answers in what they are reading. But deep down you are right. I am searching for something that the world is not giving me. . . . In a sense we are all products of a mundane world, a world without spirit. The world in which we live and the lives which we live are decidedly empty. . . . Since I have been coming to church, I have been thinking a great deal about the idea of a transcendent, something that is other than this world. It is something that you do not hear much about today, but I am finding it.
>
> One of the basic teachings that I learned from French existentialist Jean-Paul Sartre is that man is alone. We are solitary centers of the universe. Perhaps we ourselves are the only ones who have ever asked the great questions of life. Perhaps, since Nazism, we are also the ones who have loved and lost and who are, therefore, fearful of life. I certainly don't have it, but it is there. On Sunday mornings, I hear that the answer is God.
>
> You have made it very clear to me, Howard, that we are not the only ones in this world. There is something that is invisible. We may not hear the voice, but there is some way in which we can become aware that we are not the only ones in the world and that there is help for all of us.[8]

These are not the words of a man who is making a profession of faith in Jesus Christ, but they are highly significant nonetheless—note Camus's words "but I am finding it." Like the cracks and groans of a glacier under a warming sun, they are the words of a man whose worldview was shifting. Camus had built a career out of the idea that life is absurd and meaningless, but after living with that philosophy for several decades, he wasn't so sure anymore. He was willing to admit that he had found only spiritual quick-sand in the landscape of meaninglessness—and to consider that there was a God who might satisfy his thirst for meaning after all.

Another philosopher lived centuries earlier. Blaise Pascal was without equal, a brilliant French thinker, scientist, mathematician, and inventor. As a boy in Paris, his remarkable grasp of mathematics led to his involvement with the Academy of Science, where he mingled with the greatest intellectuals of his day. At fifteen, he was writing books and developing theorems that left his professors shaking their heads. As a teenager, he invented history's first digital calculating machine; other discoveries led to the invention of the barometer, the vacuum pump, the air compressor, the syringe, and the hydraulic press.

But as a young man, Pascal had trouble with the spiritual equations of life, and he soon grew disillusioned with the pleasures of his fashionable society. Everything seemed boring to him. Nothing was fresh or fulfilling.

One night Pascal picked up a Bible and turned to John 17. As he began reading, verse 3 blazed out like a spark and seemed to set the room on fire: "And this is eternal life, that they may know You, the only true God, and Jesus Christ whom You have sent." His soul instantly took wing, and he was in the permanent embrace of Jesus Christ. Taking pen and parchment, he began quickly writing snatches of his thoughts:

In the year of Grace, 1654
On Monday, 23rd of November
Fire
God of Abraham, God of Isaac, God of Jacob,

18

not of the philosophers and scholars.

Certitude. Certitude, Feeling, Joy. Peace.

Joy, joy, joy, tears of joy.

This is eternal life, that they may know You, the Only true God,

and Jesus Christ whom You have sent.

Jesus Christ. Let me never be separated from Him.

Pascal spent the rest of his life proclaiming the greatness of God. That scrap of parchment was found after his death sewed into the lining of his coat, that it might ever be close to his heart.

It was this same Pascal who echoed the words of Ecclesiastes: "There is a God-shaped vacuum in the heart of every man that cannot be filled by any created thing, but by God alone made known through Jesus Christ."[9] Anything else would be the equivalent of forcing a square peg into a round hole. None but Christ can fill that hole, though men spend their lives trying every other possibility in vain. But the moment the rightful Lord of your soul fills its vacuum, there will be a fullness such as you never knew could be possible under the sun.

And just as your heart is perfectly and joyfully filled, so will everything seem to be around you. The trees will seem to be raising their branches in heavenly praise. You will hear the very rocks cry out His glories. You will have emerged from the dark web of destruction to the light of heaven on earth.

3

Trivial Pursuits

ECCLESIASTES 1:12–2:11

O N   A   R E C E N T   E D I T I O N of the CBS television show *NFL Today,*
Deion Sanders and Dan Marino found themselves arguing on the air.
The bone of contention was Lawrence Taylor's book *LT: Over the Edge*—
a controversial account of Taylor's years in the National Football League.

"When I was on the field, I was Superman," Taylor had described in
his book. "It was almost like I operated on a higher plane. . . . But when I
came off the field, something happened. LT became Lawrence Taylor, and
Lawrence Taylor was completely clueless. Like Clark Kent on crack."[1]

Taylor admitted he had often been out of control, addicted to cocaine
and a hard-partying lifestyle that led to a bitter divorce, numerous arrests,
financial ruin, broken health, and deep depression. He went on to
describe the excesses of other NFL players.

As Sanders and Marino discussed the book on the air, Marino
expressed surprise at some of the revelations in Taylor's book and indi-
cated that such things didn't happen when he was a quarterback. When
Sanders scoffed at Marino's incredulity, Marino took offense. "Why are
you saying I'm naive?" he retorted.

Deion replied:

> Don't tell me you don't know what goes on in the NFL. You don't
> know guys get high and guys do everything under the sun?

Twenty-year-old or thirty-year-old guys with millions of dollars—that equals destruction. So you can't sit up here and tell me that you were immune to that stuff.[2]

I found it interesting that Sanders reached back three thousand years for Solomon's phrase to describe the lives of modern athletes. Whether athlete or emperor, you can try everything "under the sun," but none of it will fill an empty life. *None of it.*

To drive home his point, Solomon recounts some of his own experiences under the sun.

SEARCHING FOR MEANING IN WISDOM

I, the Preacher, was king over Israel in Jerusalem. And I set my heart to seek and search out by wisdom concerning all that is done under heaven; this burdensome task God has given to the sons of man, by which they may be exercised. I have seen all the works that are done under the sun; and indeed, all is vanity and grasping for the wind.

What is crooked cannot be made straight,
and what is lacking cannot be numbered.

I communed with my heart, saying, "Look, I have attained greatness, and have gained more wisdom than all who were before me in Jerusalem. My heart has understood great wisdom and knowledge." And I set my heart to know wisdom and to know madness and folly. I perceived that this also is grasping for the wind.

For in much wisdom is much grief,
and he who increases knowledge increases sorrow.

—ECCLESIASTES 1:12–18

Solomon ends the first chapter of Ecclesiastes by describing the futility of searching for fulfillment through learning. Was the king soured on education? Not a bit. He was the best educated man of his generation. His wisdom was legendary; he had pursued wisdom wherever it could be found. Yet to his surprise, the more he learned, the emptier he felt.

He's not alone. A few years ago, in his monthly letter from Focus on the Family ministry, Dr. James Dobson told the story of Karen Cheng, age seventeen, from Fremont, California. She achieved a perfect score of 800 on both sections of the SAT test. She also got a perfect 8,000 on the rigorous University of California acceptance index. Never before had anyone accomplished this staggering intellectual feat.

Karen, a straight-A student at Mission San Jose High School, described herself as a typical teenager who munches on junk food and talks for hours on the telephone. She even claimed to be a procrastinator who didn't do her homework until the last minute.

Karen's teachers told a different story. They called her "Wonder Woman" because of her unquenchable thirst for knowledge and her uncanny ability to retain whatever she read. But when a reporter asked her, "What is the meaning of life?" Karen's reply was surprising. "I have no idea," she answered. "I would like to know myself."[3]

T. S. Eliot once dryly remarked, "All our knowledge brings us nearer to our ignorance."[4] In other words, the more we learn, the smaller we feel.

Solomon was confused. He pursued education, wisdom, and knowledge as no one before him had done. And the fuller his mastery of these fields, the emptier they seemed. "I perceived that this also is grasping for the wind," he concluded wearily. "For in much wisdom is much grief, and he who increases knowledge, increases sorrow" (Ecclesiastes 1:17–18).

Consider the sum total of all our knowledge, all our progress, all our technology. Has any of it really made the experience of life richer? Yes, we're thankful to God for medical advances and jet travel. Most of us have more information on the hard drives of our computers than entire nations once possessed in their ancient libraries.

Yet there have never been so many unhappy people, so many illiterate, so many hungry and diseased and disowned. All our accumulated knowledge of history cannot keep us from terrorism and war and discord on every continent.

This, of course, is a global crisis. *The Star,* published in Johannesburg, South Africa, recently reported on a survey conducted among South African students. There were alarming increases in the levels of substance abuse and sexual expression. Did these freedoms bring happiness? The newspaper reports: "The survey also gave an indication of the mental health of many teenagers, showing that many had feelings of emptiness, depression, and hopelessness about their future. About 25 percent of the pupils have felt 'sad,' resulting in 19 percent considering suicide."[5]

For all its benefits, education and intellectual attainment can only speak to us about life under the sun. The rest of the story is found in God's revealed Word. When we neglect or reject the revealed truth of Scripture, even our most brilliant scientists and professors are little more than mice scurrying around inside a piano, analyzing all the hammers and strings, willfully ignorant of the musical score sitting on the stand above the keys.

To paraphrase a quaint old North Carolina evangelist Vance Havner, it is exceedingly odd that scholars master whole libraries seeking wisdom, while the janitor nearby has enjoyed it for years.[6]

Christian apologist Josh McDowell, speaking on college campuses in the 1960s and '70s, often reminded audiences that if education was the key to life, then universities would be the most moral, ethical, and spiritual centers in any nation. Education would equate to contentment. We all know that's not the case.

Paul had his era's equivalent of a wall full of Ivy League master's degrees. Yet Jesus, the Lord of life, was a self-taught peasant. The meaning of life is something discovered elsewhere.

Education is a wonderful thing, an earthly treasure to be sought. But we must realize that Western civilization has set the value of it too high. As Paul explains clearly in 1 Corinthians 13:2, knowledge minus soul amounts to a great deal of nothing. And as he says in verse 13, spiritual character trumps all other gifts every time. And as America learned in the first few years of the twenty-first century, knowledge and power in corporate offices can simply lead to more creative ways to rebel against goodness and reason.

Searching for Meaning in Wild Living

I said in my heart, "Come now, I will test you with mirth; therefore enjoy pleasure"; but surely, this also was vanity. I said of laughter— "Madness!"; and of mirth, "What does it accomplish?" I searched in my heart how to gratify my flesh with wine, while guiding my heart with wisdom, and how to lay hold on folly, till I might see what was good for the sons of men to do under heaven all the days of their lives.

—Ecclesiastes 2:1–3

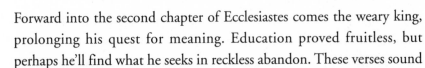

Forward into the second chapter of Ecclesiastes comes the weary king, prolonging his quest for meaning. Education proved fruitless, but perhaps he'll find what he seeks in reckless abandon. These verses sound like a report from one of our tabloids or celebrity magazines.

Solomon began with amusement: "Come now, I will test you with mirth" (Ecclesiastes 2:1). You can almost visualize the scene. His palace in Jerusalem probably resembled a tenth-century-BC version of Caesar's Palace in Las Vegas—bright lights, big city, bells and baubles everywhere. But no meaning . . . no peace . . . no happiness. The mornings-after all looked the same.

The possibilities for sensual pleasure were nearly endless in Solomon's world. And who had better access to those possibilities than the king? He had a palace and all its servants at his fingertips. He had rooms full of wives and concubines. And still he found no fullness. The emptiness of it brought him to a wise realization: "Even in laughter the heart may sorrow, and the end of mirth may be grief" (Proverbs 14:13). For many, laughter only breaks the monotony of crying, and pleasure is only an intermission to pain. Solomon was trying to be happy, but he was failing.

So many today can empathize with Solomon. They've been down the road of pleasure and found that it led nowhere but to destruction.

When amusement failed to satisfy him, Solomon turned to alcohol. "I searched in my heart how to gratify my flesh with wine," he said, "while guiding my heart with wisdom" (Ecclesiastes 2:3).

It's not that Solomon became an alcoholic; he apparently avoided being drunk. He says he was able to keep his heart with wisdom. He kept his senses about him so he could record his observations on the effects of the wine. But as he sampled the tastes of the drink before him, he found that the pleasure was fleeting and artificial. His answer was certainly not in a bottle.

The bottomless budgets of the liquor industry make drinking seem very attractive today. A wine glass or beer bottle becomes a ticket to social acceptance for our young people, and soon they feel naked without it. Campus parties and social life revolve completely around drinking and intoxication, as if these were the most glorious of pursuits, the focus of life itself. Meanwhile, the mounting tragedies of drunk driving and dissipated lives are ignored, because who can shout over the message of movies, songs, and TV commercials that glorify the emptiness?

Solomon knew the truth. Alcohol was perhaps the emptiest of pursuits.

SEARCHING FOR MEANING IN WORK

I made my works great, I built myself houses, and planted myself vineyards. I made myself gardens and orchards, and I planted all

kinds of fruit trees in them. I made myself water pools from which
to water the growing trees of the grove.

—ECCLESIASTES 2:4–6

Wisdom and wild living failed, so off to work. Perhaps through accomplishment he could find the meaning of life. Solomon turned to his genius for building. He put up houses and planted vineyards. He planted gardens and orchards and made pools to water them.

The history of that period confirms that Solomon was one of the greatest builders of any era. How could he have thought the selfish, temporal pleasures of amusement or alcohol would amount to anything? Surely the answer was in leaving a legacy—a solid monument for future generations that would say, "This was Solomon and here are his great works."

Building a monument is a glorious thing. But in these three verses Solomon refers to himself no fewer than ten times. Instead of doing all this building for God, or for the people of Jerusalem, he was doing it for himself. Why? What was he trying to prove?

Is work a valid place to find ultimate meaning in life? Certainly many of us think so, judging from the schedules we keep. But David Henderson, in his book *Culture Shift*, suggests there may be something more subtle behind our frantic activity levels:

> Our lives, like our Daytimers, are busy, busy, busy, full of things to do and places to go and people to see. Many of us, convinced that the opposite of an empty life is a full schedule, remain content to press on and ignore the deeper questions. Perhaps it is out of fear that we stuff our lives to the walls—fear that, were we to stop and ask the big questions, we would discover there are no satisfying answers after all.[7]

When I was growing up, my father was the president of Cedarville College near Columbus, Ohio. He invested fifty years of his life as president and then chancellor of that school. More recently, Dr. Paul Dixon, a dear friend of mine, served as Cedarville's president. When Dr. Dixon retired, I watched him go through the challenges of turning over all he had done for twenty-five years to another man.

A member of the college staff remarked to me, "Do you know that during Dr. Dixon's presidency, one hundred million dollars' worth of buildings were constructed on this campus?"

I was surprised, but as I walked across campus I realized it was true. Dr. Dixon was a great leader and a great builder. Were those building projects meaningful? Absolutely. Will they serve young people and educate them? Without question. But I know—and Dr. Dixon knows—that none of those buildings have vested his life with lasting meaning.

Buildings are attractive and useful, but ultimately they are no more than masses of brick plastered together. Students enjoy them for four or five years; the faculty will use them during their teaching careers. But eventually everyone who walks into those buildings will walk out again, and someday not one brick will still be standing. Solomon's great temple, as well as all of his buildings, perfect in every detail, have passed from the earth.

Ecclesiastes teaches us that our work and our projects are generally worthwhile, but if we look to them as sources of ultimate meaning we will invariably be disappointed. Remember what we have already noted: eternity is the northward compass point of our hearts (Ecclesiastes 3:11). That means we can never be satisfied with temporal-based work. We could fill the earth with skyscrapers; we could spend every hour of our lives in toil—and the emptiness would abide. Ultimate satisfaction has one exclusive source.

Ernest Hemingway was the archetypal twentieth-century man. He filled many books with reflections of his worldwide adventures. He might be found sipping champagne in Paris, hunting grizzly bears in Alaska, watching bullfights in Spain, or fishing for tarpon in the Florida Keys. He lived the fullest life imaginable—under the sun. Yet the time closed in upon him when he chose to take his own life. His suicide note read, "Life is just one damn thing after another."

We want so badly to believe that we earn our own ticket in life. We want to believe that our proud individual accomplishments will lend us distinction and significance. After all, that would imply that we are in total control, that we are the "captains of our souls," as the poet put it. But only a brief search through history is required to call the roll of those who have walked in greatness yet died in despair.

Old Testament commentator Derek Kidner makes this observation: "What spoils the pleasures of life for us is our hunger to get out of them more than they can ever deliver. Getting eternal and ultimate meaning out of temporal and temporary pursuits is destined to fail."[8]

SEARCHING FOR MEANING IN WEALTH

I acquired male and female servants, and had servants born in my house. Yes, I had greater possessions of herds and flocks than all who were in Jerusalem before me. I also gathered for myself silver and gold and the special treasures of kings and of the provinces. I acquired male and female singers, the delights of the sons of men, and musical instruments of all kinds.

So I became great and excelled more than all who were before me. in Jerusalem. Also my wisdom remained with me. Whatever my eyes desired I did not keep from them. I did not withhold my heart from any pleasure, for my heart rejoiced in all my labor; and this was my reward from all my labor. Then I looked on all the works that my hands had done and on the labor in which I had toiled; and indeed all was vanity and grasping for the wind. There was no profit under the sun

—ECCLESIASTES 2:7–11

What nation would you guess to have the happiest citizens? It's not one that you would think. According to a report on CNN, an analysis of more than sixty-five countries by the World Values Survey suggests a higher "happiness index" in Nigeria than any other country. Mexico follows, then Venezuela, El Salvador, and Puerto Rico.

The United States comes in sixteenth, Australia twentieth, and Great Britain twenty-fourth. This survey, conducted every four years by an international network of social scientists, shows that happiness has little to do with wealth or income. In fact, the researchers included this surprising sentence in their report: "Survey after survey has shown that the desire for material goods, which has increased hand in hand with average income, *is a happiness suppressant*" (emphasis added).[9]

In other words, the more we have what we want, the more we want what we don't have. We try stuffing runaway materialism into the empty pockets of our souls, but the pockets have holes in them and we never achieve a feeling of real, existential satisfaction. Jesus summed it up this way: "One's life does not consist in the abundance of the things he possesses" (Luke 12:15).

The immensity of Solomon's wealth is beyond adequate description. But we'll give it a try anyway.

In 1 Kings 10:14, we find that "the weight of gold that came to Solomon yearly was six hundred and sixty-six talents of gold." In current dollars, Solomon's annual income of gold was nearly $304 million—"besides that from the traveling merchants, from the income of traders, from all the kings of Arabia, and from the governors of the country" (1 Kings 10:15).

There were many other sources of income; silver was so abundant that it wasn't even counted (1 Kings 10:21). Therefore, we might safely round the $304 million up to $500 million—a half-billion dollars of annual income—without fear of overstatement. There are people in the world today whose lifetime net worth is counted in the billions (much of it in the form of paper, not hard assets as was Solomon's). But in this age of wealth, there are very few whose annual income approaches Solomon's.

The writer of 1 Kings sums up by saying, "King Solomon surpassed all the kings of the earth in riches" (10:23). It's easy to see why.

If we had walked into Solomon's palace during that golden age of Israel's history, we would have seen precious stones from Africa, spices from Arabia, almond and sandalwood from India, ivory from India and Africa, and cedars from Lebanon. Solomon had forty thousand stalls for his chariot horses and twelve thousand horsemen.

His awe-inspiring temple left the nation breathless. Gold was found everywhere in its design; stairways beautifully ornamented; pillars and posts, curtains and courtyards all made of rare and costly materials. A nearly infinite array of servants populated it, dressed in gorgeous clothes. Rich cuisine, costly uniforms, and expensive animals were imported from around the world. It was a building worthy of a king whose wisdom and splendor eclipsed that of all the rulers on earth. Solomon rightly claimed that he was greater and wealthier than any of his predecessors in Jerusalem.

But in the end, it was "meaningless—utterly meaningless." Solomon, in today's language, would have said, "I had it all; I had it my way, and I climbed to the highest peaks of human achievement. But the one thing I sought was never within my grasp."

Solomon made a timeless error in his quest for meaning: he sought it in things and experiences. He searched in wisdom, in wild living, in work, in wealth—all in vain. The object of his search was, in fact, unavailable under the sun.

Centuries later, another wise man, C. S. Lewis, corrected the assumption that ultimate meaning can be found in anything in this world:

> The books or the music in which we thought the beauty was located will betray us if we trust to them; it was not in them, it came through them, and what came through them was longing. These things—the beauty, the memory of our own past—are good images of what we really desire; but if they are mistaken

for the thing itself, they turn into dumb idols, breaking the hearts of their worshippers. For they are not the thing itself; they are only the scent of a flower we have not found, the echo of a tune we have not heard, news from a country we have not visited.[10]

4

Careening Careers

ECCLESIASTES 2:12–23

⁓

Tennis champion Hana Mandlikova was once asked how she felt about defeating great players like Martina Navratilova and Chris Evert Lloyd. She replied, "Any big win means that all the suffering, practicing, and traveling are worth it. I feel like I own the world."

When asked how long that feeling lasts, she replied, "About two minutes."[1]

We live in a world searching for fleeting, momentary slashes of satisfaction. British environmentalist and keen social critic Derek Ratcliffe recently wrote a compelling analysis of the Western television audience and its viewing habits. He spoke of

> the mindless, shallow hedonism that seems to be the way our society is heading: a restless search for instant gratifications, trivial and ephemeral pleasures that leave no lasting satisfaction, let alone fulfillment. TV appears to me to be feeding rather than following this trend, although its bosses will always say they are giving the public what it wants . . . a decadent media culture of soap operas, docusoaps, quizgames, police action, cooking shows, home makeovers . . . football, pornography and other expressions of the current intellectual and aesthetic development of modern western society. [2]

Some of us get off the couch and go to work. We know that we can't satisfy the soul with nonstop entertainment, but we expect a good dose of the Christian work ethic to fill the bill.

Not so fast, warns Solomon.

OUR WORK DOES NOT SATISFY US

Then I looked on all the works that my hands had done and on the labor in which I had toiled; and indeed all was vanity and grasping for the wind. There was no profit under the sun.

Then I turned myself to consider wisdom and madness and folly; for what can the man do who succeeds the king?—Only what he has already done.

—ECCLESIASTES 2:11–12

Few have more professional accomplishments than Solomon did. He excelled as a politician, a public leader, an educator, a zoologist, a biologist, and an economist. You name it, he did it. But when he took a step back from his work, viewed it objectively, and evaluated it, he was disappointed. It left him without any sense of permanent happiness. "There was no profit under the sun," he complained.

We plunge into our careers with the adrenaline of a diver off the high board, dreaming of influence and impact—of "making a splash." We want to be the best in the game. We want to be recognized as pacesetters. As one of Europe's best soccer players, Germany's Oliver Kahn, recently said, "At times . . . I think to myself that this is the worst job in the world. I remember what I felt like after losing the 1999 Champions League final against Manchester United. I felt empty and I almost had a nervous breakdown."[3]

It's not just well-known athletes who are disillusioned. Listen to an ordinary American mom: "I'm a single parent, working full time; so juggling work, home, and my social life placed me on a treadmill that left me unfulfilled, drained, and powerless. I could not see how else to live my life."

U.S. News and World Report recently devoted its cover story to this subject, saying:

> Today, work dominates Americans' lives as never before, as workers pile on hours at a rate not seen since the Industrial Revolution. Many workers are left feeling insecure, unfulfilled, and under-appreciated. . . . It's no wonder surveys of today's workers show a steady decline in job satisfaction. . . . People are feeling crushed."[4]

The magazine goes on to comment that intrusive cell phones, whirring faxes, and the relentless pursuit of e-mail have blurred the lines between work and home. Home is no longer a refuge but an extension of the office. Work just doesn't satisfy life's deepest needs. It didn't do so in Solomon's day, it hasn't since, and it never will.

OUR WORK DOES NOT SEPARATE US

> *Then I saw that wisdom excels folly*
> *As light excels darkness.*
> *The wise man's eyes are in his head,*
> *But the fool walks in darkness.*
> *Yet I myself perceived*
> *That the same event happens to them all.*
> *So I said in my heart,*
> *"As it happens to the fool,*
> *It also happens to me,*
> *And why was I then more wise?"*
> *Then I said in my heart,*
> *"This also is vanity."*

*For there is no more remembrance of the
wise than of the fool forever,
Since all that now is will be forgotten in
the days to come.
And how does a wise man die?
As the fool!*

—ECCLESIASTES 2:13–16

Now Solomon astonishes us with his conclusion. He claims that when we see things only as they are "under the sun," we discover that our work neither satisfies nor separates us; it reduces us all to the same level. Imagine for yourself a life of relentless, bone-wearying work. The man in the next cubicle puts in a career of lazy underachievement. The two of you die on the same day and are laid out in the same funeral home. No stranger could view both bodies and identify which was the go-getter and which was the slacker.

Job says, "Naked I came from my mother's womb, and naked shall I return there" (Job 1:21).

Harry Ironside once wrote, "Death is the great leveler of all men. Whether rich or poor, wise or foolish, powerful or weak, renowned or obscure—no one can rise above it, cheat it, or escape its eventual claim on his life."

The seventeenth-century British playwright James Shirley put it graphically in his famous poem "Death the Leveler."

> Death lays his icy hand on kings:
> Scepter and Crown
> Must tumble down
> And in the dust be equal made
> With the poor crooked scythe and spade.[5]

Our Work Does Not Succeed Us

Therefore I hated life because the work that was done under the sun was distressing to me, for all is vanity and grasping for the wind.

Then I hated all my labor in which I had toiled under the sun, because I must leave it to the man who will come after me. And who knows whether he will be wise or a fool? Yet he will rule over all my labor in which I toiled and in which I have shown myself wise under the sun. This also is vanity. Therefore I turned my heart and despaired of all the labor in which I had toiled under the sun. For there is a man whose labor is with wisdom, knowledge, and skill; yet he must leave his heritage to a man who has not labored for it. This also is vanity and a great evil. For what has man for all his labor, and for the striving of his heart with which he has toiled under the sun? For all his days are sorrowful, and his work burdensome; even in the night his heart takes no rest. This also is vanity.

—Ecclesiastes 2:17–23

You may not appreciate hearing it, but Solomon is simply saying aloud what we all know to be true. Build what you want; save what you might; put it in the bank; liquefy it into stocks and bonds; drop it into real estate; place it anywhere you choose. You only control your wealth for a season, and then it's out of your hands completely. As you draw your last breath, you withdraw your grip on all that you have labored to build under the sun. It's a matter for others now.

Solomon isn't telling us to forsake our children or to deny them a reasonable inheritance. The same man writes, "A good man leaves an inheritance to his children's children" (Proverbs 13:22). Providing for our loved ones after our death is part of our Christian stewardship.

No, his message here is that the accumulation of wealth doesn't produce anything that endures through time and eternity. Leaving our loved ones too much might be worse than leaving them too little.

French novelist Gaston Leroux, creator of *The Phantom of the Opera,* was almost destroyed in this way. When his father died suddenly, leaving him with a fortune of almost one million francs, Gaston abandoned his career and relaxed into a dissipated existence of gambling and pleasure in colorful Paris society. Within a year he had squandered his inheritance—another sadder but wiser prodigal.

Solomon is warning us that accumulating mountains of money becomes meaningless to us within two seconds of death. In fact, the very reality of death strips our possessions of lasting significance.

In his book *Reasonable Faith,* the brilliant apologist William Lane Craig describes the ultimate implications of that truth. He speaks from the perspective of the nonbeliever, who might say:

> I realize I am going to die and forever cease to exist. My life is just a momentary transition out of oblivion into oblivion. And the universe, too, faces death. Scientists tell us that the universe is expanding, and everything in it is growing farther and farther apart. As it does, it grows colder and colder, and its energy is used up. Eventually all the stars will burn out and all matter will collapse into dead stars and black holes. . . . Mankind is a doomed race in a dying universe. Because the human race will eventually cease to exist, it makes no ultimate difference whether it ever did exist. Mankind is thus no more significant than a swarm of mosquitoes or a barnyard of pigs, for their end is all the same. The same blind cosmic process that coughed them up in the first place will eventually swallow them all again.[6]

Who cares if we leave behind a dollar or two on the road to oblivion? Who cares if we leave millions of dollars for our children? It might merely hasten their spiritual destruction.

That's why Paul tells us to set our affections on things above, not on things below (Colossians 3:1–4). That's why Jesus tells us to lay up treasures for ourselves in heaven, not on earth (Matthew 6:19–20). That's why Paul writes these words to Timothy:

> Command those who are rich in this present age not to be haughty, nor to trust in uncertain riches but in the living God, who gives us richly all things to enjoy. Let them do good, that they be rich in good works, ready to give, willing to share, storing up for themselves a good foundation for the time to come, that they may lay hold on eternal life. (1 Timothy 6:17–19)

What Is the Answer?

Some time ago, an aspiring television star was given a shot at a network series. He went to the NBC studios, saw his name on a parking space, found the crew treating him like royalty, and admired the star on his dressing room door. The series pilot was shot in five days, but television executives rejected it. When the young actor left, no one said good-bye, the name was gone from his parking space, and his dressing room was locked.

"All the success was like smoke," he said. "I couldn't get a handle on it; like cotton candy, once it was in my mouth it was gone."[7]

Our culture is a cotton-candy world—sugary, and seductive—a pink swirl of empty calories. Today you might be the "flavor of the month," with Hollywood or Wall Street at your command. Tomorrow your pockets may be as empty as your soul.

Enjoyment Is a Gift from God

Nothing is better for a man than that he should eat and drink, and that his soul should enjoy good in his labor. This also, I saw, was from the hand of God. For who can eat, or who can have enjoyment, more than I?

—ECCLESIASTES 2:24–25

Solomon could have settled into a spirit of cynicism about life under the sun. He could have lived out his days in silent despair. But he remembered something wonderful from his youth. He recalled when life was simpler, when he had much less and enjoyed it much more. Particularly, he remembered the message of two fathers: one who taught him of heaven, the other who taught him of earth.

The last few words of Ecclesiastes 2:25 are key. The New International Version, New American Standard Version, and other modern translations get it right. For example, the New Living Translation renders verse 25 this way: "For who can eat or enjoy anything apart from him?" That is Solomon's conclusion: God is the essence of the positive life, and every moment of it is a gift from Him.

Eight times in this book we will hear this sentiment—a kind of upbeat refrain for the dirgelike verses of Ecclesiastes. And let's not miss the relief of this thought: Even under the sun, even with what is missing, what we do have is still the gift of God. The wisdom, the work, and the pleasure of a good meal are no more than appetizers, but they are good appetizers.

We can enjoy our good homes and families, the pleasure of our recreation, the chilled swim, and the grilled steak. We can feel good in connecting with our work. These things will never give us the one great pleasure that lies at the center of life, but they will complement it. They will cluster around the great shining star of godly contentment like lesser lights that point to the greatness of what is at the center.

We can smile as we watch Solomon dismantle the idea that God is in His heaven peering through the clouds to catch people having fun, so that He might put a stop to it. The God of Ecclesiastes is nothing like that; He is the Joygiver, the dispenser of pleasurable pursuits. Christ, the Bread of Life, leaves a little trail of good things like bread crumbs in the forest, leading straight to that joy that is heaven on earth: intimate fellowship with Him. Only in the aftertaste of that fellowship do these lesser tastes become truly pleasurable to us.

How important it is, then, to keep God in the middle of our bank accounts, our possessions, and our portfolios. Picture your hands out in front of you, cupped together, palms up. In your open hands are all the things He has entrusted to you—money, cars, a home, furniture, everything. All of this is His gift (James 1:17). We are the stewards, and faithfulness is our charge. That means our hands must never close over the gifts, but remain open so that He may use them as required—and refill our hands.

The human impulse, of course, is to "clutch and clench"—to close our fists protectively. We then find ourselves facing limited resources. How can God fill us when there is no opening? And as long as we can't loosen our grip, we cannot enjoy what is there.

With open hearts and open hands, however, we understand that God lacks no resources and neither will we. The more of Him we discover and enjoy, the more we find available. Our hands joyfully open wider, and He gives from His infinitely generous heart. It is not the gifts that bring the joy, but He Himself; the gifts are simply His creative expression in telling us how much He loves us. And we agree with David: "You will show me the path of life; in Your presence is fullness of joy; at Your right hand are pleasures forevermore" (Psalm 16:11).

ENLIGHTENMENT IS A GIFT FROM GOD

For God gives wisdom and knowledge and joy to a man who is good in His sight; but to the sinner He gives the work of gathering and collecting, that he may give to him who is good before God. This also is vanity and grasping for the wind.

—ECCLESIASTES 2:26

God not only gives us true enjoyment, but He gives us true enlightenment. We grow in the wisdom of using His daily blessings.

There are people who've spent decades building spacious homes, but God inhabits none of the rooms because the houses are clutched, clenched, hoarded—investments in material and financial value. These homes seem beautiful at first glance, but they come to feel empty and soulless.

There are others with spacious homes that have been opened, like their owners' hands, to the glory of God. The people who live here host Bible studies. They entertain missionaries. God inhabits every room, because they have invested it spiritually. And the joy under this roof is like a beautiful wallpaper that runs through every hall; a soft and delightful music that warms the soul.

Solomon is drawing on something he learned earlier in his life . . . that wisdom and knowledge come from God. Notice the similarity between verse 26 and Proverbs 2:6.

> For the LORD gives wisdom; from His mouth comes knowledge and understanding. (Proverbs 2:6)

> For God gives wisdom and knowledge and joy to a man who is good in His sight; but to the sinner He gives the work of gathering and collecting, that he may give to him who is good before God. (Ecclesiastes 2:26)

Would you rather be the first in line for wisdom and knowledge and joy, or would you rather be handed the heavy tools of "gathering and collecting" in service of the knowledge-and-joy-getters? It's entirely your choice. If you decide to serve God, those wonderful gifts of wisdom and knowledge and joy come with the deal. Otherwise, life is an unending round of heavy lifting.

This same interesting hierarchical arrangement is found in Proverbs 13:22: "The wealth of the sinner is stored up for the righteous." God's eye is on all the wealth of this world, and He says that the wealth of the sinner is being gathered and stored up to accomplish His purposes in due time.

Those who know God intimately will attest to the fact that life is filled with wonderful blessings from above at every turn. He wants us to know how to use His blessings, so He includes wisdom in the overflow.

Many years ago, there was a woman named Clara Tear Williams who became a circuit-riding Methodist preacher, an unusual role for a nineteenth-century woman. When a friend asked Williams for a poem to include in his book of poetry, this is what she gave him. It summarizes Solomon's message in this part of Ecclesiastes:

> All my life I had a longing
> For a drink from some clear spring,
> That I hoped would quench the burning
> Of the thirst I felt within.

> Hallelujah! I have found Him
> Whom my soul so long has craved!
> Jesus satisfies my longings,
> Through His blood I now am saved.[8]

Every longing is satisfied. Our deep thirst is quenched. And from there, life is a cavalcade of blessings—the old items of drudgery transformed, even as we have been transformed, to new and joyful gifts every morning from now to eternity.

5

Impressions About Life

ECCLESIASTES 3:1–8

Iᴛ ɪs sᴀɪᴅ ᴛʜᴀᴛ ᴏɴ ᴠᴇᴛᴇʀᴀɴ's ᴅᴀʏ, November 11, 1963, President John F. Kennedy visited Arlington Cemetery to pay his respects to America's fallen heroes. Gazing over the rolling Virginia hillside from Arlington House, he remarked, "It is so beautiful that I could stay here forever." Two weeks later he returned in a flag-draped coffin to be buried beneath an eternal flame.

Kennedy's favorite passage from the Bible was Solomon's poem in Ecclesiastes 3:1–8, which begins: "To everything there is a season, a time for every purpose under heaven: A time to be born, and a time to die."

Also in 1963, the nation was singing that same ancient passage of Scripture to a contemporary beat. Folk singer Pete Seeger adapted the words as the song "Turn, Turn, Turn," and the Byrds' rendition later sailed to the top of the charts.

Seeger stayed fairly close to Solomon's poetry in his adaptation—until the song's last line. He had come to Solomon's words, "a time of war, and a time of peace." This, of course, was a time of peace—at least to the young generation that listened to the Byrds. The folk music scene was busy providing the soundtrack for the antiwar movement, so Peter Seeger tweaked Solomon's poetry a bit. The new line was, "A time of peace, I swear it's not too late."[1]

What is it about Ecclesiastes 3 that fascinated a troubled generation and its charismatic young president? Why has this passage endured the ages as one of the oldest philosophical poems in our literature canon? It's certainly among the most pensive passages of God's Word, a beautiful meditation that casts a near-hypnotic spell over readers of any generation.

In its setting in Ecclesiastes, it follows as the next step in Solomon's unfolding logic about the futility of living the under-the-sun life.

The author was the wisest and wealthiest man who ever lived, and this book is a chronicle of his lifelong quest for heaven on earth. We've already seen in the first two chapters of Ecclesiastes how Solomon tried wealth, wisdom, work, and wild living. At the end of his wide-ranging experiments, he concluded that everything was an empty exercise in vanity. It was like trying to capture the wind in his hands.

As we come to the third chapter, we find Solomon facing an even bigger challenge, a "problem with God."

I know all about the "problem with God." A few years ago I encountered a life-threatening cancer and a life-changing adventure. I would not have chosen cancer as a path to spiritual growth, nor would I wish such fear and pain on anyone. On the other hand, I don't see my illness as a random event, some miscellaneous accident of health. And I don't believe there was a moment when God was absent from the physical, emotional, and spiritual crisis I endured.

In fact, I found Him everywhere during that time. I found Him as never before. I glimpsed His face among the doctors and nurses who cared for me so skillfully. I saw Him there in shining power among the family of my church, and intimately among the family circle of my wife and children. He met me in the private chapel of my soul, where with each passing day I felt deeper in His grace and comfort. At one bend of the road after another, I found my Lord more present and more powerful. I wrote about my experiences in a book entitled *A Bend in the Road.*[2]

Knowing there must be pain and suffering for us all, I dearly wish everyone could travel the road I did. I wish every human soul could see the face of God in the fear and turmoil. So many walk a very different path; they experience only His absence.

I was asked to participate in a debate with an individual who had shared my particular disease. He believed in God but had come to radically different conclusions than I did about God and the troubles of life. The debate was sponsored by the internationally recognized Scripps Clinic located in San Diego, California, a leading provider of healthcare for cancer patients. The individual I debated was a Jewish rabbi, a disciple of Rabbi Harold Kushner, the author of *When Bad Things Happen to Good People.*

Rabbi Kushner's book generated much interest when it was published in 1981, and again when it was rereleased on its twentieth anniversary. As a young theology student, Kushner had many questions about Job and his experience of suffering. But when his own three-year-old son contracted a rare disease that took his life at a young age, Kushner penned his conclusions about God and suffering in order to provide answers to others in similar circumstances.

Kushner's conclusion was a popularization of an ancient theological conundrum: how can God be both perfectly good and perfectly powerful? The suffering in the world suggests that if He is God, He is not good; or that if He is good, He is not God. In other words, there must be something lacking in either His love or His strength, or He would cure every little pain.

Rabbi Kushner worked through the old enigma. He concluded that God is all-loving but not all-powerful. He cares deeply about the people He created, but after creating the world He backed away and allowed it to run without His interference—again, the cosmic watchmaker who abandons his workmanship.

Kushner decided that we navigate the waters of an ocean that God does not control. That is, if you were to pray to God in your need, He would have to answer, "Sorry, that's not My job." The message of his book is supposed to offer hope and comfort to those who hurt. I've never heard it explained how that is so, because we're told we live within a kind of fence God will not enter.[3]

The rabbi I debated held Kushner's view. He admitted that he didn't pray for God's healing intervention in his life; if God wasn't involved with him getting sick, why should God get involved with making him well?

Solomon had a different view entirely. In chapter 3 of Ecclesiastes, he concludes that God is sovereign and in control, regardless of the imponderables that remain. Here Solomon sees God as being present inside the fence with us, but not helpful enough. The king wants to know why God doesn't improve the standard of life, do something about the aging process, show more favoritism to His children, and perhaps discontinue the program of human pain.

In his poem recorded in Ecclesiastes 3:1–8, Solomon presents fourteen couplets and twenty-eight statements. There are fourteen negative statements and fourteen positive ones, and they fall into three separate categories. The first describes the influence of time on our bodies, the second focuses on our souls, and the last deals with our spirits.

That is, after all, the way you and I are made. We're human beings with bodies, minds, and souls.

And Solomon's main thought? Well, it doesn't take a Hebrew scholar to notice that the word *time* occurs twenty-nine times in these verses. We rarely turn our backs on the time. You and I probably have a dozen clocks and four or five calendars in our homes. Many of us carry a timepiece attached to our wrist, and time indicators are built into our cell phones, computer screens, and PDAs. Every major corporation in America tries to teach its employees time-management skills.

When Don Regan became chief of staff for President Ronald Reagan, he was staggered by the immensity of managing the president's schedule. "It is a sobering experience to realize," he said, "that you have been entrusted with managing the time of the most powerful man in the world." Regan wrote in his memoirs:

48

A president has no more than eight years (and he may be granted half that time or even less) to keep the promises he had made to the people. Therefore it is true of the President as it is true of few other men that he hasn't a minute to waste. Every meeting, every conversation, every ceremony must have a purpose, and it must take place in the time allotted to it. What a president might fail to do for lack of time can have profound consequences. [4]

Remember that Solomon was the greatest leader of his day, a head of state to whom all of Israel and much of the known world looked for guidance. He pondered carefully the allocation of time, and he was aware of how quickly it passed.

TIME AND YOUR PHYSICAL LIFE

To everything there is a season,
A time for every purpose under heaven:
A time to be born,
And a time to die;
A time to plant,
And a time to pluck what is planted;
A time to kill,
And a time to heal;
A time to break down,
And a time to build up.

—ECCLESIASTES 3:1–3

Solomon begins his contemplation with a sobering observation: birth and death both have their appointed times.

I flew to Baltimore recently for the birth of my grandson, Ryland. As I peered through the nursery window at this beautiful new citizen of the world, it struck me that only a corridor away, some other citizen was being dispatched. Some family had gathered for the agony of farewell. It's not a lengthy walk between the nursery and the intensive care unit. We spend our own time making that trek between entrance and exit, womb and tomb.

Meanwhile, there is a time to plant and a time to harvest. Solomon refers to the food supply because he knows that God sets the boundaries of the seasons. Just as a composer of beautiful music builds certain rhythms and repetitions into his songs, so God has built certain rhythms into His world. The steady repetition of the seasons provides comfort and a workable cadence to life.

We are a bit discomforted to read that there is a time to kill as well as a time to heal. Yet our bodies are in the process of dying every moment. Scientists tell us that every seven years we replenish all the cells within our bodies. There is an ongoing maintenance department in the human machine that is constantly changing out the old for the new. And it is governed by time.

Cancer cells, infection cells, or simply worn-out cells must be killed—so even killing has its time, and we are grateful. There must be a time to kill so we might also have a time to heal.

And what of "a time to break down, and a time to build up"? We build up in our early years, and we start breaking down as we get older—painful but true. Someone said we know we're getting older when the type gets smaller, the steps get higher, the voices get softer, the muscles get weaker, and our medicine chest gets larger.

How old is old? You're old at twenty-one if you're a female gymnast. Your performance will peak in your mid- to late teens. You're over the hill at thirty if you're a professional tennis player. Do you think of forty as old? For Michael Jordan, reaching forty meant his years as an NBA star were behind him.

I was enjoying a birthday when David Todd, my six-year-old

grandson, crunched the numbers on my age. He said, "If Poppy was a dog's age, he'd be dead!" He was right. Time is relative for God's creatures, but it rules their itineraries.

There is a time for breaking down, but God is there. He is as powerful as He is loving, regardless of what the rabbi said; and you have the opportunity to experience His power all the more effectively and vividly when you turn to Him in the breakdowns of life.

Time and Your Emotional Life

A time to weep,
And a time to laugh;
A time to mourn,
And a time to dance;
A time to cast away stones,
And a time to gather stones;
A time to embrace,
And a time to refrain from embracing.

—Ecclesiastes 3:4–5

Time is also involved with the operations of the soul, the seat of human emotions. There's a time to cry, when tears flow freely; there are also times for laughter. Hopefully, the latter outnumber the former, for in another passage Solomon prescribes cheerfulness as good medicine for the soul (Proverbs 17:22). Yet tears are a part of life. The Bible says, "Jesus wept. . . . He groaned in the spirit and was troubled" (John 11:35, 33). Job states, "My eyes pour out tears to God" (Job 16:20). The psalmist asks God to store his tears in a heavenly bottle, for they are precious (Psalm 56:8). And Psalm 126:5 promises, "Those who sow in tears shall reap in joy."

Your tears are God's jewels; they are precious to Him. The greater your suffering, the greater His ministry and grace for you. We need to laugh, but sometimes we must also cry. The Lord is near us in both sadness and gladness. One day, He'll wipe away every tear from our eyes and the days of crying will be forgotten. But for now, there's a time to laugh and a time to weep.

There's a time to mourn and a time to dance. There's a time to hug, and there are times when hugging is inappropriate. God has given us a wide spectrum of emotions, and sometimes we feel we are at the mercy of our anger or depression or grief. It helps to know that each emotion is simply playing the part allotted to its own special time. We need a blue sky and green meadows; we need clouds that are willowy white. In the same way, we need our full spectrum of God-given emotions, for they are the emblems of our humanity. They mark us as children of a God who also has anger, grief, and laughter.

TIME AND YOUR SPIRITUAL LIFE

A time to gain,
And a time to lose;
A time to keep,
And a time to throw away;
A time to tear,
And a time to sew;
A time to keep silence,
And a time to speak;
A time to love,
And a time to hate;
A time of war,
And a time of peace.

—ECCLESIASTES 3:6–8

The last three verses have to do with inner decisions—the deep commitments of our lives. Sometimes we gain; sometimes we lose—money, weight, hair, loved ones, privileges, rights, responsibilities, joys, possessions.

Sometimes we store things in our garages, and sometimes we clean out our garages. We collect and we throw away.

Even large corporations do this. In periods of expansion, they swallow smaller companies; then when they need to raise cash to retire debt or enter new markets, they sell off part of what they have accumulated. Unfortunately, at the personal level we seem far more interested in accumulating than in throwing away. We need to recognize the spiritual value of both, that there is a time and a season to get rid of stuff.

Sometimes we need to speak up. Other times we need to keep our mouths shut. Solomon knew there was a "time to keep silence, and a time to speak." The assets and liabilities of words show up repeatedly in Solomon's proverbs. The father in Proverbs continually admonishes his children to pay attention to words of wisdom and instruction (Proverbs 2:1; 3:1; 4:1, 10, 20; 5:1, 7; 7:1, 24), but he also warns against talking too much (17:27) and becoming ensnared by one's own words (6:2).

The more we talk, the more likely we are to sin (Proverbs 10:19); the fire of gossip dies out as soon as the talk ceases (26:20). In short, words can contain life or death; it is up to us to choose them carefully (18:21). There is no greater wisdom than knowing the seasons of the tongue—when it is time to speak and when it is time to keep silent (26:4–5).

There is a time for love and even a time to hate. A time to hate? Yes, of course. Even Jesus hated. He hated sin. He hated its mastery over human souls. He hated the wake of its destruction. We need to learn how to hate that which is evil without hating the people who are evil. We may hate the act of abortion, but we have compassion on both the aborted and the aborting. We may hate the ravages of alcohol, but we love those who struggle with alcoholism, and we want to do whatever we can to help them.

The passage ends by reminding us that while we all long for a peaceful world, there is even a time when war is morally necessary. "A time of war, and a time of peace" (v. 8).

Peter Muhlenberg was an Anglican pastor in Virginia. In 1774, he was elected to the Virginia legislature and was present at St. John's Church in Richmond when Patrick Henry proclaimed, "Give me liberty or give me death!" Peter was so moved that he promptly joined George Washington's army.

On a bitterly sad Sunday morning, he resigned from his church and preached his farewell sermon. He read Ecclesiastes 3:1: "To everything there is a season, a time for every purpose under heaven." Looking up, he said, "There is a time to preach and a time to pray, but there is also a time to fight, and that time has now come." Then he suddenly flung off his ministerial robe to reveal underneath the uniform of a militia colonel.

He recruited other men in his church, and they became known as the German Regiment under his command. It's because of men like Peter Muhlenberg that America has been the home of the brave and the land of the free for more than two hundred years.[5]

What Solomon is teaching us in Ecclesiastes 3:1–8 is that all of life unfolds under the appointment of providence. Birth and death, sowing and harvest, joys and sorrows, acquiring and losing, speech and silence, war and peace—everything has its appointed time from God. He is sovereign, but He is always faithful.

Our lives need to reflect His divine pacing. We need the cadence of His call, the rhythm of His wisdom running through our moments, our days, and our years. Through all the seasons of life, through all the undulating circumstances of the passing years, God remains both loving and powerful. As the old Methodist hymn puts it:

> Summer and winter, and springtime and harvest,
> Sun, moon, and stars in their courses above
> Join with all nature in manifold witness
> To Thy great faithfulness, mercy, and love.[6]

6

Insights About God

W HEN ALL IS SAID AND DONE, what's the point of all I've said and done?

It sounds fatalistic. It sounds anything in the world but biblical. If you spoke up and said it at church, you might well get a lecture. But you are not Solomon; he's the king, and he can ask questions like that.

And he really wants an answer. Does all this effort make a difference? After the times and seasons and feelings have played themselves out in me—what is left?

In the king's words, "What profit has the worker from that in which he labors?"

He poses a fair question. If God controls the peaks and the valleys of life, if *He* has it all covered, then what is the point of *my* work? Why should I even bother to punch in on time when tomorrow morning rolls around?

I have known friends to spend twenty years building a secure home for their families, only to see it quickly evaporate through some disaster or financial crisis. Were all those years a total waste?

The *Times* of London recently carried a profile of Philip Guston, the Canadian/American abstract-expressionist painter who died in 1980. The article was entitled "Exposing a Futile Existence." It was a profile of a man who managed, through his art, to show the meaninglessness of every little thing people do.

The art reviewer described Guston as a man who, being expelled from school, "went on to smoke three packets of untipped Camels a day, and eat and drink so much, and who somehow succeeded in making noble, even heroic art about these excesses." To Guston, life was empty—have another smoke.

The *Times* writer added this despairing line: "Most modern lives do, indeed, unravel and then stop, like a stair-carpet being unrolled."[1]

That's rather vivid, isn't it? It's simply the more modern version of Macbeth's famous soliloquy:

> To-morrow, and to-morrow, and to-morrow,
> Creeps in this petty pace from day to day,
> To the last syllable of recorded time. . . .
> Life's but a walking shadow, a poor player,
> That struts and frets his hour upon the stage,
> And then is heard no more; it is a tale
> Told by an idiot, full of sound and fury,
> Signifying nothing.[2]

GOD'S PLAN IS GOOD

What profit has the worker from that in which he labors?
I have seen the God-given task with which the sons of men
are to be occupied.
He has made everything beautiful in its time.

—ECCLESIASTES 3:9–11

Solomon faces this attitude of futility and despair head-on, and the middle of chapter 3 gives us three answers to ponder.

In verse 10, Solomon says our busywork can obscure the true meaning of life unless we stop and take a close look. In so doing, we realize that God's plan is good. The truth is, "He has made everything beautiful in its time" (3:11). If we allow the meaning of this statement to sink in, we will realize that *everything* is beautiful in God's sight; *everything* in life has a purpose.

Life is not empty and random and godless, but full and precisely aligned and God-ordained. It's not that your most important work is meaningless; it's that your most trivial movements are also significant.

Ruth Bell Graham used to have an inscription over her kitchen sink: "Divine service conducted here three times a day." She understood that whatever we do—even washing a dirty pot—is worthwhile if done in God's will and for Christ's glory.

One man who understood this well was Nicholas Herman, otherwise known in history as Brother Lawrence. He was born in Lorraine, France, in 1605, but little is known of his early life. He reached his teen years at the onset of the Thirty Years' War. He fought for the French army, was seriously wounded, and was lame for the rest of his life. Converted at eighteen, he went to work as a footman for a local official in the treasury.

Nicholas, however, had a nagging fear of living an insignificant life. At the age of fifty, he joined a Carmelite monastery in Paris where he was dubbed Brother Lawrence and assigned to the kitchen. It was a task that struck him as insulting and humbling. For the next several years, he went about his chores, miserable but dutiful.

Then one day he began thinking about his attitude. He started reminding himself that God's presence continually permeated him. Even the most menial tasks, if undertaken for God's glory, are holy. And that means the heat of a kitchen, the sweat of the unplowed field, even the stench of the gutter are holy ground because God goes there with us.

Many years passed. Brother Lawrence's countenance and demeanor gradually changed, until others began asking him a reason for his radiance. His thoughtful message began to have a profound influence on those around him, and it was preserved in the little book entitled *The*

Practice of the Presence of God. Thus the simple message of a simple kitchenhand has had a worldwide impact, because Lawrence understood the full implications of God's invisible presence.[3]

What profit has the worker? Much profit, if our tasks are God-given and Christ-centered. The real question is, "Am I doing what God wants me to do? Am I in the place, above all others, that He wants me to occupy?"

Solomon goes on in verse 11 to add this beautiful sentence: "He has made everything beautiful in its time." Everything that happens in our lives has a purpose. God makes it beautiful in its time. This verse is the Old Testament counterpart of Romans 8:28: "We know that all things work together for good to those who love God, to those who are the called according to His purpose."

In our churches we used to sing a chorus based on this verse:

> In His time, in His time,
> He makes all things beautiful in His time.
> Lord, please show me every day,
> As You're teaching me Your way
> That You'll do just what You say in Your time.[4]

We have no problem connecting with that truth in the nice moments. What sets the true saint apart is his ability to apply it during moments of unpleasantness. When young couples fall in love and get married, they are convinced that God has made everything beautiful in His time. But ten years later, when little children are underfoot, bills are due, a job has been lost, and a medical scare has been diagnosed—we wonder what happened to all that beauty. Marriage has lost a little luster, parenthood is less glorious, and homebuilding is more sweat than sweet.

Men and women leave their marriages in times like these simply because they're unaware of God's presence in the rugged times as well as the smooth. Our challenge is to recognize that everything has a time, a season, a reason, and to trust God to bring sense and unity on His schedule. Then not only will the beauty be there, but it will be far more beautiful for the hard polishing.

When I was sick with cancer, people would ask me, "Pastor, why did you get cancer? You're a godly man, serving the Lord in full-time ministry." It's true that I'm a pastor. But on a deeper level I'm just another human being. And human beings get cancer. The game of Monopoly offers a "Get out of jail free" card, but God offers no such card to Christians. We must take the rain with the sun, the dark with the light, and know that God is painting a beautiful picture which requires all the tones, all the colors, all the depths of suffering as well as joy.

Years ago, British media expert Malcolm Muggeridge, who became a committed follower of Christ, wrote the following in his book *A Twentieth Century Testimony:*

> Contrary to what might be expected, I look back on experiences that at the time seemed especially desolating and painful with particular satisfaction. Indeed, I can say with complete truthfulness that everything that has truly enhanced and enlightened my existence has been through affliction and not through happiness, whether pursued or attained. In other words, if it ever were to be possible to eliminate affliction from our earthly existence by means of some drug or other medical mumbo jumbo, as Aldous Huxley envisaged in *Brave New World,* the result would not be to make life delectable, but to make it too banal and trivial to be endurable. This, of course, is what the Cross signifies. And it is the Cross, more than anything else, that has called me inexorably to Christ.[5]

In other words, if life were like drawing a picture, and your pencil included a nice eraser, you might rub away all the darker marks in the picture. In the end there would be no real picture at all, for it is what happens at those junctions between light and darkness that tells the final story.

Civil War–era devotional writer E. M. Bounds wrote many great books on the subject of prayer. He also penned this little poem:

> Why should I fear tomorrow? The Lord directs my way.
> Why should I trouble borrow? I live but for today.
> Whenever I am weary, in God I find my rest,
> And when my path seems dreary, I know it's for the best.

In his autobiographical book, *A Turtle on a Fencepost,* business leader Allan Emery tells of accompanying his friend and mentor Ken Hansen to visit a hospitalized employee. The patient lay very still, his eyes conveying anguish. His operation had taken eight hours, and recovery would be long and uncertain.

"Alex," said Ken quietly, "you know I have had a number of serious operations. I know the pain of trying to talk. I think I know the questions you are asking. There are two verses I want to give you—Genesis 42:36 and Romans 8:28. We have the option of these two attitudes. We need the perspective of the latter."

Hansen turned to the passages, read them, then prayed and left. Allan Emery never forgot those two verses, nor should we.[6]

The choice is this: to be beat up, or to be upbeat. To say with Jacob in Genesis 42:36: *All these things are against me.* Or to say with Paul in Romans 8:28: *All things work together for good to those who love God.*

The perspective you choose will color your life completely and thoroughly—will it be gentle tones of grace and providence, or harsh slashes of despair and emptiness?

Missionary Hudson Taylor sometimes quoted this Frederick W. Faber poem when afflictions came his way:

> Ill that God blesses is our good,
> And unblest good is ill.
> And all is right that seems most wrong,
> If it be His sweet will.[7]

This is where faith comes into play, of course. We walk by faith, not by sight. If our faith only works when everything is rosy and upbeat, it's not worth very much. Faith kicks in when the roof falls in. We keep up our spirits and fortify ourselves by trusting in God's presence and promises despite the dismal circumstances.

We have to understand that God's plan is good, and that includes even the negative things that come into our lives. I know we are left with some serious questions: What about the Holocaust? What about 9/11? What about genocide in Bosnia? I can't answer all those questions. But I can say this: *When you stand back and view the great cavalcade of human experience from the divine perspective, God's fingerprints cover everything— the places of misery and tragedy most of all.*

In Tommy Nelson's book on Ecclesiastes, he shares an object lesson he used in his church. He had his pianist come to the piano. He asked her to play "Jesus Loves Me" using only the white keys on the piano— the "do-re-mi" notes of the diatonic scale. Then he asked her to play it again, adding the black keys—the sharps and flats. Then he asked his congregation, "Which version did you prefer?" There was no contest; it took "light music" and "dark music," major and minor, sharps and flats to make a melody.[8]

If you don't learn to trust God, you will do one of two things: You will invent a god who has no basis in fact, as my friend the rabbi did. Or you will believe in the true God but live in a constant state of agitation because He doesn't act the way you think He should or explain to you what you think you deserve to know.

We must trust God to be God.

God's Purpose Is Clear

Also He has put eternity in their hearts.

—Ecclesiastes 3:11

A missionary-scholar named Don Richardson wrote an award-winning book called *Eternity in Their Hearts,* based on Ecclesiastes 3:11. He presented more than twenty-five examples of missionaries all over the world who had discovered cultures completely cut off from Christianity in which vestiges of truth about God existed.

The people were looking for God, indeed were *hungry* for God, since knowledge about Him had been passed down in their culture for generations. Leading them to Christ required little more than explaining how the God they had been searching for had come to earth in the person of Christ to save them from their sins. Richardson set forth the idea that every human being has eternity in his heart, that winning people to Christ is a matter of discovering what piece or part of eternity they were familiar with and connecting the dots to Christ.

God has put something in our hearts—a taste or longing for eternity that cannot be discovered through the experiences of life. There will always be a longing within us for something more than we have experienced until we know God personally.

And even after we come to know Christ, there will still be an ache, for the Bible says the whole creation is groaning, waiting for the day of redemption (Romans 8:22). Planet Earth was not fitted to carry a curse of sin, and we were not created to live with a sin nature. We will never find ultimate satisfaction in this life because we were made for eternity.

C. S. Lewis, in his classic *Mere Christianity*, says it this way:

> Creatures are not born with desires unless satisfaction for those desires exists. A baby feels hunger; well there is such a thing as food. A duckling wants to swim; well there is such a thing as water. Men feel sexual desire; well there is such a thing as sex. If I find in myself a desire which no experience in this world can satisfy, the most probable explanation is that I was made for another world. If none of my earthly pleasures satisfy it, that does not prove that the universe is a fraud. Probably, earthly

pleasures were never meant to satisfy it, but only to arouse it, to suggest the real thing.[9]

I wonder if Saint Augustine had Ecclesiastes 3:11 in mind when he wrote, "Thou hast made us for Thyself, and our hearts are restless until they learn to rest in Thee" ? That says it as succinctly as it could be said. The unrest we see in our world and in our own hearts tells us we have not found our rest completely in God. And we will not experience that rest completely until we enter the realm for which we were created—*eternity.*

Once again, C. S. Lewis's words help us: "Our Heavenly Father has provided many delightful inns for us along our journey, but He takes great care to see that we do not mistake any of them for home."

As we make these stops along the road, we can only wonder about the mansions He is preparing for us.

HIS PROGRAM IS MYSTERIOUS

Except that no one can find out the work
that God does from beginning to end.

—ECCLESIASTES 3:11

God's plan is good; His purpose clear. But the last part of verse 11 tells us that His program is mysterious. Nobody can figure it out.

If you've picked up this book thinking that I have answers to all of life's imponderable mysteries and miseries, I must apologize. I'm not God, and I can't understand it all. I try to figure it out just as you do, and I often wish God would be more forthcoming with the answers. The evangelist Vance Havner used to say, "God writes over some of our days: *'Will Explain Later.'"*

The word *why* occurs 430 times in the Bible—and you and I have asked it that many times or more. Catherine Marshall, the eloquent writer and wife of U. S. Senate chaplain Peter Marshall, wrote about her anguish over the death of a beloved grandchild. For quite a while, Catherine felt anger and depression toward God for allowing such a thing, when she had earnestly prayed and trusted for the child's healing.

Then one day she was reading through Isaiah 53, a poignant passage about the suffering of the Messiah.

> I had read this passage many times before, even since Amy Catherine's death, but it had not affected me as it did now, particularly the tenth verse. God made His own Son suffer, but it was a "good plan." More than "good." It was perfect, as only something from God could be. It was terribly important to the future of the human race that Jesus Christ have His dark night experience on the cross. Yet what a desperately dark night it had to be for Him to have cried out, "My God, my God, why hast though forsaken me?"

Catherine concluded:

> When life hands us situations we cannot understand, we have one or two choices. We can wallow in misery, separated from God. Or we can tell Him, "I need You and Your presence in my life more than I need understanding. I choose You, Lord. I trust You to give me understanding and an answer to all of my whys, only if and when You choose."[10]

God is God, and He doesn't owe us every answer to every question on demand. Someday we'll understand, but right now we live by faith and peer through a glass darkly. It's like looking through the back window in the foggy morning mist. You can't make out every detail of the fields and trees, but you have faith that things will clear up, and the world will be beautiful—a little heaven on earth—all the lovelier, somehow, after a good rain or fog.

7

Read the Instructions

ECCLESIASTES 3:12–15

SEVERAL YEARS AGO, there was a bestseller entitled *Life's Little Instruction Book*. The title said it all. We all want profound insights about living, given in bite-sized chunks that we can digest. It was Solomon who invented this form of teaching, and these verses in Ecclesiastes 3 could be considered the original *Life's Little Instruction Book*. Having given us his impressions about life (verses 1–8) and his insights about God (verses 9–11), Solomon ends this section by sharing some instructions about living (verses 12–15).

Watch out: These verses are heavy loads in small packages. It's best to take them one at a time.

DON'T FORFEIT ENJOYMENT BECAUSE OF WHAT YOU CAN'T UNDERSTAND

I know that nothing is better for them than to rejoice, and to do good in their lives.

—ECCLESIASTES 3:12

You enter the world's greatest amusement park. You have the whole day to spend there. Which amazing roller coaster will you ride first?

None! You sit on the bench, pull out a laptop computer, and dedicate yourself to computing the precise mechanical configurations of every attraction. You figure that mastery of the nuts and bolts will enhance the roller coaster experience.

Eight hours later, it's time to go home. The laptop is humming . . . but you haven't experienced a single thrill.

That's what happens in life when we become preoccupied with looking over God's shoulder. You'll never understand even a small portion of His program, so you might as well enjoy a larger portion of His provisions. If He tried to explain the science of providential mechanics, it would be like you trying to explain your job to a flea. Better to let the flea find a dog and do what it does best.

Life—the awesome gift of God—shouldn't be afflicted by the paralysis of analysis. We'll either be frozen in fear over what comes next, or we'll become so confused over the meaning of it all that we won't notice the joy leaking out through the seams of everyday living.

There comes a time to "lighten up" a bit, as people sometimes say. Do we take God, His Word, and His laws any less seriously? Not at all. We simply acknowledge the boundaries defined by His greatness and our smallness.

He cannot be put into any convenient box of our design. As Archie Bunker once said (with painfully mangled theology), "That's how He got to be God." Besides, poking too far into the matter is how we got to be in *our* present state.

The Eternal One says in Isaiah 55:9, "For as the heavens are higher than the earth, so are My ways higher than your ways, and My thoughts than your thoughts."

"God moves in a mysterious way /His wonders to perform," hymnist William Cowper wrote.[1] Some people want to master every corner of the God question before they make a commitment to believe in Him, and they miss the heart of the issue—the issue of the heart.

Jesus says, "I have come that they may have life, and that they may have it more abundantly" (John 10:10). In telling us that, Jesus uses a great old Bible word to describe the way God wants to bless our lives. He *abundantly* pardons our sins (Isaiah 55:7). His grace is exceedingly *abundant* (1 Timothy 1:14).

Psalm 37:11 promises us an abundance of peace. The apostle Paul says that out of the abundance of God's grace and righteousness, we can reign in life through Jesus Christ (Romans 5:17). We have abundant labors in His kingdom (2 Corinthians 11:23), but also abundant joy (Philippians 1:26) and abundant mercy (1 Peter 1:3).

I think when most Christians approach the end of life, they're going to wish they had served God more faithfully. But I think they'll have another regret—that they didn't fully take advantage of the wonderful abundance in life that Christ offers us.

God enjoys our enjoyment! He filled the world with good things for a reason. Go to a football game. Spend time with your family. Take a vacation. Pursue an enjoyable hobby. Relax in the sauna. Do a little something for yourself every day, and thank God for the blessings He has abundantly poured into your life.

Author Jim McGuiggan has observed:

> Some saints can't enjoy a meal because the world is starving. They can't joyfully thank God for their clothing and shelter because the world is naked and homeless. They're afraid to enjoy an evening at home with their families because they feel like they ought to be out saving souls. They can't spend an hour with an unforgiven one without feeling guilty if they haven't preached a sermon or manifested a sober Christian spirit. They know nothing of balance and they're miserable because of it. . . . They think the gospel is good news until you obey it. And then it becomes an endless guilt trip.[2]

The Westminster Catechism has it right: "Man's chief and highest end is to glorify God, and fully to *enjoy* him forever." (emphasis mine)."[3]

Don't Forget to Be Thankful for God's Gifts

And also that every man should eat and drink and enjoy the good of all his labor—it is the gift of God.

—Ecclesiastes 3:13

Luke 17 is a healing story of Jesus. He restores ten lepers to perfect health, but only one has the good manners to come back and say thank you. Why was this leper different? We have no clue, but it's logical to believe that long before Jesus came to town, this one showed evidence of a different heart. And we can imagine the other nine grumbling, rumbling, dwelling in the considerable misery of their lives.

This one leper must have been different—thanking God for the sunshine and the blue sky, bowing before meals to offer thanks. Disease is a terrible thing, but its power to inflict misery over us is, to a great extent, within our control. Godly people cope with amazing adversities by simply refusing to bow to misfortune. The most powerful weapon in the attitudinal arsenal is gratitude: "In everything give thanks, for this is the will of God in Christ Jesus for you" (1 Thessalonians 5:18).

The best-known evangelist in the world during the early 1900s was Billy Sunday, a former professional baseball player who preached with acrobatic vigor and powerful results. His wife, Helen, was heavily involved in his ministry. On November 19, 1935, Billy died in her arms, and she felt she had lost both her husband and her life's work. But the following week at a memorial service in Buffalo, her subject was "Things I'm Thankful For." She had a long list, but she began like this:

> Folks, it's surprising how many things God can reveal to you to be thankful for, if you really want to know and ask Him to help you. I had no idea there were so many! But when I prayed and asked God to help me write them down, they came into my

mind one after the other—the very first one was: If Billy had to go, oh, how thankful I was to God Almighty that He called him away in an instant. . . . He just cried out to me, "I'm getting dizzy, Ma!" and he was gone! How wonderful to be here one second, and up in heaven the next second! Never knowing any real pain or any real suffering of that type—I think God was so good to take Billy that way, and I thank Him for it.[4]

Life is like one of those Rorschach tests administered by psychiatrists. Some look at it and see the black inky stains. "It's a monster, preparing to attack me," they say. Others look at the same blot and define it by the whiteness that encloses the ink. "It's a heavenly cloud and a hovering angel," they say.

Optimistic people see blessings amid burdens. They realize the sun always breaks through sooner or later. It refuses to be defined by the presence of dark clouds. After all, the dark clouds are nothing but mist; the sun is built to last.

We have the opportunity to look at life through the powerful eyeglasses of God's promises, which magnify blessings and keep trials in perspective. The more we peer through those spectacles, the more we want to send thank-you notes, the more we want to commit random acts of kindness, the more we want to stop during the day and offer silent thanks for the subtle blessings that cover us all the time.

Don't Fear Life—Fear God

I know that whatever God does,
It shall be forever.
Nothing can be added to it,
And nothing taken from it.
God does it, that men should fear before Him.
That which is has already been,

And what is to be has already been;
And God requires an account of what is past.

—ECCLESIASTES 3:14–15

God deals exclusively in *forever* and *flawless*. If God made it, you can't add to it, subtract from it, or put a stop to it. Though even a sunset over the Rockies is not forever, you have these feelings as you stand in its presence: "This is a work of perfection; a masterpiece. I can add nothing to it, nor can I detract from it one iota. Therefore I simply stand, humble and speechless."

God's design for your life is every bit as awe-inspiring as tomorrow's sunset. What? You have your doubts about that plan? It is perfect; it's a forever thing; it can't be edited. We should rest in the knowledge of His perfection, but we should also respond in a healthy fear.

Did you read that correctly? Fear? Even though that word appears less frequently in today's sermons and Bible studies, it remains in God's perfect, uneditable Word. The phrases "fear God" or "fear the Lord" occur more than 114 times in the Bible. For example:

> You shall fear the LORD your God and serve Him.
> (Deuteronomy 6:13)

> Now therefore, fear the LORD, serve Him in sincerity and in truth, and put away the gods which your fathers served. (Joshua 24:14)

> The fear of the LORD is clean, enduring forever. (Psalm 19:9)

> You who fear the LORD, praise Him! (Psalm 22:23)

[Walk] . . . in the fear of the LORD and in the comfort of the Holy Spirit. (Acts 9:31)

Therefore, having these promises, beloved, let us cleanse ourselves from all filthiness of the flesh and spirit, perfecting holiness in the fear of God. (2 Corinthians 7:1)

Does this imply that we should cower in fear of God—tremble as we enter the church or begin our morning prayer? Not in the way we fear any force of malevolence, such as a wild animal or a disaster or a misfortune for someone in our family. No, this kind of fear we feel in the presence of something too marvelous for words.

Have you ever visited Niagara Falls and ridden the *Maid of the Mist* right out into the basin of that thundering cataract? It's a bit terrifying to stand there, only a few yards from such power, deafened by the roar of six million cubic feet of water bursting over the cliff every minute and falling 170 feet into the basin before you. The spray hits you, and you can literally feel the sound waves beating against your face. You look at the awesome power of the pounding waters, and you feel small and fragile in your sense of wonder.

When you look at the sun setting over the Rockies, painting the sky in a spectrum of reds and oranges, you reflect on the size and heat of that solar star, and the fact that in a millionth of a second you would cease to exist if you were in its near presence. You feel small, fearful, and awestruck.

The One powerful enough to set that sun in space, and to create that waterfall, is far more worthy of our fear and wonder. He holds all of space and time within His fist, and how small are we in that context?

This is a fear caught up in love—the way we may have once feared our earthly mothers and fathers, but to the trillionth power. It is a fear that inspires worship as the heat inspires warmth. Life? We have no reason to fear it. God? We have every reason. We fear His magnificence,

His infinity, His wrath, and therefore we fear the prospect of ever wandering from His friendship, ever turning from His presence, ever losing His power, as Solomon did.

We fear the thunderous power of a love so relentless it could send One's own Son to die. We fear the utter blackness of God turning away, as endured by Christ on Calvary. We stand before the cross and realize we can add nothing. We can take nothing away. The act is perfect and forever, and our fear turns to abounding love and devotion.

8

When Justice Isn't Just

ECCLESIASTES 3:16–22

T HE MISTY IMAGE OF AN EAR sealed his fate.

In 1998, Mark Dallaher was convicted of killing a ninety-four-year-old woman in England. The key testimony was an expert witness who stated that the intruder had pressed his ear against the glass window of the woman's house, listening quietly before slipping into the room to murder her. The earprints matched those of Mr. Dallaher, said Cornelius Van Der Lugt; in fact, he was "absolutely convinced" of the match.

The trial made headlines around the world because it was the first time ear-prints had been used to convict a killer. Dallaher was sentenced to life behind bars in England's notorious "Old Bailey" prison.

It turns out that the evidence against Dallaher was flawed. A DNA profile obtained from the earprint proved it didn't belong to Dallaher at all. Instead, a new suspect has been implicated. Dallaher has been set free.

"I've waited seven years for this day," he told British newspapers as he left Old Bailey. "I've spent six of those years in prison, protesting my innocence to deaf ears. The last nine months has been a terrible ordeal, all as a result of the prosecution's reliance on discredited expert evidence."[1]

If there is a God of love, justice, and power, how do you explain the fact that life isn't fair, and cruel injustices may stand? It's a story as old as humanity. The guilty walk free while the innocent suffer.

INJUSTICE UNDER THE SUN

Moreover I saw under the sun:
In the place of judgment,
Wickedness was there;
And in the place of righteousness,
Iniquity was there.

—ECCLESIASTES 3:16

This deeply bothered Solomon—injustice under the sun. The wicked prosper in their sins while the righteous suffer in their integrity. People with money can oil the wheels of justice, making them turn in their direction and in their favor, while the poor often find themselves at the mercy of an overburdened court nearly bursting at the seams. A new survey shows one of every seventy-five men in the United States is in jail or prison.[2] The odds dictate that a few of these are surely innocent, but it is even more certain that the streets are filled with as many evildoers as ever.

Solomon uses a unique literary technique to make his point. With characteristic honesty, he tells it exactly as he sees it, using the phrase "I saw" no fewer than four times in this section (Ecclesiastes 3:16; 4:4, 7, 15). He takes a look around, records his observations, and draws his own conclusions. He thinks in his heart (3:17), he perceives (3:22), and he considers (4:1).

We do the same. We see the innocent suffer, and it cuts us deeply. There but for the grace of God go we. In time, we become angry, and we stand with Solomon to demand: Why must justice be so unjust?

Thousands of upright souls are suffering in filthy prisons under the tyranny of communism, militant Islam, and totalitarianism. The "crime" may well be that of bearing the name of Christ.

Few governments have been more brutal to Christians than that of North Korea. Soon OK Lee was a prisoner in North Korea from 1987 to 1992. She did not become a Christian, however, until she escaped to

South Korea. When she first received Christ, she was overwhelmed by her memories of what she had seen and heard in prison. It was the simple things, like the Christians who sang as they were being put to death. At that time, she did not understand and had thought they were crazy. She was not allowed to talk, so she never had the chance to speak with a Christian. She does remember hearing the word, "Amen."

While she was there, she never saw Christians deny their faith. Not one. When those Christians were silent, the officers would become furious and kick them. At the time, she could not understand why they risked their lives when they could have said, "I do not believe," and done what the officers wanted. She even saw many who sang hymns as the kicking and hitting intensified. The officers would call them crazy and take them to the electric-treatment room. She didn't see one come out alive. It was the singing that stuck with her. Perhaps it was the singing of those precious saints that planted a seed in her spirit and eventually led her to Christ.

As Solomon pondered the problem of faulty justice, he proposed a series of profound answers in verses 17–21.

And yes, there *are* answers.

JUDGMENT IS COMING

I said in my heart,
"God shall judge the righteous and the wicked,
For there is a time there for every purpose and for every work."

—ECCLESIASTES 3:17

Times are just, Solomon said—but just wait, for here comes the Judge. And when He sits behind the bench, the rulings will be according to the secrets of men's hearts. Furthermore, there will be no partiality; no favoritism or influence peddling. The date has been set, and each of us will have his or her day in court.

As Ecclesiastes 8:6 puts it, "Because for every matter there is a time and judgment." Again, a time for every purpose under heaven.

We hate it when someone "gets away with it." Solomon tells us that in truth, nobody gets away with it. Paul Harvey illustrated this point when he told about a man named Gary Tindle who was charged with robbery. While standing in the California courtroom of Judge Armando Rodriguez, Tindle asked permission to go to the bathroom. He was escorted upstairs to the bathroom, and the door was guarded while he was inside. But Tindle, determined to escape, climbed up the plumbing, opened a panel in the ceiling, and started slithering through the crawl space, heading south.

He had traveled some thirty feet when the ceiling panels broke under him, and he dropped to the floor—right back in Judge Rodriguez's courtroom![3]

When the guilty seem to have escaped judgment, it's only for a short moment and a short crawl. They will find themselves before the Judge once again in due time. Sooner or later, the wheels of God's righteousness will right every wrong, balance every scale, and correct every injustice in the world. James Russell Lowell's famous poem, "The Present Crisis," describes this truth:

Truth forever on the scaffold. Wrong forever on the throne—
Yet the scaffold sways the future and behind the dim unknown
Standeth God within the shadow, keeping watch above His own.[4]

William Wadsworth Longfellow elaborated on Lowell's original sentiment, saying:

Though the mills of God grind slowly
Yet they grind exceedingly small,
Though with patience He stands waiting
With exactness He grinds all.[5]

Small and all—good ways to characterize the extent of God's present and future judgment. As someone has said, "In the choir of life, it's easy to fake the words—but someday each of us will have to sing solo before God."

DEATH IS CERTAIN

I said in my heart, "Concerning the condition of the sons of men, God tests them, that they may see that they themselves are like animals." For what happens to the sons of men also happens to animals; one thing befalls them: as one dies, so dies the other. Surely, they all have one breath; man has no advantage over animals, for all is vanity. All go to one place: all are from the dust, and all return to dust. Who knows the spirit of the sons of men, which goes upward, and the spirit of the animal, which goes down to the earth?

—ECCLESIASTES 3:18–21

Here is Solomon's point: A man and his dog romp through the same field, breathe the same air, die on the same acre, and fade to dust together in the earth. They are more alike than different.

Some liberal interpreters of the Bible claim this passage argues against the eternal nature of the human soul. But Solomon is referring to issues of flesh and bone. These bodily temples are not built to last any more than was Solomon's temple of gold. Both topple someday; both become one with the dust.

But the issues of the soul are a separate discussion. Eternity is set in our hearts and engraved in our destiny—but it is not so for the animals. We are made in the image of God, and we are His children—but it is not so for the animals.

So death is certain. The criminal may run free today, but Death wears excellent running shoes and cannot be outrun.

In recent years, doctors and social scientists have been studying deathbed scenes and interviewing people who have had near-death experiences. Dr. Maurice Rawlings, a Chattanooga cardiologist, has written about his research. He observes that death survivors tell us that the moment of death is absolutely painless, regardless of every instinct we have about it. "Feels like fainting," survivors say, or "like a missed heartbeat" or "a lost breath." Many have a sense of their souls leaving their bodies on a tranquil voyage down what seems to be a tunnel.

But not all the stories have happy endings. Dr. Rawlings was an agnostic and a cynic when something happened to him that changed his life. One day he was examining the heart of a forty-eight-year-old mail carrier named Charles McKaig, from LaFayette, Georgia. McKaig was on the treadmill when his heart monitor became erratic, then flatlined.

Surprisingly, Charlie continued to talk for a moment, unaware that his heart had stopped. Four or five seconds later, he looked suddenly dumbfounded. Then his eyes rolled up in his head and he fell, the tread-mill sweeping his body away like so much trash, as Dr. Rawlings later put it.

Rawlings immediately began applying CPR. As Charlie's heart began beating, he screamed, "Don't stop! I'm in hell! I'm in hell!"

Rawlings thought the man was having hallucinations. But Charlie continued, "For God's sake, don't stop! Don't you understand? Every time you let go, I'm back in hell." Charlie begged Rawlings to pray for him, but Rawlings told him to shut up. "I'm a doctor," he said, "not a minister."

The nurses gave Dr. Rawlings such terrible looks that even while applying CPR he said, "All right. Say it! Jesus Christ is the Son of God. Go on and say it." Charlie said those words, and a strange thing happened. He was no longer a wide-eyed, screaming, combative lunatic. He was relaxed and calm and cooperative. He survived the experience, a changed man from that moment on. He went on to live a committed Christian life.

The experience shook Rawlings deeply. He began a long-term study into near-death experiences, and out of his research Rawlings himself became a Christian. What he discovered in his research is that near-death experiences are often horrifyingly negative and terror filled when the person has no relationship with God.

Dr. Rawlings summed up his findings, saying, "Most people are deathly afraid of dying. They say, 'Doctor, I'm afraid of dying.' But I have never heard one of them say, 'Doctor, I'm afraid of judgment.' And judgment is the main concern of patients who have been there and returned to tell about it."[6]

We need to be careful about building our theology on the ambiguity of near-death incidents. Even so, it is interesting that such information often harmonizes with what the Bible tells us. "And as it is appointed for men to die once, but after this the judgment," says Hebrews 9:27. And one chapter later we read this sobering verse: "It is a fearful thing to fall into the hands of the living God" (Hebrews 10:31).

Life Continues

So I perceived that nothing is better than that a man should rejoice in his own works, for that is his heritage. For who can bring him to see what will happen after him?

—Ecclesiastes 3:22

Let's get personal here. Have you ever been the victim of injustice? Perhaps you received a speeding ticket when, in fact, you were well within the speed zone. Perhaps a co-worker slandered you, preventing you from getting the promotion you deserved. Maybe an associate or family member accused you falsely.

What should you do about it? Grow bitter? Get even? Complain to everyone who will listen? Brood over the injustice until the bitterness springs forth like a weed? No. Just leave it in God's hands and get on with your life.

I heard of a pastor whose car was sideswiped by a speeding motorist. The stranger shot off down the road, never to be seen again. While he wasn't hurt physically, the young pastor was devastated financially. He was just getting started in ministry and his little church could pay him only a small stipend. He didn't have comprehensive car insurance, so he had to bear the cost of the repairs himself. He also knew he could easily have been killed.

The more this pastor thought about it, the angrier he became. For several days, he drove around his neighborhood, searching for the offending car, primed to confront the driver with his fists, if necessary.

Then he began to regain his perspective, saying to himself, *It was God who spared my life. It will be God who cares for me financially—and it will be God who sees that justice is done. I'll leave the matter in His hands.*

And so, for the pastor as well as for you and me, there is wisdom and comfort in realizing that because life goes on, we can go on with life. Yes, injustices will go on as well on this side of eternity. Life isn't fair—never was, never will be.

But justice *is* coming, whether today, tomorrow, or in a thousand lifetimes; it is as certain as death. Living in bitterness is not worth the trouble, while joy is worth any price.

Therefore life goes on; we move on, and even with its entire catalog of inequities—life is good.

> God holds the key of all unknown, and I am glad:
> If other hands should hold the key, or if He trusted it to me,
> I might be sad,
> I cannot read His future plans, but this I know:
> I have the smiling of His face, and all the refuge of His grace,
> While here below.[7]

9

From Oppression to Obsession

ECCLESIASTES 4:1–6

Sᴵᴹᴏɴ ᴡɪᴇsᴇɴᴛʜᴀʟ ꜱᴜʀᴠɪᴠᴇᴅ the Holocaust of World War II, but his faith in God died somewhere in a Nazi concentration camp.

He told the story of watching a Nazi commander shackle two Jews together, back to back. The commander pushed his revolver into the mouth of one of the victims and pulled the trigger. One bullet killed both men.

The Nazi turned to his corporals and said, "See, I told you there's no need to waste bullets. You can kill two with one."

Wiesenthal concluded, "When I saw the oppression and the wickedness and the injustice of that [act], I couldn't comprehend it, and I turned from God."[1]

THE OPPRESSION OF THE POOR

Then I returned and considered all the oppression that is done under the sun:

And look! The tears of the oppressed,
But they have no comforter—
On the side of their oppressors there is power,
But they have no comforter.

81

Therefore I praised the dead who were already dead,
More than the living who are still alive.
Yet, better than both is he who has never existed,
Who has not seen the evil work that is done under the sun.

—ECCLESIASTES 4:1–3

The loss of faith is tragic, but in Wiesenthal's case, somewhat understandable. He simply lacked the perspective that Solomon offers you and me.

Yet the wise king must have seen a few atrocities too. Here he suggests that the oppressed—people like the two Jews in Nazi Germany—would be better off if they'd never been born. Job once thought the same thing about himself. After he lost his children, he said,

> May the day perish on which I was born,
> And the night in which it was said,
> "A male child is conceived ." . . .
> Why did I not die at birth?
> Why did I not perish when I came from the womb?
>
> —JOB 3:3, 11

Have you ever cursed the day you were born? Many of us have endured terrible times and unthinkable trials. There are more than a few of us who have, in rock-bottom moments, wished the Lord would go ahead and take us home. Others simply say, "I wish I were dead."

The suicidal impulse, of course, is a very serious emotional issue and requires professional care. But most of us have endured midnights of the soul. In such moments we can thank God that we know He has a better place for us; we need only be patient. But what about those with no belief in heaven? What can we say to the temporally oppressed and eternally hopeless?

Through my years in ministry I've come to the conclusion that sometimes it's best to simply say, "I don't know. I wish I could give you a full and satisfying answer to your question." We would be foolish to claim an understanding of all the intricacies of God's ways, when in truth we comprehend so little of them.

Psalm 73 offers a compelling take on this particular matter. I've returned to this passage again and again to draw on the fount of its wisdom and to lead others there. The psalmist tells us, "But as for me, my feet had almost stumbled; my steps had nearly slipped . . . when I saw the prosperity of the wicked" (verses 2–3).

The psalmist has had enough of the "haves" ravaging the "have-nots." The more wickedness he has seen, the bleaker his perspective has become. The psalm grows darker and more troubled until a tentative ray of sunshine breaks through in the middle portion. That's when something happens that shifts the psalmist's perspective:

> When I thought how to understand this,
> It was too painful for me—
> Until I went into the sanctuary of God;
> Then I understood their end.
>
> —Psalm 73:16–17

Comprehension came to him through the act of worship.

We look at our jobs, our governments, and everything else through our own hazy viewpoints. Then, perhaps in church, perhaps in prayer, perhaps on some other holy ground, we gaze through the portal of "the sanctuary of God." The picture changes, like a kaleidoscope of dark colors shifting into a beautiful moonlight landscape. The colors all remain, but we begin to get the picture too. God's perspective is based on different parameters—His love, His grace, His eternal purposes— and the moment we begin to account for these, we make wiser judgments about what we see under the sun.

Charles Tindley was one of the greatest African American preachers of the twentieth century. He had been born into slavery in 1851. After the Civil War, he moved to Philadelphia, where he began attending church and found Christ as his Savior. He was called into the ministry and made the impressive vocational journey from church janitor to senior pastor.

His congregation grew just as radically. Thousands eventually came to hear him preach each Sunday. Most of them were poor and black, in a time when there was particular oppression for the poor and the black. Tindley himself died in poverty, despite his fame, and was buried in an unmarked grave.

He faced great oppression in life: racial injustice, false accusations, plain mistreatment. When he was a candidate for a bishop's position, a competing minister told him to his face, "You are an unlettered ignoramus. You know you are not educationally fit to be a bishop." An anonymous letter accused him of immorality, and he was denied the position. Tindley's wife died; his son was killed during World War I. His ministry was a midnight landscape.

Tindley channeled the burden of his suffering into wonderful music. His hymns endure. "I'll Overcome Some Day," for example, became "We Shall Overcome," the basis for the great theme of the civil rights era. He also wrote "Stand by Me," "Nothing Between My Soul and the Savior," and "Take Your Burden to the Lord and Leave It There." That was what Tindley himself had learned to do.[2]

But one of his hymns has a special place in our hearts. "We'll Understand It Better By and By" goes hand in hand with Solomon's insight:

> We are often destitute of the things that life demands,
> Want of food and want of shelter, thirsty hills and barren lands;
> We are trusting in the Lord, and according to God's Word,
> We will understand it better by and by.

> Trials dark on every hand, and we cannot understand
> All the ways that God could lead us to that blessed promised land;

But He guides us with His eye, and we'll follow till we die,
For we'll understand it better by and by.

Temptations, hidden snares often take us unawares,
And our hearts are made to bleed for a thoughtless word or deed;
And we wonder why the test when we try to do our best,
But we'll understand it better by and by.[3]

Solomon's message for you and me is, "As we look upon the oppressed, our hearts are broken. We'd rather not see; we'd rather fix our minds on pleasant subjects. But how can we turn our backs on God's beloved children? We must look hard and accept that we don't have all the answers. Our Lord does, and we'll understand it better by and by."

Suffering Solomon aches for the huddled masses of the poor and hungry because he knows that God aches for them. But the down-and-outers aren't the only objects of his pity. We watch him shift his gaze, and we're shocked to see him looking toward the rest of us—those who covet.

THE OBSESSIONS OF THE PROSPEROUS

Again, I saw that for all toil and every skillful work a man is envied by his neighbor. This also is vanity and grasping for the wind. The fool folds his hands and consumes his own flesh. Better a handful with quietness than both hands full, together with toil and grasping for the wind.

—ECCLESIASTES 4:4–6

Basketball coach Pat Riley, in his book *The Winner Within,* tells the story of the 1980 World Championship and the Los Angeles Lakers. After they became the NBA champions, they were thought to be unbeatable. As the

1980–81 season approached, sports pundits agreed that the Lakers were sure to repeat their league domination.

Then, within weeks of the opening game, Magic Johnson tore a cartilage in his knee and faced three months of recuperation. He was the star. He was the playmaker. The team and its fans were crushed, but they rallied. The Lakers reached within themselves, found their courage and intensity, and brought their team's game to a new level. They played their hearts out.

Magic was on the bench, but there was fresh magic on the court. The Lakers were winning at an amazing 70 percent clip as Johnson's return drew near. The fan anticipation mounted. During time-outs, the public address announcer would say, "And don't forget to mark your calendars for February 27. Magic Johnson returns to the lineup of your World Champion Los Angeles Lakers!"

Johnson's teammates would hear the announcement and grumble, "Hey, we're on top of our game *right now*. What's so special about February 27?"

But even as they continued to overachieve, all the attention shifted toward the one player who hadn't yet seen the court. On the twenty-seventh of February, 17,500 ticket holders pushed through the turnstiles and were handed buttons reading "The Magic Is Back!"

At least fifty press photographers crowded onto the floor while the name of each player was called. Normally only the starters were introduced, and Magic was going to be on the bench when the game began. But he was nevertheless included in the introductions. At the mention of his name, the arena rocked with a standing ovation. Flashbulbs burst like popcorn. Magic Johnson was hailed as a returning conqueror, as if the games without him really hadn't counted.

The other Lakers burned with resentment. That night their games were off, and they barely overcame the worst team in the league. As the season progressed, team morale plummeted. There was finger-pointing and recrimination among what had been a tight-knit family of players. The coach was fired. The Lakers' win-loss record collapsed, and they took a quick exit from the playoffs.

"Because of greed, pettiness, and resentment," Riley later said, "we executed one of the fastest falls from grace in NBA history. It was the Disease of Me."[4]

The Web site PersonnelToday.com, a resource for human resource managers in the workforce, recently reported their survey on this subject. The headline read "Professional Jealousy Grips the Nation." The article under the headline gave the evidence:

> Almost nine out of ten office workers suffer from "professional envy" of colleagues they perceive to have more glamorous or better paid jobs, according to a survey by Office Angels. The survey of 1,500 office workers by the recruitment consultancy found more than two-thirds of respondents felt professional jealousy toward friends who made their own working life appear bland in comparison. Almost a third envy a partner or spouse's job, while a fifth feel jealous of a work colleague who is further up the career ladder.[5]

Solomon shifts his gaze to envy, jealousy, and the drive to outdo others. The ancient king could have been writing for the *Wall Street Journal* as he summarized the driving motivation in today's workplace.

Most of us work hard at our jobs. But our motivations are ambiguous. Many workers push themselves simply because they want others to envy and admire them. They want the corner office, not because it has a nice view, but because their coworkers will be jealous. And the main reason for buying the high-end car is the hungry look they long to see on the faces of the Joneses next door.

We like being one step ahead. It's normal to want approval, but we want more than that—we want admiration and envy. Competitive drive is a deeper motivator for many of us than we realize.

Erwin Lutzer says that envy is basically a rebellion against God's plan. We don't want others to be blessed more than we are, regardless of God's master plan. J. I. Packer notes that envy is dangerous because it's fed by pride, "the taproot of our fallen nature." Billy Graham has pointed out that envy ruins reputations, splits churches, and even incites murder. It is the precise opposite of love, for love rejoices in the good fortune of others.

Some of us realize the truth of this and determine that we'll be different. We don't want to be the kind of people who step on everyone else on our climb up the corporate ladder. But we must also avoid the opposite extreme, as Solomon points out in verse 5. "Foolish people refuse to work and almost starve" (NLT).

During the 1960s, and on into the '70s, some young people decided to abandon what they called "the establishment." We called them "flower children." They sold what they had, piled what was left into their old VW buses decorated with psychedelic paint schemes, and moved into communes.

Naturally, this is less a rejection of competition than an excuse for laziness. And because we are designed to be fruitful, laziness doesn't sit well with the human spirit. Lethargy sets in, self-respect plummets, and relationships weaken. And don't forget that for every lazy person, society pays a price. The unproductive become social burdens in various ways.

Neither overcompeting nor underperforming is the answer. Solomon suggests the true solution in 4:6: "Better a handful with quietness than both hands full, together with toil and grasping for the wind." Translation: *Seek balance.* One hand filled with prosperity, contentment, and quietness is far better than two hands filled with envy and rivalry. Compete but cooperate; rest but resume.

Most of us would agree that our society has erred on the side of overwork. That's why a recent Associated Press article details the growing numbers of young adults who are scaling back their lifestyles. They are moving into smaller homes, selling their expensive cars, and often quitting their high-pressure jobs. "It's true among people of all ages," said Bruce Tulgan, a Connecticut-based consultant who tracks generational relationships and trends in the workplace. "But it's much stronger, much more notable among the younger generations." Tulgan said these young adults want more time for "the *life* part of life."[6]

I have enjoyed using a daily devotional resource called *Daily Light,* an updated version of what was first compiled by Samuel Bagster in the nineteenth century. The plan is simple: exclusively Scripture, with one collection of verses for morning, another for evening, and a topical index. I call it the "Starbucks" of devotional time because it's pure spiritual caffeine—a powerful jolt of truth that comes from the all-Scripture program. I've developed a discipline of putting myself in the Scripture passages and offering them as my own prayers to God. Here's an example, recorded in my journal, for the topic of financial stewardship:

> Lord, I ask that You give me neither poverty nor riches—please feed me with the food allotted to me; lest I be full and deny You, and say, "Who are You, Lord," or lest I be poor and steal, and profane the name of my God. Give me this day my daily bread.

> Lord, help me not to worry about my life, what I will eat or what I will drink; nor about my body, what I will put on. Isn't my life more than food and my body more than clothing? . . . So Lord, let my conduct be without covetousness; help me to be content with such things as I have. . . . for You yourself have said, "I will never leave you nor forsake you."

If you're familiar with the Bible, you'll recognize the verses I was reading on those days. The Scriptures were speaking to me about financial contentment, and this was my way of replying to God in the power of His Word. I realize the crucial nature of contentment in life. Every one of us involved in a race to accumulate the most toys will come out the loser in the end. Solomon, the world's richest man, knew this and knew it early on. As a younger man he wrote, "Better is a little with the fear of the LORD, than great treasure with trouble" (Proverbs 15:16), and along the same lines, "Better is a little with righteousness, than vast revenues without justice" (Proverbs 16:8).

Help us indeed to be content, Lord, in the pleasant valley between too much and too little; between slavery and sloth; between overcompeting and underperforming. There, in that valley where heaven meets earth, we can walk with our hand in Yours rather than grasping at the wind.

10

When 1 + 1 > 2

Ecclesiastes 4:7–16

⌒

Sticks and stones may break my bones, but words will never hurt me." It has a nice memorable ring to it, but I'd guess whoever said it had very few close friends.

The fact is that the worst hurts of all come from people, their words, and the pains we suffer simply in trying to get along together in some semblance of a social life.

You twist an ankle—*ouch!* The immediate pain is considerable. You feel it for a few days, and you may even go to the doctor. But a year from now, maybe two years from now, will you even remember the incident? When someone mentions the day you twisted your ankle, will your face darken as you feel a jolt of fresh pain and sadness? I doubt it.

But consider a relationship wound—and we're not even considering divorces, lawsuits, or the truly serious issues. Just think about the last time someone you care about said something that *really hurt.*

As with the ankle, the immediate pain was considerable. You felt it with intensity for days. But there was no medical doctor who could help you, and few could even understand your pain. This was nothing as generic as a twisted ankle—this was *personal.* Someone hit a nerve of the emotional variety, and I would predict that in one year, two years, maybe even a decade, you'll remember exactly what was said and how you felt. Only time and God heal wounds like that.

Solomon knew this. Certainly he was king, and there were probably very few who chanced a biting remark in his direction. Still, he came from a family that had its share of discord. Absalom was his half brother; David was his father. Solomon had plenty of opportunity to observe the profound suffering that can result from the fact that we always hurt the ones we love. Many of us struggle all of our lives to overcome the pain arising from early family life, even after we have committed the problem to God. The first cuts in life are the deepest.

T. S. Eliot provided a cynical definition for the typical family in one of his poems:

> Two people who know they do not understand each other,
> Breeding children whom they do not understand
> And who will never understand them.[1]

Yes, families are also beautiful, wonderful gifts from God. If they can be monstrous, they can also be marvelous through the bountiful blessings of God.

But you and I know the truth, don't we? Several times each year we are shocked at the hurtful things that happen to godly families we know. This teenager, so active in the youth group, ran away; that child, raised in Sunday school, got into some trouble; this couple, pillars of the church, are getting a divorce. We hurt with them. We whisper, though we should not. But the wiser ones among us throw no stones; we may be living in glass houses of our own. We know that life's most perilous task may well be that of maintaining an emotionally and spiritually successful family.

Solomon knew it, too, and within the fourth chapter of Ecclesiastes he begins to reflect on the terrible pain of relational discord.

RICHES OVER RELATIONSHIPS

Then I returned, and I saw vanity under the sun:
There is one alone, without companion:

He has neither son nor brother.
Yet there is no end to all his labors,
Nor is his eye satisfied with riches.
But he never asks,
"For whom do I toil and deprive myself of good?"
This also is vanity and a grave misfortune.

—ECCLESIASTES 4:7–8

Solomon perceives that a problem arises when people choose riches over relationships. Perhaps he took a walk and studied the construction crew busily toiling over the temple. He looked off toward the valley and saw workers laboring in the fields even after sundown. He saw them arrive for worship and he looked at their eyes, full of weariness within and dark circles beneath.

These people were working their fingers to the bone, putting in hundreds of extra hours. They weren't having much fun—they simply refused to leave time for it. Many of them, from farmers to bricklayers, were amassing fortunes. Their labors were paying in the way labors pay: financially.

But there is a cost as well as a payout to our work. We all begin with the same number of minutes, and we invest them however we choose. If the bulk of our investment is in work, our relationship portfolio will be very weak. Solomon looked at a particular laborer, "alone, without companion," and said, "He has neither son nor brother."

What a lonely picture. We see images of the unforgettable character of Ebenezer Scrooge, created by Charles Dickens, sitting up by himself on Christmas Eve, eating his soup before a fire small enough for one. All the rich furnishings around him are slowly going to dust and mold, for who is there to share them with? Why polish the windows when no one looks in or out? He was a rich man, but money bought him no friends; in fact, it seemed to do the very opposite.

Do the math and you'll discover that 1 + 0 = 0.

RELATIONSHIPS OVER RICHES

Then Solomon turns to a happier image. It's one of the better-known passages in Ecclesiastes, but have you ever studied it in context? Solomon implores us to keep our relationships first. I'm indebted to Warren Wiersbe, who came up with perfect titles for these truths about friendship, and I've appropriated them in the following four points.[2]

TWO ARE BETTER THAN ONE FOR WORKING

Two are better than one,
Because they have a good reward for their labor.

—ECCLESIASTES 4:9

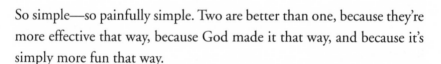

So simple—so painfully simple. Two are better than one, because they're more effective that way, because God made it that way, and because it's simply more fun that way.

Have you ever noticed the strong friendships that blossom over shared labor? A small group from church goes overseas for a mission project, or they build a house for Habitat for Humanity. There is something about the environment of the hammers and the heavy lifting, the mortar and the muscle, that forces us to drop our usual inhibitions and let people really know us. You can know someone for twenty years in an office or a church environment and hardly know him at all. But spend an afternoon of yard-work together and you may become inseparable friends for life.

Work is a sacrament of sweat by which God reconciles us one to another. It works for both sexes, married and single, family and strangers, and across the races. When it comes to labor, "two are better than one."

Two human souls combine their strength, creativity, talent, and ambition. Synergy (the intangible chemistry of working together) takes over. You share the work but you also share a greater reward.

The whole can be greater than the sum of its parts. When you do the math, you find that 1 + 1 adds up to some value greater than two.

Two Are Better Than One for Walking

For if they fall, one will lift up his companion.
But woe to him who is alone when he falls,
For he has no one to help him up.

—Ecclesiastes 4:10

Life is, as Eugene Peterson once put it, "a long, slow obedience in the same direction." It's a marathon, an epic journey. They who walk together, walk farther. The path can get steep and rough, and walking with another brings help should we stumble and fall. I pity the person who has no friends to lean on when life gets hard. Not only does he face the difficulties of life, but he faces the discouragement and loneliness of confronting those challenges alone.

Have you ever noticed that even the Lone Ranger had Tonto? He would have been more honest to call himself the Almost-Lone Ranger. He must have known that a campfire with one can be lonely and depressing, but a campfire with two is lively and fun. That's just the way God made things for us. The modern emphasis on being "independent" and "going one's own way" is not a biblical one. We were made to work, walk, and live together, for God understood that it wasn't good for us to be alone (Genesis 2:18).

Loneliness is a warning light on an inner gauge that confirms we're running short on a primary fuel we require to run efficiently. We were made for relationships. Otherwise, who would want to be married?

Who would want to have an evening out with the guys or the girls? Who would enjoy family reunions or Bible study groups, as opposed to individual study? We crave all these groups because we need each other, and we need each other daily in the same way we need food, water, air, and shelter.

In truth, Solomon shouldn't even have to remind us of such obvious facts of life. But there are many who try to go it alone as much as possible, and it is for these true lone rangers that Solomon makes his point. "Woe to him who is alone when he falls."

Two Are Better Than One for Warmth

Again, if two lie down together, they will keep warm;
But how can one be warm alone?

—Ecclesiastes 4:11

Does your spouse have cold feet?

When we lie down for the night, warmth becomes much more important, because our bodies go into cold storage. We're almost completely sedentary for eight hours. Few calories are being burned, and therefore even in the summertime we need to be covered by some kind of sheet when we sleep. No one likes those cold feet or the chilly floor tile when we walk into the bathroom early in the morning; everyone likes warmth.

And as we all know, two bodies create more heat than one as we sleep. There's something pleasant and secure about having someone sleep beside you.

In Solomon's time, cold was a much more serious issue. When forced to sleep in the open, or even in a tent, the more bodies that huddled together, the warmer all would be. It reminds me of the Australian aboriginal phrase, "a three-dog night," that refers to a freezing cold night in the outback. One requires at least three dogs sleeping around him to ward off the chill.

So Solomon says that two are better than one in staying warm. Love is a warm blanket of affection and affirmation that keeps us safe from life's bitter chills.

Two Are Better Than One for Watchcare

Though one may be overpowered by another,
two can withstand him.
And a threefold cord is not quickly broken.

—Ecclesiastes 4:12

Notice the pattern? Solomon begins his discourse by speaking of one, then two; he ends with three, a number that signifies perfection and holiness. A friend is a treasure; two friends is a treasure-house.

The emphasis here is safety in numbers. One is not only the loneliest number, but the riskiest. Surely that's partially why Jesus sent His disciples out "two by two" to preach the Gospel (Luke 10:1). Imagine those groups of two young men each, spiritually unconfident, walking into strange towns with such a message. The good news was really good but really *new;* they were certain to encounter hostility, and the "buddy system" made sense not only for working and walking together, but for watching out for each other.

And if our own world is so much more civilized, why do we have pepper spray, alert whistles, and personal defense classes? Through the nighttime cityscapes of today, you'll never walk alone—if you have good sense. As Solomon says, however, "a threefold cord is not quickly broken."

We can be attacked physically, but also spiritually, emotionally, or financially. The world is filled with snares, and there is wonderful security in the feeling of community we have. It's heartbreaking to read of people who grow old without the comfort of friends and family. One day the police or a neighbor force open the door to find the lonely old soul passed away several days ago, and there were no loved ones to notice the silence. How any normal person can get by today without a church family, I'll never understand.

The great hymnist Charles Wesley isn't as famous as his brother John, the founder of Methodism; but Charles's hymns are far better known than John's sermons. All over the world, Christians still sing "O, for a Thousand Tongues," "Christ the Lord Is Risen Today," "Hark the Herald Angels Sing," and "Jesus, Lover of My Soul."

Charles wrote hymns day and night, sometimes jumping off his horse to run into nearby houses, shouting, "Pen and ink! Pen and ink!" He reportedly composed 8,989 hymns during his lifetime, an average of ten poetic lines every day for fifty years. He was still writing hymns on his deathbed.

When Charles fell in love, he wrote his love letters in the form of hymns. As he pondered his love for Sally, and as he studied Ecclesiastes 4, he brought the two together in this hymn that began:

> Two are better far than one
> For counsel or for fight;
> How can one be warm alone,
> Or serve his God aright?
> Join we then our hearts and hands,
> Each to love provoke his friend;
> Run the way of his commands
> And keep it to the end
> Woe to him whose spirits droop,
> To Him who falls alone!
> He has none to lift him up,
> To help his weakness on:
> Happier we each other keep,
> We each other's burdens bear;

Never need our footsteps slip,
Upheld by mutual prayer.

Are you struggling to make and keep friends? Are some of your relationships going sour? Don't worry so much about *making* friends; work at *being* a friend. Solomon writes elsewhere: "A man who has friends must himself be friendly"(Proverbs 18:24).

Dale Carnegie observed that we can make more friends in two months of showing interest in others than in two years of trying to get them interested in us. And Andy Rooney has said that good old friends are worth keeping, whether we like them or not!

All that we see around us will pass away, but every person you ever meet is an eternal creature. Treat people with profound love and respect as the fellow citizens of heaven they are, or could become. Guard your friendships as you would guard the world's largest diamond, because you can be certain the least of your friends is infinitely more valuable in the eyes of God than any jewel.

Relationships over Popularity

Better a poor and wise youth than an old and foolish king who will be admonished no more. For he comes out of prison to be king, although he was born poor in his kingdom. I saw all the living who walk under the sun; they were with the second youth who stands in his place. There was no end of all the people over whom he was made king; yet those who come afterward will not rejoice in him. Surely this also is vanity and grasping for the wind."

—Ecclesiastes 4:13–16

Solomon takes one more look at the industrious workers hauling great stones into place as they build the temple. He sees them helping each other instinctively, hardly thinking about it; protecting each other; bolstering each other through the heat and perspiration of the day. He looks at the great edifice being built, then at the little people doing the building. And Solomon suddenly realizes that as great as this temple will be—surely the world's finest and holiest building—it is worth less than the people for whom and by whom it is built, because the God of this temple loves every one of those souls with an everlasting love. And He made it possible for us to love, support, encourage, and protect in the same way.

It's all about people, the older and wearier Solomon reflects in his later years, as he composes Ecclesiastes. *People needing people.* And what is needed from those people is true, sincere love and friendship, not the power that comes through fame or envy. That's the point Solomon drives home in these verses.

Fame is like a lover to avoid: beautiful to the eye, seductive to the spirit, and fickle to the end. Fame is expensive, requiring obsessive pursuit. Once apprehended, its attractions are not only fleeting but profoundly disappointing.

Winning the Super Bowl is the professional dream of every NFL player. It isn't the money they make; the winner's earnings from a Super Bowl appearance amount to less than a full game's check for the average NFL player. It isn't the Vince Lombardi trophy, which they don't get to take home. It's the fame, the respect, that moment of supreme glory.

The players do receive a ring, and the Super Bowl ring is perhaps the most coveted prize in the world of sports—on par with an Olympic gold medal.

But even such a ring may not last. Charlie Waters of the Dallas Cowboys found that out when his *five* Super Bowl rings were stolen from the closet in his home.

Joe Gilliam won two Super Bowl rings as a member of the 1974 and 1975 Pittsburgh Steelers, but he later pawned them for a few dollars after being caught in a vicious cycle of drug addiction and homelessness.

Another former Steeler, Rocky Bleier, sold his four rings to cover divorce and bankruptcy proceedings.

The Cowboys' Thomas Henderson had his Super Bowl XII ring seized to pay back taxes. Former Raiders All-Pro cornerback Lester Hayes sold his to pay for dental work. Mercury Morris of the Miami Dolphins sold his to raise money to clear his name during a drug-trafficking case.

That ring, symbolic of months and years of hard work crowned by a season at the top, is as fleeting as the glory it supposedly stands for. The hype may be spectacular, the TV ratings may be the biggest of the year, the commercial time may cost millions . . . but the glory is fool's gold. Its ephemeral luster is quickly tarnished. As Houston sportswriter Steve Campbell puts it, "One of the dirty secrets about the Super Bowl is that the winner's high often has less of a shelf life than a container of cottage cheese."[3]

With those insights in mind, we take another look at Ecclesiastes 4. We find mysterious references to certain individuals:

A poor but wise youth; which one?

An old and foolish king; hmm, who might that be?

The second youth; dare we venture a guess?

Most authors, as we all know, write what they know (the first law of literature). Naturally, they use their own family experiences, perhaps changing the names or using some other literary subterfuge. I think the shady characters in this passage are members of Solomon's family circle.

For example, he points out that a poor and wise youth is better than an old and foolish king. We quickly think of Saul, the first and ill-fated king of Israel. When Saul was crowned, he had palatial fame and acclaim. His approval ratings soared. For Saul, it was good to be king. He ascended in glory but eventually went down in flames.

That would identify the poor and wise youth for us as David, born a peasant shepherd from a small town, destined to bestride the Old Testament like a Colossus, to build a kingdom, to ensure military supremacy, to write psalms and become a man after God's own heart.

But verse 15 speaks of "a second youth who stands in his place." I believe that young man is David's son, Solomon himself, who replaced his father on the throne. Solomon got off to a fast and promising start as a leader, relying on God's wisdom and his own considerable gifts. He extended the empire for which his father had laid the foundation. People all over the world knew about Solomon and the ascendancy of the children of Israel—once slaves in Egypt, now rulers of the Mediterranean world.

But what does Solomon say about this second youth? "I saw everyone rally to the rule of this young successor to the king. Even so, the excitement died quickly, the throngs of people soon lost interest" (MSG).

Fickle, fleeting fame. Solomon knew that his footprints in the sand of time may be deep at the present, but the tide of history would quickly wash them away. His father had reminisced over the days when he rode through the streets to hear people singing, "Saul has slain his thousands, and David his ten thousands" (1 Samuel 18:7). It was a lovely hit tune if you were David, but if you were Saul it was a funeral dirge.

Saul died and was quickly and happily forgotten in the glory of David's prowess as a military king over Israel. But like his predecessor, David's approval rating couldn't soar forever. The young Solomon had to realize that his newfound glory had bittersweet taste for his aging father.

Now Solomon himself was growing old. He could already hear the people preparing their hearts for a new hero.

Super Bowl rings, Oscars, and chart-topping songs are like the flavor of the month at your local ice-cream parlor. They're smooth, delicious, and they go down easy. But they'll be replaced shortly enough. The apostle Paul would refer to a much better crown than any the world could offer. This was a crown worth striving for, one that can only be applied by nail-scarred hands.

I believe Solomon would have appreciated the wisdom offered in 1 Corinthians 9:25: "And everyone who competes for the prize is temperate in all things. Now they do it to obtain a perishable crown, but we for an imperishable crown." We seek the crown not of supreme fame but supreme faith.

11

A God Who Can't Be Used

ECCLESIASTES 5:1–7

⁓

THERE I SAT, IMMERSED IN THOUGHTS of the ancient king and his quest for meaning. As I worked on this chapter, our community was swept by one of California's largest and most destructive fires ever. Several of our church members lost their homes, and many of the rest—including my own family—were evacuated for safety.

We were beneficiaries of God's severe mercy, as our home was spared. But to this day I take little comfort in that. Again and again, God has allowed my preaching itinerary to overlap with events in the wider world.

After great natural disasters, people walk among the rubble and ask the big questions: *Why did this have to happen? What was the meaning of our years building this home, only to see it literally go up in smoke? What could possibly be God's purpose for all this? Pastor, are you listening? We'd like some answers!*

I turn to my Bible and find that it happens to be opened to Ecclesiastes this week. That's the way I planned it—at least I *thought* it was me. But here is Solomon, walking among the rubble of his own devastated life, asking all the same questions from a distance of three thousand years. Again the point comes home to us: This is a book for all seasons.

Still, we are left with questions that demand good answers.

Solomon has already spent two chapters discussing the emptiness of a life apart from God. Then, in the third chapter, he has admitted that even so, the stubborn questions remain. But Solomon stands boldly on the declaration that God has a plan, and that even when it is cloaked in several layers of mystery, it is a good plan—a trustworthy plan.

Now we come to Ecclesiastes 5 and the rubble around our ankles. This is the site where all that we built once stood: our hopes right here, our dreams in that pile over there. You can still reach your finger down and find wet traces of our blood, our sweat, and our tears. But now all of that has been leveled. It lies in ruins around us, and nothing is left standing but these towering questions—questions too tall for us to see past, even when we stand on tiptoe.

In times like these, life is hard, spirits are low, and faith is hanging by the adhesive on its bandages. God? A no-show. And maybe that's for the best, because what would we say to Him right now, anyway?

DON'T BLAME GOD

Author John Killinger tells about the manager of a minor league baseball team who got so frustrated with his center fielder's performance that he jerked him out of the game and played the position himself. The first hard-hit ball that came to the manager took a bad hop and smashed into his mouth. His next play was a high fly ball that he lost in the sun—until it smacked him in the forehead. The third ball that came his way was a hard line drive that flew between his hands and popped him in the eye.

Furious, he ran off the field to the dugout, grabbed the center fielder by the shirt and shouted, "You've got center field so messed up, even I can't play it!"[1]

God is the subject of more than His share of fingerpointing. As a matter of fact, a seventeen-year-old was accused recently of burning down a church in Nashville, Indiana. At his trial, he explained that he took a cigarette lighter to the nearly century-old building because "I was angry with God."

One woman, having lost both her husband and son in separate accidents, posted a notice on the Internet: "I am ANGRY at God. I am VERY ANGRY!" She dared to say out loud what you and I really feel sometimes.

God understands our anger, and when we pray, it's a good thing to tell Him what we honestly feel. But sustained bitterness toward the Lord who loves us is irrational and unwise.

The *Journal of Health Psychology* recently reported an interesting study. Social psychologist Julie Juola-Exline and her team of researchers found a link between anger toward God, and anxiety and depression. Those who couldn't get beyond their resentment toward God were more likely to experience problems with negative emotions. The good news, according to Juola-Exline, was that "those who were able to forgive God for a specific powerful incident, reported lower levels of anxiety and depression."[2]

"Forgiving God" is a term I'd rather avoid. It implies that God has done something wrong that requires our pardon. We should underline the statement that by the perfection of His nature, He will not and cannot do wrong. What seems like misdeed is mystery. The important thing to remember is that His love and compassion are perfect, unbroken, and forever.

Just the same, it's all too easy to blame God for our losses and sorrows. Here in Ecclesiastes 5:1–2, Solomon gives us some pointed instruction.

Walk Carefully Before Him

Walk prudently when you go to the house of God;
and draw near to hear rather than to give the sacrifice
of fools, for they do not know that they do evil.

—ECCLESIASTES 5:1

Imagine stumbling into the house of God loaded down with a heavy burden. It's the dead weight of all your sorrows. You're certainly bringing them to the right place, but you need to bring them in the right way. When you're overloaded, it's important to watch your step.

We want to lay them carefully at the altar rather than violently at His feet. That is, we need to give Him the burden, but not the blame. There's a difference. That's why we need to tread carefully in the house of the Lord.

Remember that Solomon was the builder of the temple, the most beautiful building on earth in its day. There had never been such a place to bring God and His children together. It was, in a sense, the one place for heaven on earth. The architect understood that such a place should not be entered carelessly or thoughtlessly—particularly not resentfully.

We must decide which side we're on: Do we honor God as the Lord of life, or not? Do we trust Him in the rough times, or only when it's convenient? Our modern expression, "Watch your step!" comes from Solomon's warning: "Walk prudently." Literally, the Hebrew says, "Keep your foot."

You may remember a time when you heard that phrase from your parents. You were angry, and your words were approaching the territory known as *disrespect* when Mom or Dad said, "Watch your step, young man" or "young lady."

Due respect for parents and for God is a sufficiently urgent issue to be enshrined in the Ten Commandments. Life without boundaries is chaos, and when we treat God as if He is not in control and not loving, when we cut Him down to our size through a petty approach, when we wander outside of the boundaries between us, we invite chaos into our lives.

When we come into the house of God, we're to draw near to hear, to understand, to learn, and to worship. We're to cultivate an attitude of reverence, expectation, and a holy sense of resignation to His will.

TALK CAUTIOUSLY TO HIM

Do not be rash with your mouth,
And let not your heart utter anything hastily before God.
For God is in heaven, and you on earth;
Therefore let your words be few.
For a dream comes through much activity,
And a fool's voice is known by his many words.

—ECCLESIASTES 5:2–3

Now that we've walked the walk, we have to talk the talk. We must talk cautiously to Him as well as walk cautiously before Him—always keeping in mind that we are speaking from a basis of ignorance.

I think about the terrible fire that has burned a path through our community. We often don't know how such a blaze begins. An electric storm could send a bolt of lightning. Some disturbed individual could engage in a conscious act of arson. A careless person could innocently start a great fire without realizing it.

What about God? Could He start a fire? *Of course.*

Could He also prevent or suppress one? *Yes.* Could it be that He has done so many times in many places without any human being realizing it? *Yes!* That's something we seldom consider. We see every fire God allows but none that He prevents.

So when we philosophize about His character based upon our limited observations, we speak from ignorance. On a given day, His intervening hand may have prevented some horrendous act of global terrorism—then five minutes later, a single automobile with a drunk driver crashes, and all who knew the victim are giving God a tongue-lashing.

Nothing illustrates this insight more vividly than a widely watched episode of television's *The West Wing* in which the fictional president, Josiah Bartlet (played by Martin Sheen) lashes out at God. Bartlet, battling multiple sclerosis, is anguished over the death of his longtime secretary in a drunk-driving accident. After attending her funeral in the National Cathedral, he waits until everyone leaves, then orders the doors sealed so that he is alone. Standing before the altar, Bartlet, a Roman Catholic in the television series, lashes out at God. "She bought her first car and You hit her with a drunk driver," shouts Bartlet into the cavernous cathedral. "That's supposed to be funny? Have I displeased You, You feckless thug?"

The angry president then launches into a tirade in Latin. Translated, his words are: "Am I really to believe that these are the acts of a loving God? A just God? A wise God? To hell with your punishments!" Then, in a gesture of contempt, the fictional president lights a cigarette and crushes it on the cathedral floor.

The reaction of viewers was predictable. While some were shocked at Bartlet's anger and blasphemous words, others commended him for his expression of brutal honesty and for representing thousands of people in his anger toward God.

Solomon would feel differently. He reminds us that God knows the time and appointed season of every life. He counts the very hairs on your head, and a sparrow doesn't plummet to earth without His awareness. And as Jesus tells us, "You are of more value than many sparrows" (Matthew 10:31). Moreover, God knows every implication of every event: positive, negative, or neutral. We live in the goldfish bowl of time and space, with all the limitations imposed by that habitation. God is outside that bowl entirely, and He sees past, present, future, and all across every inch of His creation simultaneously. We can't wrap our minds around that one any more than a goldfish can understand a map of your county.

Seeing, hearing, knowing, and planning all things, and based upon His own mysterious purposes, God governs the affairs of this planet. There will be a time for intervening and a time to refrain from intervening. To feel angry and frustrated is human; but to chastise God is to make a cosmic spectacle of our own folly in the presence of the Alpha and the Omega, the King of kings who loves us so much that He bears the nail marks in His hands, in the presence of the seraphim and cherubim, and all the heavenly realm.

Solomon counsels us to be men and women of few words, for the mark of a fool is his airy gust of reckless speech. Verse 3 is difficult to translate, but Solomon seems to say that a fool babbles on relentlessly, like a man who has had a busy day and experiences dream after dream all night long. And we do sleep better when we don't dwell on our short-sighted grievances against a loving Father.

Don't Bribe God

When you make a vow to God, do not delay to pay it;
For He has no pleasure in fools.
Pay what you have vowed—
Better not to vow than to vow and not pay.
Do not let your mouth cause your flesh to sin, nor say before the
messenger of God that it was an error. Why should God be angry at your
excuse and destroy the work of your hands? For in the multitude of
dreams and many words there is also vanity. But fear God.

—ECCLESIASTES 5:4–7

As a troubled young man walked through a field in Germany, a terrible electrical storm filled the sky. A lightning bolt struck a nearby tree, and he instantly took it as a sign from God. "Help me!" cried the young man, "and I will become a monk." That sudden vow changed the life of Martin Luther.

Another young man, a disreputable character named John Newton, made a similar promise to God in the middle of a deadly storm at sea. "Help me," he prayed, "and I will change my life." Out of that prayer came a gradual transformation that led Newton into the ministry and made him a world-class hymnist, the author of "Amazing Grace."

There are times when God uses a storm or crisis to awaken us, and we make life-changing vows and commitments to Him. The problem is that most of us are quicker to make a commitment than we are to keep it. We live in an age of halfhearted vows and ill-kept promises. If every single person kept the promises they made to God in a pinch, then Africa and Asia would be swarming with millions of missionaries.

We sometimes call this "foxhole Christianity." It's the ultimate expression of using God. Bargaining with God is an extremely questionable activity, generally one to be avoided. But if you do put yourself on the line, don't even think about not making good, for God is not mocked. What is vowed before Him is *binding,* just as He is bound by His many promises in the Scriptures.

Solomon is teaching us that vows are serious. They are lasting and, in the eyes of God, not subject to "on second thought" revocations.

I love what David says in the Psalms as he thinks about a vow he had made to God. "I will go into Your house with burnt offerings; I will pay You my vows, which my lips have uttered and my mouth has spoken when I was in trouble" (Psalm 66:13–14).

We don't know exactly what kind of trouble David was in, but whatever it was, God apparently got him out of it. And in the process, David made a vow to God. Vows were not uncommon in the Old Testament, nor was breaking them. Otherwise, Solomon wouldn't have warned against it, nor would Jesus have commented on it when bringing a spiritual perspective to what had become pharisaical traditions surrounding the Mosaic Law (Matthew 5:33–37). But David kept the vow he made to God.

Eva J. Alexander was born to believing parents in Chennai, India, and was born again at age twelve during a Billy Graham meeting. In 1963, she married R. D. Alexander, and the two took positions with the government of India. Eva's job exposed her to the plight of women in her country, and she began speaking out about their status and suffering. For a while, she became so socially active that her spiritual life suffered. Politics became more important than her faith.

But the Lord sent a serious illness that brought her to her knees, where she made a solemn vow before the Lord. As she hovered near death in the hospital, she prayed, "God, if You're real, do not allow me to die. I will serve You."

Eva ultimately recovered from her illness. When she returned home, she began reading her Bible again. Two words in Matthew 21:31 tore through her mind like torpedoes, the words *and harlots.* Jesus said, "Tax collectors *and harlots* enter the kingdom of God before you." Our Lord wants to bring *harlots* into His kingdom.

A week later, a nearby pastor told her of a prostitute who had run away from the brothels, and he asked Eva to provide a room for her. "I can't," Eva said. "You keep her." Eva had a husband and four children at home, including two teenage sons. But once again the Lord brought Matthew 21:31 to mind, and Eva relented.

Her family was aghast: "What is this? You're turning our house into a brothel!" But their attitudes soon changed, and they accepted this ministry as coming from God. Other girls began showing up, and the Alexander home became a rehabilitation center. Police officers and prisons referred troubled women to Eva, and today up to fifteen women live in the Alexander home at any one time. The Alexanders provide medical treatment, job training, and a strong gospel witness.

As a result of her vow made to God when she was near death, Eva has started a home for the children of prostitutes. In this home, sixty children—ages twelve months to thirteen years—find refuge. Her husband and children joined her work and, spurred on by that passage in Matthew, they are bringing many harlots into God's kingdom.[3]

We've seen it throughout church history. A promise to God, honored by the one who made it, can lead to a touch of heaven on earth. But a vow in danger of being broken is an idea that should make us shudder with fear. At this moment, when the flames are at the door, a vow comes easily to the lips; but tomorrow, when a cool rain drives calamity from memory, it's too easy to double-cross God. The soul implications could be far worse than the original danger that brought about the vow.

My recommendation? Keep your mouth shut when your back is to the wall, and keep the faith with God. Then keep on keeping on. That's the only vow He's really looking for.

12

Governments Never Change

ECCLESIASTES 5:8–9

N IKITA KHRUSHCHEV stood in a high Kremlin window and glared in the direction of the West, home of democracy and freedom. He shook his fist in defiance and shouted, "We will bury you!"

Another translation of his Russian phrase reads, "We will be present at your funeral." He spoke of a time when Soviets would rule the world, and they would see the last Christian of the last free nation taken to his execution.

Translation aside, his meaning was clear and unambiguous. The Union of Soviet Socialist Republics had reached its zenith. It measured one-sixth of the world's land mass—two and one-half times the size of the United States of America. Its mastery of science and military technology forged ahead of American progress. And on a clear evening in 1957, North Americans stood on their roofs and watched *Sputnik,* the first satellite, take a victory lap around the very planet that some felt would be overrun by Soviet Communism.

Within thirty-five years—little more than a generation—that same proud Communist government lay in ruins, one more casualty of political hubris. What had happened? The demise of the USSR is a complex matter and not to be oversimplified. There were many factors, including a changing world-economic climate. But historians agree that one of the largest contributors to the toppling of Soviet Communism was the incredible personal corruption of government officials. They used their positions, not to serve the nation's starving farmers and factory workers, but to line their own pockets. They exploited the system, nibbling at its foundations until the whole edifice teetered and collapsed from the inside.

Remember, this empire was the shining fruit of an idealistic revolution. It was to be a socialist organism that would prefigure a new world order, according to Lenin and its champions. Production and prosperity would be in, of, and for the working classes. So went the pledges of the insurgents.

But in December of 1991, when Gorbachev signed the papers that dissolved Lenin's dream, all of that was long gone. The ideals-driven government of the worker classes had quickly given way to the most totalitarian of regimes. As we have long observed, today's revolutionaries become tomorrow's bureaucrats—or, as rock philosopher Pete Townsend put it, "Meet the new boss—same as the old boss."

To which Solomon, presiding over his own idealistic regime, would nod vigorously in agreement.

Imperfect Institutions

If you see the oppression of the poor, and the violent perversion of justice and righteousness in a province, do not marvel at the matter, for high official watches over high official, and higher officials are over them. Moreover the profit of the land is for all; even the king is served from the field.

—Ecclesiastes 5:8–9

A timelier passage cannot be imagined—and as we have seen, it is timely for any era. If you poke your nose too far into government, Solomon says, don't be shocked at what you find: graft, injustice, exploitation. The great palace of state always has a termite problem. As *The Message*

words verse 8, "Exploitation filters down from one petty official to another. There's no end to it, and nothing can be done about it."

How's that for a bleak summary of the wheels of state that make the world go round?

The church is imperfect because it is made of flesh and blood, not bricks; it is the same with government. Human institutions always fall prey to corruption, and—because of the presence of wealth and power—governments most of all.

So we must retain a certain realistic level of pessimism. We expect the system to fail occasionally, and we have to wash out the stains every now and then, keeping the laundry of state as pure and clean as possible. Therefore, we cheer on the honest representatives and leaders, and we use the system to uproot those who break the trust. But we cherish no illusions of keeping the machine in perfect repair. This is Solomon's point: creeping corruption cannot be prevented.

In England, the established church persecuted those who identified with Martin Luther's Reformation movement throughout the sixteenth and seventeenth centuries. The "divine right of kings" was the unbiblical doctrine used by monarchs to establish their will as the will of God.

Against such tyrannical rule in the British Isles rose the thunderous voice of John Knox. And from this Scot's inspiration came the writings of Samuel Rutherford. His book, *Lex Rex: or The Law and the Prince* (1644), resulted in his own sentence of death, though he died of natural causes before the sentence was carried out.

Lex Rex stated the biblical view of kings: they and their laws are subject to God and His laws. Everything God is, earthly kings should be: just, righteous, good, merciful, generous . . . everything the established kings of the period were not. Rutherford's treatise was consistent with the New Testament teachings about civil rulers: that they are an extension of the hand of God on earth to carry out His will (Romans 13:1–7; 1 Peter 2:13–17).

With that kind of philosophy, it's easy to see why Rutherford gained the disfavor of kings who asserted their "divine right" to rule.

Unfortunately, the kings of the post-Reformation period in England are not the only government rulers who failed to rule with God's priorities. Even in the United States, the most successful government in the history of the world has had to constantly remind itself of its obligations and responsibilities to the governed.

And long before American, English, or any other governments lost sight of their priorities, rulers in Solomon's day had lost the vision for good government. Solomon says the poor were oppressed, and justice and righteousness were perverted. Corruption followed the trickle-down rule as it flowed through one layer after another of back-scratching rulers.

In the 1980s, there was a succession of benefit concerts held by the "glitterati"—rock stars and film idols concerned about issues such as hunger, disease, famine, or the plight of the farmer. They raised huge sums of money, only to discover that the money too often had to be funneled to the third world through corrupt governments. Instead of serving as humble stewards to the people, officials siphoned off large amounts for personal gain.

We spend a great deal of energy railing about these things, and well we should. Righteous anger is natural, but Solomon tells us it is simply naive to be surprised.

In good times, people look at government as their protector, and in bad times as their savior. The failings of governments are nothing more than the failings of men. Why should we expect government to be any different from other segments of society since all are populated and over-seen by sinners? Anyone who puts his hope in the government is surely bound to be disappointed. That doesn't mean we don't appreciate the righteous things government does. It just means that our ultimate hope for protection and salvation is in a God who never disappoints.

Russian author Alekandr Solzhenitsyn says, "The line dividing good and evil passes not through states, nor between classes, nor between political parties either—but right through every human heart."[2]

The government is nothing but human beings gathered together for a particular purpose. Sometimes they make good decisions, sometimes they don't. In that regard, looking at the government is like looking in a mirror. If you feel the government should be doing a much better job of governing the people, what about the job you are doing governing your life? Are there integrity issues? Health issues? Effective use of time and resources?

The problem is the same with principalities as it is with princes: *sin.* We are foolish to expect the work of government to be any more effective than the lives of its people.

GOD, GRACE, AND GOVERNING

We sometimes forget the wonderful idea of the providence of God. Someone has defined this as "God's hands behind the headlines." A preacher named T. DeWitt Talmage once said, "Despots may plan and armies may march, and the congresses of the nations may seem to think they are adjusting all the affairs of the world, but the mighty men of the earth are only the dust of the chariot wheels of God's providence."[1]

Providence is the belief that God will have His way in the end. He rules over land and sea, and He guides the course of history toward His appointed ends. Benjamin Franklin admitted this when he said, "The longer I live, the more convincing proofs I see of this truth, that God governs in the affairs of men."

King David referred to providence when he wrote, "The kingdom is the LORD's, and He rules over the nations" (Psalm 22:28). Proverbs 8:15–16 says, "By me kings reign, and rulers decree justice. By me princes rule, and nobles, all the judges of the earth."

These are particularly difficult promises for us to claim in these days. We know more about the governments of the world. Secrets are harder to keep. Just the same, the Bible assures us that God is in control. We cannot and should not expect the government to be the highest court of appeal or trust. Every ruler in this world serves at God's pleasure—and so do you in your own position, for that matter. Our God is in control of everything; why should we think His divine authority ends on the Capitol steps?

So our first response to the political and governmental sphere should be to trust in the sovereignty of Almighty God. In doing so, we will sleep much better.

Second, we are to pray for our officials. Paul commands, "Therefore I exhort first of all that supplications, prayers, intercessions, and giving of thanks be made for all men, for kings and all who are in authority, that we may lead a quiet and peaceable life in all godliness and reverence" (1 Timothy 2:1–2). How often do you actually pray for your president, your elected representatives, your governors, mayors, and councilmembers? Pray for them, then take one extra step: write them to encourage them, and let them know you're girding their work with prayer every day. Perhaps if we all did these things, we would begin to see a positive effect on the people who toil to serve us.

INVOLVEMENT AND INSURRECTION

Third, Peter tells us to be good citizens—actually *excellent* citizens: "Therefore submit yourselves to every ordinance of man for the Lord's sake, whether to the king as supreme, or to governors, as to those who are sent by him for the punishment of evildoers and for the praise of those who do good" (1 Peter 2:13–14). We obey our leaders loyally, knowing that in serving them we serve God. An ordinance is a law. Many of us have grown cynical about our laws and our duties toward them. Be an upholder of the law, and a proactive servant of the public good in your community. Get to know your policemen and other public servants. Ask them how you can help.

It's troubling to see Christians withdraw from public discourse. Our influence needs to be present in every event that occurs in this world. Linda Ellerbe wrote:

Civilization is a stream with banks. The stream sometimes is filled with blood from people killing, stealing, shooting, and doing things historians usually record, while on the banks, unnoticed, people build homes, make love, raise children, sing songs, write poetry, and even whittle statues. The story of civilization is the story of what happened on the banks. Historians and journalists are pessimists because they ignore the banks for the river.[2]

Some of that activity on the riverbanks regrettably reminds us of church activity: singing songs, having covered-dish dinners, enjoying our evangelical culture as we build steeples high enough to block our view of the stream. We need to dive in and make our presence known!

Fourth, take a stand for God when the government clearly defies Him. Peter and John were faced with such a choice. The gauntlet was thrown down when the authorities commanded them not to preach the name of Jesus. They replied, "Whether it is right in the sight of God to listen to you more than to God, you judge. For we cannot but speak the things which we have seen and heard" (Acts 4:19–20).

There was a time when Christians looked into the depths of that stream and saw the evils of slavery. In eighteenth-century England, for example, Christian voices were among the few that spoke out against it. Of course, some Christians defended it with passages from the Bible, such as when Paul tells slaves to submit to their masters. But the conviction of the Holy Spirit was giving a different interpretation. Slavery was a disgraceful plight that needed to be addressed. Many believers devoted their lives to combating the outdated institution. They collected data on the mistreatment of the human cattle who were being exploited for the sake of economic growth. These concerned believers began to build a following that raised an outcry. Still, they needed someone in power to take up their cause. They needed a voice within the seat of government.

William Wilberforce became a believer in 1785, five years after his election to Parliament. Interestingly, the work of former slave trader John

Newton was a factor in Wilberforce's conversion. Newton was a man with a burden of guilt; he had piloted vessels filled with groaning, bleeding, dying souls. "Amazing Grace" was the first legacy of Newton's wretchedness; Wilberforce was the second. Under Newton's influence, Wilberforce began to fight in Parliament for the abolition of slavery.

This was no election-year stunt; it was a twenty-year pursuit of a godly vision. The proslavery lobby had terrible clout in the government. At every turn Wilberforce spoke of God's heart against such inhuman exploitation, until Lord Melbourne sniffed, "Things have come to a pretty pass when religion is allowed to invade public life."

The army of Christ won the victory when the slave trade was abolished in 1807.

We are inspired by Wilberforce, who persevered against the Goliath of slavery. We are inspired by Martin Luther King Jr., a martyr to the Goliath of racism. And we realize that Christians must walk the tightrope of respecting government (as both these men clearly did) while working within it to the glory of God. Following their example, we can make a difference. We can weed out the corruption Solomon warned us about and strike a blow for the kingdom of God.

But never, never expect utopia to come to a Capitol near you. Heaven on earth cannot be established at the ballot box, but only through the hearts of men. One day we will see the descent of the New Jerusalem, and there will be at last, one Governor before whom we'll bow, with no more use for intermediaries; one Party to serve, with no more use for debate or dissension; one Lord, one faith, one baptism into the world that has always been our destiny as His divine constituency.

13

Dollars and Sense

ECCLESIASTES 5:10–20

Y OU MIGHT AS WELL ADMIT IT: you've had those fantasies. You can't grow up in this country—or perhaps any country—without having them.

I'm talking about those dreams of unbounded riches. You've visualized winning the lottery, or perhaps having Ed McMahon walk up to your door with the cash prize for the Publisher's Clearinghouse. You've watched those TV shows about the lifestyles of the rich and famous, and you've wondered what it would be like to have just a little of that for yourself.

You've daydreamed about April 15 being just another day, when that tax deadline no longer looms like a predator over your home, of having an army of servants who fix the meals and do the laundry, of cruising up to your mansion in a brand-new luxury car.

We all build castles in the air, but Solomon warns us not to get too carried away. It's all an illusion, he says, no matter how it appears—and today's magazines and TV cameras can make it appear pretty lovely!

Solomon wants us to understand that the deepest desires within us are for heaven, and that they'll never materialize on earth through the paper paradise of wealth.

Wealth underachieves when it comes to bringing happiness, but it overachieves when it comes to bringing misery. It's true now, it was true in old Jerusalem, and it will always be true under the sun.

CNN recently covered a story about a man with stomach pain. The report said, "French doctors were taken aback when they discovered the reason for the patient's sore and swollen belly: He had swallowed around 350 coins: $650 worth."

The sixty-two-year-old man came to the emergency room of Cholet General Hospital in western France, having a history of psychiatric illness. His family warned doctors that he sometimes swallowed coins, and a few had been removed from his stomach in past hospital visits. Still, doctors were astounded by what they saw on the x-ray. There was an enormous opaque mass in the patient's stomach that weighed twelve pounds. It was so heavy that it had forced his stomach down between his hips. Five days after his arrival, doctors cut him open and removed his badly damaged stomach and its contents, but the man died a few days later from complications. Doctors said he was suffering from a rare illness that makes people want to eat money.[1]

But that's simply *insanity.* You and I are nothing like this mentally unhealthy fellow, are we? We'd never become consumers of wealth— well, at least not literally. But what about spiritually?

In the realm of faith, we require a certain kind of nourishment. As the body thirsts for water and the lungs yearn for air, so the soul is hungry for heaven. We feed ourselves through His Word, His presence, His service, and His vision for us—so many good and healthy nutrients. He has set a full table before us, and we need only share the banquet.

Instead, the world seduces us away from His table. It draws our hungry gaze toward its shiny trinkets until we become ravenous consumers of the American Dream. We feed the hunger of the soul with the empty calories of the world, and we end up as bloated and unhealthy as the man in the CNN story. Perhaps the only difference is that this man's price was $650. What is ours?

We are spirits in the material world, ghosts in the machine, as someone has said. We live on earth, but our true home is heaven, and that creates a dissonance in the soul. We will never be at peace until we find the bridge between the two worlds. So we continue to search for the things that really matter in life—for heaven on earth.

So thoroughly have we been hypnotized that no matter how many times we tell ourselves that wealth is *not* contentment, no matter how many times we witness the utter bankruptcy of that myth in real life, no matter how many miserable millionaires walk the earth, and no matter how powerfully our own experience points to the truth—we keep returning to the empty dream, mesmerized by the mirage.

And when life goes wrong, we look first to the financial remedy. Her marriage fails, and she wonders if a bigger house would have made the difference. He faces depression, so he goes out and buys an expensive sports car. They're losing their kids, so they shower them with gifts.

Very simply, *wealth is not the answer.* Don't you think it's significant that this idea permeates the whole Word of God, from Moses to Paul? Isn't God urgently trying to tell us something?

The illusion is powerful, persistent, and deadly. It promises heaven but delivers heartbreak. In this chapter of Ecclesiastes, Solomon offers us five points on finance, then two profound truths about God.

FIVE THINGS WE SHOULD KNOW ABOUT MONEY

1. The More We Have, the More We Want

> *He who loves silver will not be satisfied with silver;*
> *Nor he who loves abundance, with increase.*
> *This also is vanity.*
>
> —ECCLESIASTES 5:10

Look up the richest tycoons in town. Meet them at the country club for a game of golf or tennis; discuss their dreams. I predict you'll discover that they are focused on getting *more.*

You can be the poorest peasant or the richest land baron, yet it seems you'll always want *more*. The more we get, the more we want. The fire is fed but never quenched.

Jesus said, "Take heed and beware of covetousness, for one's life does not consist in the abundance of the things he possesses" (Luke 12:15).

There aren't many "Uncle Bud" Robinsons among us. Robinson, a well-known holiness preacher of an earlier generation, was taken by friends to New York and shown all the sights of the city. That night in his prayers, he said, "Lord, I thank You for letting me see all the sights of New York. And I thank You most of all that I didn't see a thing that I wanted."[2]

Wouldn't it be wonderful to be truly content? To be eased of the burden for more accumulation, and to be at peace with where we are in life? Why do we make ourselves miserable over what has no track record of satisfying?

Part of Paul's incredible power in his ministry comes from this trait: "I have learned in whatever state I am, to be content: I know how to be abased, and I know how to abound. Everywhere and in all things I have learned both to be full and to be hungry, both to abound and to suffer need" (Philippians 4:11–12).

There is wisdom and power in knowing how to be content with much or little.

2. The More We Have, the More We Spend

When goods increase,
They increase who eat them;
So what profit have the owners
Except to see them with their eyes?

—ECCLESIASTES 5:11

The big promotion comes through with its expected raise. We could simply keep the same lifestyle and use the extra money wisely, but in a microsecond we are salivating over the prospect of new cars, new furniture, perhaps a second home. Solomon says that when possessions get thick, so do we. He wants to know, what's the point of having more money? We'll just go out and spend whatever we get.

The Message puts the concept this way: "The more loot you get, the more looters show up."

Author William MacDonald says, "When a man's possessions increase, it seems there's a corresponding increase in the number of parasites who live off him: management consultants, tax advisers, accountants, lawyers, household employees, and sponging relatives."[3]

The more you have, the more you want. The more you want, the more you spend. The more you spend, the more you need. The more you need, the more you have to have. Stop the world—I want to get off!

3. The More We Have, the More We Worry

> *The sleep of a laboring man is sweet,*
> *Whether he eats little or much;*
> *But the abundance of the rich*
> *will not permit him to sleep.*
>
> —ECCLESIASTES 5:12

When the San Diego County fires began approaching our neighborhood, the order came to collect our valuables and evacuate our homes. Driving down the hill from our home, I turned to my wife, Donna, and said, "Do you realize it only took us ten minutes to collect our valuables? Everything else is just 'stuff.'"

When you can fit all your life's valuables in the backseat of your car, you can sleep well at night because you've cut down your "worry field." By God's grace I can say I've never lost a night's sleep over the status of my investments. Many people think that the more money they have, the more soundly they'll sleep at night, but the opposite is true. The more they get, the more they worry about preserving it.

When money is your shield and bulwark, you'll spend all your time worrying about what will happen if you lose your shield. Thankfully, my Shield and Protector is One who has already said, "I will never leave you nor forsake you" (Hebrews 13:5).

When he was fifty-three years old, John D. Rockefeller was the world's only billionaire. His income was one million dollars per week. But he was a sick man who lived on crackers and milk and could not sleep because he worried so much about his money. Eventually, he learned how to give money away, and his health improved radically. As a philanthropist, he lived to celebrate his ninety-eighth birthday.

Elderly couples reminisce about the box of macaroni days in the tiny apartment. They conclude that those may have been the best times in their marriage. The Great Depression was a severe time for people, yet many folks have remembered those same years fondly.

Lack of money flushes us out of self-satisfied isolation. It forces us to go out and meet people and to need some of them. As we grow richer, we draw away from community. We miss a lot of the little graces and relational encounters that make life real and satisfying—and we replace them with trinkets that never live up to their shiny allure.

4. The More We Have, the More We Lose

There is a severe evil which I have seen under the sun:
Riches kept for their owner to his hurt.
But those riches perish through misfortune.

—ECCLESIASTES 5:13–14

Let me be clear on this point, because it's easy to misunderstand what Solomon is saying. The essence of his message is this: You can't lose what you don't have.

We shouldn't avoid seeking things just because we could lose them. But we realize from the very beginning that we are adding one more element to our lives, one more dependency, one more responsibility. Anyone who has ever bought a home for the first time understands that concept. We become attached to our possessions at our own risk because we now have so much more to lose.

5. The More We Have, the More We Leave Behind

> *When he begets a son, there is nothing in his hand.*
> *As he came from his mother's womb, naked shall he return,*
> *To go as he came;*
> *And he shall take nothing from his labor*
> *Which he may carry away in his hand.*
> *And this also is a severe evil—*
> *Just exactly as he came, so shall he go.*
> *And what profit has he who has labored for the wind?*
> *All his days he also eats in darkness,*
> *And he has much sorrow and sickness and anger.*
>
> —ECCLESIASTES 5:14–17

We all know the modern translation of this one: *You can't take it with you.*

It's just common sense. You pay sweat and toil for the things you accumulate. But you never own anything permanently; you only rent it for a season, until you pass from this earth. Your precious possessions, even if they outlast you, will belong to someone else.

The flip side of that coin is positive: Much good has been done by sizeable bequests to charities, Christian ministries, or individuals. Accumulation can work hand in hand with goals for God's kingdom. For now, we only need to remember that in eternal terms, there is no *own*—only *loan*. Jesus reminds us to act wisely, therefore, and invest in the treasures that are indeed permanent, for they are fixed in heaven. "But lay up for yourselves treasures in heaven, where neither moth nor rust destroys and where thieves do not break in and steal. For where your treasure is, there your heart will be also" (Matthew 6:20–21).

One way we find heaven on earth is to make investments in it from earth. And that bank is accessed through what we set our hearts upon.

Two Things You Need to Know About God

Now Solomon turns to insights about God.

1. Our Ability to Earn Money Is a Gift from God

Here is what I have seen: It is good and fitting for one to eat and drink, and to enjoy the good of all his labor in which he toils under the sun all the days of his life which God gives him; for it is his heritage.

—ECCLESIASTES 5:18

It's the American tradition to be a self-made man or woman. The Horatio Alger stories of the late nineteenth century, about impoverished boys who achieved wealth and respect through hard work and virtue, instilled a work ethic in the burgeoning industrial culture of America that has never faded.

We can't say anything negative about hard work or virtue; Scripture promotes personal industry (Proverbs 6:6–11; 2 Thessalonians 3:10). But motives tell the tale, and the American tale lacks a spiritual premise, for there is no such thing as a self-made man or woman. Every person who ever earned a dime did so with a heart, mind, soul, strength, talents, and opportunities supplied by God. And what God gives, God can take away (Job 1:21).

Solomon says you've worked for what you have, so go ahead and enjoy it. "Knock yourself out," he would say in modern terms. "You've got it coming to you." But remember that every gift is from God, and those gifts are not ends in themselves but reminders of His goodness. He gives us things for the same reason you buy birthday presents for your children. It makes them smile. God, too, enjoys our pleasure—which increases exponentially when we see His gifts for what they are; maintain hearts of humility, contentment, and gratitude; and thank and praise Him daily as the source of all that is good in life.

2. Our Ability to Enjoy Money Is a Gift from God

As for every man to whom God has given riches and wealth, and given him power to eat of it, to receive his heritage and rejoice in his labor—this is the gift of God. For he will not dwell unduly on the days of his life, because God keeps him busy with the joy of his heart.

—ECCLESIASTES 5:19–20

God gives us not only the gift, but also the ability to enjoy it, the food and the mouth to eat it, the art and the mind to appreciate it, the beautiful earth and the feet to run upon it. Every component of life, down to the smallest molecule, is part of His gift. But we cannot enjoy any gift properly without reference to the Giver.

As I prepared to preach this particular chapter of Ecclesiastes, God offered me a living illustration in the fires that our community endured.

Material things that people had spent a lifetime accumulating were consumed in mere moments. People came through it well if their hearts were set on the Giver rather than the gifts. Those people knew that what went up in smoke was little more than smoke to begin with. Life itself is a vapor that lingers a moment before evaporating (James 4:14). But for those whose hearts were set on their material possessions, the devastation of the loss was terrible indeed.

We have mentioned John D. Rockefeller, who learned the life-giving therapy of generosity before it was too late. In a 1905 interview, he said:

> God gave me money. I believe the power to make money is a gift from God . . . to be developed and used to the best of our ability for the good of mankind. Having been endowed with the gift I possess, I believe it is my duty to make money and still more money and to use the money I make for the good of my fellow man according to the dictates of my conscience.[4]

God is a loving and generous Father, but He doesn't want our things to possess *us*. What a joy to learn the lesson Rockefeller learned: money and possessions are not evil as long as they don't enslave us. Instead of destroying lives, wealth can serve the kingdom of God. Every good and perfect gift comes from God and has a good and perfect use. As long as we can find it and honor it, we honor Him. And we are one step closer to heaven on earth, rather than one foot deeper into the golden mirage of a fool's paradise.

14

Money Without Meaning

ECCLESIASTES 6:1–6

W HAT HAPPENS AFTER "HAPPILY EVER AFTER?" Where do you go after your dream comes true? Three lottery winners had the chance to find out.

Carl D. Atwood of Elwood, Indiana, appeared on the Indianapolis TV show called *The Hoosier Millionaire.* They gave him the good news, and he was ecstatic. "I'm very thankful," the seventy-three-year-old told viewers. "I must admit that I never expected to be leaving the show with this amount of money. Now I can purchase a very nice car."

Hours later, Atwood took a walk to the same grocery store where he bought the winning ticket. He was struck by a truck and killed.[1]

A winning lottery ticket brought Rosa Grayson of Washington four hundred dollars a week for life. Now she hides in her apartment and suffers nervous disorders. "People are so mean," she said. "I hope you win the lottery and see what happens to you."[2]

Then there was Jack Whittaker, winner of the richest undivided lottery jackpot in U.S. history: $314.9 million. The West Virginia construction contractor, already owner of a multimillion-dollar business, took the lump-sum, after-tax payout of $113 million in December 2002.

Whittaker's fondest wish was to help the people of his home state. He, his wife, and his daughter held a press conference on national television where he announced he would give a tithe of his winnings to his church and start a foundation to help the poor of West Virginia.

That's when reality came crashing in. Floods of letters and visitors to the door of his office and home have yet to subside. Thousands of pleas for help, enough to fill file cabinets lining three walls in the conference room of Whittaker's new office, still arrive in the mail every day.

Security guards watch his house and office around the clock, and visitors from all over the country bring their hard-luck stories. Most of them have to be met and handled at the front door of their home by Whittaker's wife, Jewel.

Jewel says she's going to write a book on how to handle the limelight, to help others whose lives will likely be changed from sudden financial fortune. His granddaughter, sixteen-year-old Brandi, has lost almost all her friends. "They want her for her money," says Whittaker. "She's the most bitter sixteen-year-old I know. She doesn't communicate with anybody but me. I'm working on it, though."

There have been some positive results of his win. Jack's expanded his business, spent about $14 million on charity work, and established the Jack Whittaker Foundation to help West Virginians find jobs, buy food, and get an education. The three-employee foundation had to hire private investigators to check out approximately half of the nine hundred families helped so far. He has also donated more than $7 million to three of his denominations' pastors.

The one goal he hoped the lottery would allow him to reach has not happened: spending more time with his family. Whittaker, who worked fourteen-hour days before winning the lottery, is now busier than ever. "I was hoping I could start taking naps in the afternoon," he said. "But that hasn't happened yet."[3]

One study claims that instant millionaires have about the same level of happiness as accident victims. Story after story can be cited of people whose newfound fame and fortune have made them more miserable than when they were just average citizens. Some people manage to keep heart and home together, but their stories are few and far between. Yet people still line up at convenience stores and gas stations across the nation to put down their money for a chance at unhappiness.

If we were to hold a convention of lottery winners, I have a hunch they would agree with Solomon's five truths from the last chapter:

1. The more we have, the more we want. (Ecclesiastes 5:10)

2. The more we have, the more we spend. (5:11)

3. The more we have, the more we worry. (5:12)

4. The more we have, the more we lose. (5:13–14)

5. The more we have, the more we leave behind. (5:14–17)

I would hope those lottery winners would agree that it is God who gives us our ability to earn money (5:18) and to enjoy money (5:19–20). We think we're talking about something very material, but actually it's all about God. Without reference to Him, money cannot be enjoyed.

Ecclesiastes 6 shows the results of violating that principle. Without Him, there can be no meaning, joy, or answers. Wealth in itself is not evil; wealth apart from God is another thing entirely.

Solomon's Insights

There is an evil which I have seen under the sun, and it is common among men: A man to whom God has given riches and wealth and honor, so that he lacks nothing for himself of all he desires; yet God does not give him power to eat of it, but a foreigner consumes it. This is vanity, and it is an evil affliction.

—Ecclesiastes 6:1–2

Ecclesiastes, we are again reminded, is a kind of veiled memoir. Solomon's conclusions about the world are colored by his own fortunes and misfortunes. It isn't surprising that wealth becomes an important subject in this book.

Running the numbers on Solomon's net worth is a chore of some complexity, but we know he was the wealthiest man alive. And we know how he acquired his fortune. When he was twenty, the Lord appeared to him as he worshiped and invited him to ask anything he desired. Solomon asked for wisdom, and God was pleased.

> Then God said to Solomon: "Because this was in your heart, and you have not asked riches or wealth or honor or the life of your enemies, nor have you asked long life—but have asked wisdom and knowledge for yourself, that you may judge My people over whom I have made you king—wisdom and knowledge are granted to you; and I will give you riches and wealth and honor, such as none of the kings have had who were before you, nor shall any after you have the like." (2 Chronicles 1:11–12)

It is characteristic of God to give us more than we ask. He knows we possess neither the wisdom nor the boldness to ask what we should of Him. Our little minds cannot fathom all that He longs to bestow upon us, so He always gives us more than we request. He blesses us "exceedingly abundantly above all that we ask or think, according to the power that works in us" (Ephesians 3:20). Our cups overflow, and goodness and mercy follow us all the days of our lives.

Solomon asked God for wisdom and got it—but so much more came along with the blessing: wealth, success, power, fame. With God in His rightful place at the center, the young king and his empire flourished as never before. He built the temple in Jerusalem, a place for God to dwell in the midst of His people. He developed trade and commerce initiatives that had an economic trickle-down effect throughout the land as money flowed into and out of Israel. Solomon was a kind of King Midas for Israel; everything he touched turned to gold.

But even blessings from God come wrapped in the trials and temptations by which He develops our character. Like the rest of us, Solomon had to conquer his own appetites to attain the godliness his Lord wanted for him. But he began to fail these tests.

He established relationships with neighboring pagan countries. As part of that diplomatic process, he took wives from these countries—something he had been specifically warned by God not to do (1 Kings 11:1–8). These foreign women brought their idolatrous worship into Solomon's life. Tragically, the king's spiritual center, God Himself, gradually was moved more and more to the sideline of his life. "For it was so, when Solomon was old, that his wives turned his heart after other gods; and his heart was not loyal to the LORD his God" (1 Kings 11:4).

Solomon began to compromise his commitment. He went so far as to build centers of worship for his wives' idols on a hill overlooking Jerusalem.

As Solomon later looked back over his life, he wrote about his own frustration of trying to find meaning in life through money and godless marriages. It reminds me of a poignant sentence by Jerry White in his little book *The Power of Commitment:* "Christians have never worn the clothes of affluence well."[4]

The same Solomon who wrote, "As for every man to whom God has given riches and wealth, and given him power to eat of it, to receive his heritage and rejoice in his labor—this is the gift of God" (Ecclesiastes 5:19), later rejected God's banquet table of provision and decided instead to go out for fast food.

As Solomon began to lean on his financial wealth to the exclusion of his spiritual wealth, his life and his national empire quaked. He permitted and abetted idolatry, introducing a deadly virus into the kingdom of which God had made him shepherd. It would take four centuries for that virus to run its course.

David began as a shepherd and had to learn to be king; Solomon began as a king and had to learn to be a shepherd. Allowing other gods was tantamount to letting in wolves among his sheep.

Author Warren Wiersbe summarizes the lesson we should learn from this failure:

> To enjoy the gifts without the Giver is idolatry, and this can never satisfy the human heart. Enjoyment without God is merely entertainment, and it doesn't satisfy. But enjoyment with God is enrichment and it brings true joy and satisfaction.[5]

SOLOMON'S ILLUSTRATIONS

If a man begets a hundred children and lives many years, so that the days of his years are many, but his soul is not satisfied with goodness, or indeed he has no burial, I say that a stillborn child is better than he—for it comes in vanity and departs in darkness, and its name is covered with darkness. Though it has not seen the sun or known anything, this has more rest than that man, even if he lives a thousand years twice—but has not seen goodness. Do not all go to one place?

—ECCLESIASTES 6:3–6

Solomon uses two illustrations to drive home his point about the vanity of money and pleasure apart from God.

First, he offers us the eye-opening comparison of a stillborn child and a two-thousand-year-old man who fathers one hundred children. One enjoys the full rich feast of life and comes back for about twenty-five second helpings; the other doesn't quite make it to the table.

Solomon exaggerates to make his point. The longest life span recorded in Scripture is Methuselah's, and he lived to be "only" 969 years old (Genesis 5:27). Imagine the man who lives more than twice that long, to be two thousand years old, and has a hundred children in the process? I know of no one who has fathered one hundred children, though Solomon's own son Rehoboam came close. According to 2 Chronicles 11:21, Rehoboam had eighteen wives and sixty concubines, and he fathered twenty-eight sons and sixty daughters!

In the Old Testament, a Jewish family was considered blessed by God if the patriarch lived long and had lots of children (Psalm 92:14; 127:3–5). Solomon's point here is obvious: you could live twice as long as anyone else and have more children than anyone else—but if God is not involved, it's all worthless.

Notice that Solomon afforded his fictional geriatric no burial. For a Jewish person to have no burial was a sign of disrespect and dishonor. Jeremiah 22 tells about a king named Jehoiakim who was not given a burial, which illustrated how disrespected he was by the people. Solomon's fictional character lived a long time and had lots of children. But in the end, his family didn't want anything to do with him; and when he died, they didn't even give him a funeral.

King Solomon now travels to the other end of the spectrum, using a stillborn baby as his illustration. According to Solomon, such a child never sees the light of day, never experiences the disappointment the rich man has known. The stillborn baby knows only the bright shadow of time, while the other greets twenty centuries.

We all want long lives. But imagine for a moment twenty centuries of loneliness, twenty centuries of never finding what really counts in life. We want heaven on earth, but that would come close to the equivalent of hell. It's like the story of a man who is granted the gift of immortality only to be apprehended for some crime and locked up for life in prison. What value would eternal life be in a tiny cell?

As I wrestled with this text, I told Donna that this might be the hardest passage in the book of Ecclesiastes. But with Scripture, the strongest boxes bear the richest treasures. This one yields a profound point: life without God and without meaning is worse than never having been born at all.

On the other hand, life *with* God is deeply satisfying, whether one has little or much. It's not the years in life but the life in the years. Only

God can give us the wisdom to know what to do with what we have. As Jesus says:

> Don't hoard treasure down here where it gets eaten by moths and corroded by rust or—worse!—stolen by burglars. . . . It's obvious, isn't it? The place where your treasure is, is the place you will most want to be, and end up being. . . . You can't worship two gods at once. Loving one god, you'll end up hating the other. Adoration of one feeds contempt for the other. You can't worship God and Money both." (Matthew 6:19, 21, 24 MSG)

I have talked with more than a few individuals who have a lot more money than I will ever see in this life. Many of them discuss wealth as a great burden. Jesus once talked about those who hear the Word of God but become distracted by wealth, as Solomon did. "Now he who received seed among the thorns," said Jesus, "is he who hears the word, and the cares of this world and the deceitfulness of riches choke the word, and he becomes unfruitful" (Matthew 13:22).

My friend Adrian Rogers tells of a man who loved gold. When he inherited a fortune, he decided to redecorate his bedroom to reflect his first love. He hung gold parchment wallpaper, highlighted by yellow curtains, a golden rug, and a yellow bedspread. He even bought some yellow pajamas. But then he got sick and came down with yellow jaundice. He died because when the doctor came to treat him, no one could find him!

A lighthearted illustration, but the sad truth is that many great people have disappeared into their wealth. They have built railroads and restaurant chains, mills and malls, empires of every variety. But instead of ruling over those empires, they woke up one day to find themselves in shackles. J. C. Penney, having built a flourishing business, became filled with despair, checked himself into a hospital, and waited to die. No doctor could do a thing for him.

One evening, the certainty of impending death flooded across

Penney's troubled soul. He was writing farewell notes to his wife and his loved ones when he heard the singing of nurses in a chapel down the hall. "No matter what may be the test," they sang, "God will take care of you."

To Penney these were the voices of white-clad angels. Something was suddenly born within his soul: an absolute assurance that the old faith was true—that he was completely in the loving hands of Jesus, and need fear no more.

J. C. Penney climbed out of his bed immediately—fully cured physically, emotionally, and spiritually. He was a brand-new creation. He left the hospital immediately, rebuilt his sagging business empire to unprecedented heights, and served God magnificently all his days. We need not disappear into the golden quicksand of our wealth, as Solomon did, and as countless other lost souls have done.[6]

That quicksand is a valley of lost souls. It is among the most treacherous tests we face on the trail to finding what counts in life. But we can get through it as long as we cling to the knowledge that whatever the test, God will take care of us. Then, when we get beyond that golden trap, we will see the true cities of gold on the horizon—the heaven on earth we have longed for. We will see the eternal wealth of a life ruled over by the God who gives us the ability to earn, to enjoy, and to finally, quite happily, lay it all at His feet for His use.

That's a life of richness beyond imagining.

15

Employment Without Enjoyment
ECCLESIASTES 6:7–9

STAN COLLYMORE'S DREAM CAME TRUE. Not only did he want to make it as a world-class soccer player, but he signed the most lucrative contract in British soccer history. His fans called him "Stan the Man," and he was powering forward to peak career performance.

Then something unexpected happened. England was rocked with reports of strange, public sexual antics on the part of "Stan the Man," who abruptly checked into a clinic to be treated for depression. He told reporters:

> I remember one day sitting in the bath feeling empty inside. It was as if my energy levels had gone from 100 percent to flat battery overnight. I lost all interest in my appearance, and my self-esteem was low. There was this terrible void and emptiness inside. I couldn't even cry.[1]

"Stan the Man" had a clear field before him, but he instead encountered a pit of quicksand, not far from the deathtrap of wealth without God. He discovered the hazard of work as the meaning of life.

Work is not, in fact, our greatest adventure, and most of us are okay with that proposition—particularly when we're burned out on the job, or lazy, or simply not up to giving our very best to the task. It seems like

143

a good time to say, "Solomon tells us that work is vanity, and that's good enough for me. My boss is not God, so why give Him my all?"

Not so fast, my friend. Solomon isn't critical of work in itself. The world wouldn't be much of a place to live in if everyone started calling in sick a couple of times a week because they just didn't care. Would you like to use the services of a surgeon who felt that way? Would you trust your financial investments to a stockbroker whose mind is on his next ski trip?

I find genuine joy in my job, and I hope you do too—whether you're a governor or a garbage collector. We stand with Solomon to assert that work is one more gracious gift from God. Work makes life compelling. It teaches us about ourselves. It gives us the pleasure of fruitfulness. But if you approach your job as the reason for being here, you'll come to one more dead end.

Jobs are earthly, and joy is heavenly. A job is not what really matters in life, but it offers a number of clues to what does. It's not the whole picture, but one more jigsaw-puzzle piece that fits into the vast panorama we are developing of heaven on earth.

According to Solomon, here are three reasons your job cannot supply ultimate joy in this life.

YOUR JOB CAN'T SATISFY YOUR SOUL

All the labor of man is for his mouth,
And yet the soul is not satisfied.

—ECCLESIASTES 6:7

Solomon tells us that work is about food for the stomach rather than the soul. Who could say it any better? Your work is based in the tangible world—the world of material things—and it pays in that same coin. You receive money, which translates to food, shelter, clothing, and other material needs. In itself, your work does not pay in the currency of heart fulfillment, nor is there any exchange rate between the two worlds.

I have many friends who work hard, grueling weeks. They put in sixty hours, barreling right on through evenings and weekends. Occasionally I talk to a friend about church, and he tells me, "I'm really in over my ears with the job right now. This is a crucial time in my career, and I can't really stop for worship or Bible study."

Five years later, I talk to him again and discover it's *still* a crucial time in his career. He's five years older, five years wearier, not noticeably happier, but he's given his all to that company. And is the company grateful? Actually, I find that often my friend isn't even working for the same company; that one chewed him up and spit him out a few months back, and now it's a crucial time with this new one.

On and on goes the cycle until my friend might look and sound like Solomon: tired, cynical, and possibly deeply angry about a life that somewhere took the wrong turn.

We can and should work hard, and all of us do at times. But don't miss the caution flag Solomon is waving here. Trade those minutes and hours of your life carefully, for they repay you in the coin of the realm, which does not satisfy the hunger of the soul.

God is the ultimate worker. "We are His workmanship, created in Christ Jesus for good works, which God prepared beforehand that we should walk in them" (Ephesians 2:10). That means we are wired to work in the manner He previously arranged.

We recently had our grandson, David Todd, at our house. My wife had purchased a computer toy for David to play with when he came to visit us. It worked through our television and it was a pretty cool little game. As I was about to leave for my office, Donna stopped me. "I can't get this thing to work," she said. "Can you help me with it?"

After a few moments' inspection, I said, "Honey, I don't think this thing has any batteries in it. It's not heavy enough." I got the Phillips screwdriver, removed the top, and sure enough, it needed four batteries. It was in perfect working order and it looked like it would be a lot of fun, but it wouldn't work without the batteries.

As I came to my office to finish my study on this passage in Ecclesiastes, I couldn't help thinking that's the way life is for us. We're complicated, impressive, and made for a specific purpose. But we don't "work" because there is no power source deep inside. We are empty shells without the battery of the Holy Spirit's power.

Men in particular must take heed. We are made to find our meaning in work, but we had better have the right kind of voltage powering us.

YOUR MIND CAN'T REPLACE YOUR HEART

For what more has the wise man than the fool?
What does the poor man have,
Who knows how to walk before the living?

—ECCLESIASTES 6:8

A wise man with the greatest education in the world has no ultimate advantage over a fool when God is absent from his life. On the day when we all stand before God, He is not going to ask to see anyone's diploma. He's not going to inquire about the number and source of academic degrees. He's not going to ask about IQ, SAT or GRE scores, or bank balances. All He's going to ask about is our hearts.

The problem is that our work begins by requiring our strength. We do it during the best hours of our day, and we find that we need to be rested and at our physical best. Then we find that our work requires our minds, if we are going to do better at it. We're soon mulling over challenges and problems, even when we are away from work. We begin to come up with some solutions, and we become emotionally involved in the work before us. It has taken a piece of the heart. And finally, when we are completely sold out to the world of nine to five, we discover that our work has required our very souls.

But Jesus says the number one commandment includes loving God with all your heart, soul, mind, and strength (Luke 10:27). Work, in short, becomes another idol that displaces (and displeases) God.

Forty miles south of downtown London is a tiny village named Piltdown. One day in 1908, a lawyer named Charles Dawson, a member of the prestigious British Geological Society, claimed to have discovered an ancient skull. More bones were soon discovered, and suddenly the world had "proof" of Darwin's theory of evolution: Piltdown Man. The scientific literature that came out about Piltdown Man was enormous, with more than five hundred doctoral dissertations written about the discovery. School children were shown pictures of what Piltdown Man looked like and where he fit into the evolutionary chain.

Sir Arthur Keith, one of the world's greatest anatomists, wrote more about Piltdown Man than anyone else. His works include the widely acclaimed book *The Antiquity of Man,* based on the Piltdown discoveries. He had based a lifetime of work on his faith, and he was fascinated by the Piltdown development.

Sir Arthur was a frail eighty-six years old when Kenneth Oakley and Joseph Weiner paid a sad visit to his home. They were breaking the news that after a half-century of study, Piltdown Man was a hoax, nothing more than an old human skull, the jawbone of an orangutan, and a dog's tooth.

For forty years, the brilliant scientist had trusted in a fraud.

> Keith was a rationalist and a profound opponent of the Christian faith. Yet in his autobiography he tells of attending evangelistic meetings in Edinburgh and Aberdeen, seeing students make a public profession of faith in Jesus Christ, and often feeling "on the verge of conversion." He rejected the gospel, because he felt that the Genesis account of Creation was just a myth and that the Bible was merely a human book. It causes profound sadness to know that this great man rejected

Jesus Christ, whose resurrection validated everything He said and did, only to put his faith in what proved to be a phony fossil.[2]

The Bible warns about those who think they are wise but are really fools (Romans 1:22). While a good education is desirable, it's not as important as a heart that knows God through Jesus Christ our Lord. The Bible says, "The fear of the LORD is the beginning of knowledge" (Proverbs 1:7). Your mind cannot replace your heart.

YOUR DREAMS CAN'T REPLACE REALITY

Better is the sight of the eyes than the wandering of desire. This also is vanity and grasping for the wind.

—ECCLESIASTES 6:9

Solomon is comparing the vanity of living in a fantasy world with the wisdom of living in the real world. Proverbs 28:19 says, "He who works his land will have abundant food, but the one who chases fantasies will have his fill of poverty" (NIV). There is nothing wrong with dreaming and vision-casting. But if we live in a fantasy world, we live in a world that will likely never come to pass. Too many people say, "We'll take the children there when . . ." or "We'll start saving for retirement when . . ." and the "when" is always tied to something big that is "just around the corner." People who are continually talking about the future never seem to get around to enjoying the present.

If your career is the determining factor in your life—you're constantly waiting for the next raise, the next promotion, the next assignment, the next transfer—then you are living with the "wandering of desire." Keep your dreams and goals, but stop and smell the roses! Today is the day the Lord has made, and you ought to stop and rejoice in it (Psalm 118:24).

Solomon is saying something over and over again in Ecclesiastes: between now and the time you go to heaven, enjoy what God has given you. Don't be so caught up in earning money and building a career that you don't have time to enjoy your life. What happens if you take a "surprise day off" for your family? You'll be one more day behind on the job, but think of the memories you'll make with your wife, kids, or grandkids. Twenty years from now, which will matter more? One touches godly relationships with heavenly companions; the other is simply another acre plowed, another clock punched, another day, another dollar.

Perhaps Solomon gained some insight on these issues by thinking about his father, David, the king of Israel before Solomon. David's Psalm 16 so captures the spirit of what Solomon is advising that I am going to reproduce it in its entirety here, in this paraphrase of *The Message:*

> Keep me safe, O God,
> I've run for dear life to you.
> I say to God, "Be my Lord!"
> Without you, nothing makes sense.
> And these God-chosen lives all around—
> what splendid friends they make!
> Don't just go shopping for a god.
> Gods are not for sale.
> I swear I'll never treat god-names
> like brand-names.
> My choice is you, God, first and only.
> And now I find I'm your choice!
> You set me up with a house and yard.
> And then you made me your heir!
> The wise counsel God gives when I'm awake
> is confirmed by my sleeping heart.
> Day and night I'll stick with God;
> I've got a good thing going and I'm not letting go.
> I'm happy from the inside out,

and from the outside in, I'm firmly formed.
You canceled my ticket to hell—
that's not my destination!
Now you've got my feet on the life path,
all radiant from the shining of your face.
Ever since you took my hand,
I'm on the right way.

People talk about "mission statements" these days. I can't think of a better one than Psalm 16. Try adopting it as your personal creed for your lifework.

George Young was a carpenter. He and his wife were dedicated to following the Lord wherever He led. "He does the leading," they often said, "and we do the following." God led the Youngs to the rural Midwest, and they traveled from church to church in revival efforts. Their finances were always tight, but "through the many years we never went hungry!" as Mrs. Young said years later. "Oh, sometimes we didn't have too much of this world's goods, but . . . we always had so much of Jesus."

Finally they saved enough to buy a small piece of land on which George built a cottage. Though humble, it was the fulfillment of a life's dream, and when they moved in they dedicated the house to God and sang the Doxology. But some time later, when the Youngs were away on a ministry trip, a thug who had been offended by George's preaching set the house afire. Returning home, the Youngs found a heap of ashes. All their worldly goods and cherished possessions were gone.

As George gazed at the ruins, he recounted the precious possessions fire could never destroy—his family, his relationship with Christ, his ministry, his eternal home. There and then, the words of a hymn began forming in his mind. Within a few days, he had written all three stanzas of the great hymn "God Leads His Dear Children Along." The chorus says:

Some thro' the waters, some thro' the flood
Some thro' the fire, but all thro' the blood.

Some thro' great sorrow, but God gives a song
In the night season and all the day long.[3]

Years later, music publisher Dr. Harold Lillenas decided to track down George's widow. Driving to the small Kansas town where she resided, he stopped for directions and was alarmed to hear that Mrs. Young was living in the rundown county poorhouse. Lillenas was deeply troubled that the widow of the author of such a hymn about God's guidance should spend her final days in the poorhouse.

Mrs. Young only smiled and said,

> One day God took my sweet husband home. Oh, how I missed him, for we had always served the Lord together. In my heart I wondered, where will God lead me now? Dr. Lillenas, God led me here! I'm so glad He did, for you know, about every month someone comes into this place to spend the rest of their days, and Dr. Lillenas, so many of them don't know my Jesus. I'm having the time of my life introducing them to Jesus! Dr. Lillenas, isn't it wonderful how God leads?[4]

Some people are so caught up with their jobs, careers, and acquisitions that their song is, "God, leave me alone!" But others keep Christ in the center of their lives, and they sing, "God leads me along."

Which song are you singing?

16

Solomon Answers Your Questions

ECCLESIASTES 6:10–12

⁓

T IME OUT! You and I have handled some big ideas in the last couple of chapters, haven't we? Heavyweight contenders for the battle of the soul, a great load of issues in a small number of pages. We've plunged deep into our study, and it's time to come up for air.

We talked about the place of money in your life. I don't know anyone who wouldn't consider that a central matter to be confronted on a daily basis.

Then we discussed the place of your work. Whoever you are, CEO or CPA, student or homemaker, your work is at the very core of your life experience.

And above all, we've taken on one towering monolith of an issue: the matter of God's role in your life. That's the biggest one of all, the great sea into which all the little rivers of your life expressions flow.

This book is a thirty-one-day study, but at times it's like touring Europe in a week—"If it's Tuesday, this must be Belgium." We have a wonderful and thought-provoking book by Solomon, but I want to be certain we're making the most of it. Are you still there? Have you absorbed all that Solomon is saying? How is all this coming across to you, and what changes are being forged in the way you see the purpose of your life?

Readers will come to these pages from many different points on the spiritual compass. Some of you have grown wise in the seasons of life. You nod in recognition of these truths and could probably add a few insights of your own to every chapter in the book.

Others come from a direction of ongoing struggle. You, too, recognize the frustration and the disappointment of dead-end pathways. But at this juncture of life, you're stuck. You've come to one of the many walls that define the geography of living.

Or perhaps you're just one of those many who are found somewhere in-between. For you it's fairly smooth sailing through the voyage of life right now. You have a few instruments on the boat that need adjustments. But for the most part, your ship is moving full speed ahead, on course for a destination you feel good about.

Where do you fit? What particular life issues do you bring to this book? I believe that there are many key moments in life: whenever the sermon begins, whenever you read the first page of a book, whenever you find yourself in a thoughtful conversation about life with a trusted friend. I don't believe these moments are random and coincidental, but that in some important way they are divine appointments, potential crossroad moments.

God is speaking to us all the time, and He will use whatever megaphone catches our attention. His wisest children have figured that out, and they are always discerning what He is trying to tell them in those instances of inspiration.

That's why I firmly believe that your reading of this book, like many of your other experiences, represents a "message moment" for you. What you come away with will depend upon what you're willing to take seriously about this moment.

For example, what does God want you to see about the search for heaven on earth? What key life decisions can you make because of the insights the Holy Spirit is even now implanting in your heart? Are you countering the enemy's distractions, knowing he'd rather you look the other way than think seriously? Do you feel him trying to "fiddle with the remote control" of your attention span, put other thoughts in your mind, convince you this is, after all, just another book, no different than a good novel?

Okay, that's a lot of questions! I'll stop right there. But I hope you'll stop right here, too, and reflect a bit on what is happening in your life between God, His Word, this book, and your future. I would predict that if you are facing some of the serious issues about your life and your values, you will find yourself encountering some personal turmoil. You could be saying, "My approach to God needs to change" or, "I've been making wealth the center of my life."

The still, small voice will be guiding you toward the life that God has always wanted for you: the embracing of what really matters in your life. But another part of you will argue, will come up with objections, will question whether this is just another wild-goose chase, will roll its eyes and say, "What does Solomon know about anything?"

Solomon has anticipated the kind of arguments we might have. And as we come to the middle of our book, he offers us four reasons that competing arguments about the purpose of life will fail. These are not four separate arguments, but four ways to approach one bedrock truth. If you hold up a spectrum to the sunlight, you'll see that all the colors come together to make what we call light. Solomon is going to offer us four colors that form one core argument: *your life without God is meaningless.*

This is your time to take stock of your own life as Solomon nails down the great theme of his book, and what should be the theme of life on earth for you and me.

God Has Ordained Life As He Desires It to Be

Whatever one is, he has been named already,
For it is known that he is man.

—Ecclesiastes 6:10

The *New English Translation* is right on target: "Whatever has happened was foreordained, and what happens to man was also foreknown" (Ecclesiastes 6:10).

In the last chapter we talked about the soccer player "Stan the Man." He went wrong when he began to think he was the Man; what he discovered was that he was only "Stan, *a* Man"—just another man created by God to do greater things than simply play good soccer. "For it is known that *he is man*," says Solomon. And God planned how life will be for a man—and for a woman.

Success and riches won't satisfy us because God didn't design us to be satisfied that way. He made horses for galloping gracefully, He made eagles for soaring spectacularly, and He made us purely for himself, as His special companions. When we try to live some other way, we're like horses trying to fly or eagles trying to gallop.

He made us creatures who enjoy work because He enjoys it. He made us as creatures who enjoy gathering wealth because He owns the cattle on a thousand hills. But He didn't make us to *exist* for these things—only to recognize Him more clearly through them.

Solomon says this is simply the way God planned it, from the foundation of eternity. It's useless to try living outside of the parameters He created for us.

Arguing with God Is an Exercise in Futility

And he cannot contend with Him who is mightier than he.

—Ecclesiastes 6:10

So you've come to the middle of this book, and you find yourself facing a far greater commitment to God than you're prepared to offer. You begin to argue with Solomon, but he cuts you off in midsentence. "I don't make the rules," he says. "I just work here."

You scratch your head. "I thought you were king."

"Yeah, well, not *the* King," says Solomon. "*A* king—same deal as Stan the Man." Solomon points upstairs. "Your argument is with *God.*"

And that quiets you down, because you realize the obvious: arguing with God is an exercise in futility.

> But indeed, O man, who are you to reply against God? Will the thing formed say to him who formed it, "Why have you made me like this?" Does not the potter have power over the clay, from the same lump to make one vessel for honor and another for dishonor? (Romans 9:20–21)

Job had the same conversation with God one day. Even when facing the devastation of his entire life, as Job did, he was in no position to argue with God. There are no circumstances in which the clay gets the last word over the sculptor. Many characters in the Bible argued with God, from Abraham to Jonah. God was always willing to talk it over, but He made the decisions. He is the Lord, and His vision and justice and providence are perfect. The right approach is to discover the plan of God and live it out; it is arrogance of a cosmic intensity to try to change the plan.

God Is Willing to Bring Meaning to Life

Since there are many things that increase vanity,
How is man the better? For who knows what is good for man in life,
all the days of his vain life which he passes like a shadow?

—Ecclesiastes 6:11–12

Solomon asks a simple question. Any child could answer it. He says, "There are so many ways to completely foul up my life. Who has the best idea about what will actually work?"

Any child could answer it, but only the wisest will follow it. The fact is that deep down, we each think we have better ideas. We wait for the really big decisions in life to ask God's opinion, and then only after we've weighed all the options ourselves.

Parents know what it's like to watch a child struggle to make life a success. We, the veteran life-livers, know a lot of the answers. When they are tested, we can't help but try to pass them the answers. "Honey, popularity is not the highest priority in junior high school," we say. Or, "Son, don't make your college decision based on where your girlfriend goes. Down the road you may wish you had looked at the bigger issues."

To which our kids may well roll their eyes and say, "Sure, Pop," or "Whatever you say, Mom." And we wish they would trust us just a little more, the way they did when they were younger. Hey, we're not on a power trip, trying to run anyone's life. We love our children. We want them to be happy, and when they stumble we often hurt more than they do.

That's just the way God looks at us. We think we're pretty sharp and that we already have the answers. And God patiently keeps speaking to us through His Word, through His Spirit, through our believing friends, wishing we would trust Him just a little bit more than we do.

The secret of life is not some exotic puzzle to work out. It is right there in front of our noses, just as the Promised Land was for the Israelites— only a couple of weeks' walk in their case. Heaven on earth is near, but the problem is not the lack of a treasure map. It's our disobedience.

GOD ALONE IS IN CHARGE OF THE FUTURE

Who can tell a man what will happen after him under the sun?

—ECCLESIASTES 6:12

Who knows the future?

Americans went through a time of fascination with horoscopes—the ones printed in the daily newspaper on the comic page. People generally took them no more seriously than the comic strips themselves, but these columns paved the way for astrology and other New Age philosophies for divining the future.

Now it seems the pendulum has swung back the other way toward a more cynical view of the future—a fatalism that says, "Whatever will be, will be." For people who embrace the postmodern view that life has no controlling theme or story, the future is a game of chance. The idea that today is all that matters is a repackaging of the existentialism of the 1950s.

The Bible has a great deal to say about the future. First and foremost, it says that God is in control of the future and has already determined what it will be. The best way to be ready for the future is to stick close to God. He's the One in charge of it. Solomon says that trying to figure out the future for oneself is an exercise in vanity: "Nor can anyone tell [a man] what the future will hold for him on earth" (Ecclesiastes 6:12 NET). For that reason, arguing with Him will change nothing.

Solomon's points in these verses are logical and clear:

- God created all of us to find meaning a certain way.
- Ultimate meaning is not found in money or in vocation.
- Ultimate meaning is found only in God.
- To argue with God about this arrangement is an exercise in futility.

I have already described the impact of the San Diego County fires on my neighborhood, including some who are members of our church. My friend Lee and his family were in our church when I first came. They have given themselves in service to the Lord for years. They're known and loved throughout our congregation, and they lived near the church.

While our church and college campuses survived, Lee's home was totally consumed. I talked to Lee shortly after the fire, and he told me he only had time to dash into his home and grab three books related to his job, his Bible, and a daily devotional book he was reading. Everything else was lost. Lee was alone when the house went up in flames because his wife was in Virginia visiting their daughter, a cancer patient. When he told me about placing the phone call to his wife, it took my breath away.

This couple, fighting to save their daughter from cancer, lost their house and all their worldly goods to a wildfire. He said, "Pastor, you know, my wife and I have talked about what's happened to us in these last days. God has been wonderful to us. We've experienced very few difficult times in life. For some reason that we don't understand, He has trusted us with some trouble right now. We know He's going to be with us in the midst of it and help us through it. So we're just honoring Him through this time and trusting Him for everything that we need."

As I listened to the voice of this humble, godly man, I knew his family was going to come through the furnace of life. They were like Daniel's three friends who were in conversation with an angel as the flames should have broiled them. Lee and his wife, because they stick closely to God, were ready when the future came.

We don't know what the future holds, but we do know who holds the future—and that is enough. It ends every argument or objection we can pose. And coming to the end of all the questions, we can only bow before the One with all the answers.

Praise God, for knowing Him is better than knowing the answers.

17

The Joy of Misery

ECCLESIASTES 7:1–4

WHILE WE'RE HERE AT THE MIDDLE OF THE BOOK, halfway through our search for heaven on earth, it seems like a good time for a midterm exam.

Don't worry. No grades will be sent out, and it's a short test. No trick questions. No essays or multiple choices. No pressure. Just five simple true/false statements for you to consider:

T or F—I like laughter better than crying.

T or F—I like weddings better than funerals.

T or F—I like thinking of my birthday better than my dying day.

T or F—I like compliments better than criticisms.

T or F—I like shortcuts better than the long way around.

T or F—I like the good old days better than the way things are now.

If you marked *true* on any or all of those statements, Solomon would flunk you. If he were giving the test, all these questions would be answered *false*. That is, he prefers crying, funerals, death reflections, criticism, the harder way, and the bad old days.

You may be asking yourself, what kind of man is this Solomon? Is he a glutton for punishment? But as we read Ecclesiastes 7:1–10, we begin to catch on. Solomon teaches us the lessons most teachers would avoid. This is the TV infomercial you're not likely to come across late at night: "The Joy of Misery."

The key word in Ecclesiastes 7:1–10 is *better.* It was also the key word in your test. The Lord shows us that some of the medicine that tastes the worst has the best cure. In these verses, Solomon is going to goad us into thinking outside the box.

The first thing he tells us is that sorrow is better than laughter. No kidding—*literally.*

Funerals Are Better Than Festivals

A good name is better than precious ointment,
And the day of death than the day of one's birth.

—Ecclesiastes 7:1

Okay, you had decided this is an odd chapter. But now you feel like throwing the book against the wall. *Death, better than birth? Come on.*

Just humor me for a moment (even if sorrow is better).

It's not that Solomon is buying into the philosophy of despair. If that were true, he wouldn't tell us eight times in this book to enjoy life. I've underlined those passages in my Bible; it's clear that Solomon—and the Lord—are in favor of joyful and abundant living.

In his book of Proverbs, I counted at least thirty verses emphasizing the goodness of enjoying life. A few examples:

A merry heart makes a cheerful countenance, but by sorrow of the heart the spirit is broken. (Proverbs 15:13)

All the days of the afflicted are evil, but he who is of a merry heart has a continual feast. (Proverbs 15:15)

A merry heart does good, like medicine, but a broken spirit dries the bones. (Proverbs 17:22)

Solomon liked to have a good laugh, just like you and I do. So what's all this about preferring funerals? Warren Wiersbe has said that laughter is medicine for a broken heart, but sorrow is a hearty meal for the soul.[1]

There are two phrases in verse 1, and the first explains the second: "A good name is better than precious ointment, and the day of death than the day of one's birth."

This was originally written in the Hebrew language, and Hebrew scholars tell us something interesting about this verse. The word "name" in Hebrew is *shem,* and the word "ointment" in Hebrew is *shemen.* So Solomon is saying a *shem* is better than a *shemen.* He gets a Hebrew reader's attention with a play on words.

There are two days in our lives when our name is prominent: the day we receive our name at birth, and the day our name appears in the obituary column. What happens between those two determines whether our name is a lovely ointment (a *shemen)* or a foul stench.

The late Bill Bright, founder and president of Campus Crusade for Christ, International, told about growing up in Oklahoma in the 1920s and '30s watching his father and grandfather conduct business affairs with other men. It was all done on a handshake (which is almost unheard of today) because of his grandfather's reputation in the area. He didn't realize exactly how respected his grandfather's name and word really were until years later.

In 1948, Bill was driving from California to Oklahoma to marry his sweetheart, Vonette Zachary. As he passed through Okmulgee, Oklahoma, where his grandfather had lived for many years, he remembered that he had forgotten to purchase gifts for several members of the wedding party. Stopping at a jewelry store, he asked if he could make a purchase with an out-of-state check and was told no, that it was against store policy.

As he turned to leave, the owner asked him, "Do you know anyone in Okmulgee?" thinking someone might be able to vouch for his honesty.

"No, I don't," Bill replied. "My grandfather used to live here, but he died a few years ago."

"Who was your grandfather?" the store owner asked.

"Sam Bright."

"Are you Sam Bright's grandson?" the store owner asked, his face lighting up as he approached Bill. "Why, Sam Bright was the most honorable man I have ever known! If you're anything like your grandfather, I'll sell you anything in the store—and I'll gladly take your check."[2]

As a result of looking back to his grandfather's honorable life and standing on the name he had established in his community, Bill Bright was able to accomplish what he needed to do. That's an example of what Solomon means when he says, "A good name is better than precious ointment, and the day of death than the day of one's birth."

Notice the way we mark a person's life span. We'll write a person's name, and below it we'll put something like this: 1934–2003. We list the year of birth and the year of death. Between the two is what? *A dash.*

Solomon might agree that this life is a quick dash between birth and death—just a vapor. All we'll ever do on earth, all the influence we'll ever garner, all the reputation we'll ever build is summarized in a simple line between one year and another. It's not much time to serve God, but plenty of time for making a huge mess of things.

Solomon was suggesting that if you die with a good name, you can no longer do anything to tarnish it. But on the day of your birth, you have an entire life before you yet unwritten. In that respect, if you have a good reputation, the day of your death is better than the day of your birth. Looking back on a life well lived is better than looking forward to a life unlived. Ending a good life is better than beginning an unknown life.

MOURNING IS A BETTER TEACHER THAN FEASTING

Better to go to the house of mourning
Than to go to the house of feasting,

164

For that is the end of all men;
And the living will take it to heart.
Sorrow is better than laughter,
For by a sad countenance the heart is made better.
The heart of the wise is in the house of mourning,
But the heart of fools is in the house of mirth.

—ECCLESIASTES 7:2–4

Solomon doesn't want you to spend daily time thinking about your death. What he wants us to see is that wisdom is forged in the fires of mourning, trouble, and disappointment. Fools with a frivolous, carefree attitude don't learn from the experiences of life. When wise men and women face adversity like death, disease, and destruction, they learn fresh lessons from God, they take the lessons to heart, and they become better instead of bitter. It is a choice.

This has been one of the deepest secrets of the greatest saints. Listen to this passage from the founder of the China Inland Mission, Hudson Taylor:

> The great enemy is always ready with his oft-repeated suggestion, "All things are against me." But, oh, how false the word! The cold, and even the hunger, the watchings and sleeplessness of nights of danger, and the feelings at times of utter isolation and helplessness, were well and wisely chosen, and tenderly and lovingly meted out. What circumstances could have rendered the Word of God sweeter, and the presence of God so real, and the help of God so precious.[3]

Have you ever had a day where you missed every green traffic light, spilled your coffee on your best jacket, saw your baseball team lose in the ninth inning, and generally seemed to be living out an audition for poster child for Murphy's Law? You grumble, "Everything is against me! It's all set up to make my life miserable!" Taylor is saying it's precisely the opposite. God desires to lovingly use every inconvenience, every bad day, every trial, to make us stronger and wiser and closer to Him.

There's an old clipping from the devotional magazine *Our Daily Bread* that illustrates this in a practical way. During World War II, a man in Sussex, England, sent some money to the Scripture Gift Mission. He enclosed a letter saying that he longed to give more, but the harvest on his farm had been very disappointing because of a lack of water. He was also fearful because German bombs were being dropped in the area, and his family and farm were at risk. He asked the workers of Scripture Gift Mission to pray that no bombs would fall on his land.

Mr. Ashley Baker wrote back from the mission and said that while he didn't feel led to pray that exact prayer, he had prayed that God's will for their lives would prevail. Shortly after, a huge German missile crashed down on the farm. None of the man's family or livestock were harmed, but the bombshell went so far into the ground that it liberated a submerged stream. The stream yielded enough water to irrigate the man's farm as well as neighboring farms. The next year, due to a bountiful harvest, the man was able to send a large offering to the mission.[4]

Sometimes even bombs are blessings. They fall from heaven, make a lot of noise, and liberate something wonderful within us—streams of living water that refresh us and draw us closer to Christ.

Of course, we never seek the bombs or the burdens. We like festivals—parties. The truth is that no one grows wiser who lives the party life. The year in your life when everything goes well is the year you'll gain the *least* maturity. As someone says, if we learn from our mistakes, we ought to be Ph.D.'s by now. We should also be all the wiser in our faith.

I can speak by experience. The richest and most probing time in my life as an adult has been these last ten years when cancer has been a part of my vocabulary. I never sought it, I never welcomed it, but I've never doubted the blessings that God has indeed showered upon me through it.

There are things I simply could never have learned with an unmitigated, unbridled, uninterrupted success pattern in my life.

That's why God isn't as concerned about our being momentarily happy as He is about our being mature. We wonder why He doesn't seem to answer the prayer by the side of the road, when the tire is flat, or why He is silent during this or that crisis. God seems cruel and unfeeling at those moments, but the truth is that even though He hurts for us, He knows that if He protected us from every inconvenience we would never cease being infants. There must be rain, and there must even be a few tornados and wildfires. Such is the university of life.

We are beginning to see the light. The highest purpose of life is *not* happiness. But as we take the blows that life brings us on the way home from the festival, as we suffer the unpitying rain that falls on the just as well as the unjust, as we keep right on moving down the road toward heaven on earth, often not happy at all—*miserable* is more like it—we begin to see the light in the distance. We begin to realize that, when we reach that final destination, *then* we will be paid richly in the coin of happiness. We will realize that, until now, we never knew what happiness was—and never could have enjoyed it so richly now without the sorrow that was preparing our hearts all along the path.

18

The Pleasure of Rebuke

ECCLESIASTES 7:5–6

M ARK TWAIN SAID, "I can live for two months on a good compliment." And it's probably true. But he could have gotten more out of those two months on a good criticism.

Do you agree?

I'm just like you. I get a lot more pleasure from people telling me the things I want to hear. After a church service, I appreciate people who tell me the sermon was absolutely perfect—the jokes funny, the quotes compelling, the Scripture selection powerful, and the stories inspiring. Music to my ears. Just once I'd like to preach such a good one that the deacons carry me out of the sanctuary on their shoulders, cheering!

But then there's that one fellow who says, "You may have slam-dunked your first outline point, Pastor, but you had to rush the next three. And I noticed how you slipped your final outline point into the closing prayer."

Ouch. Now I'm *still* thinking they'll carry me out of the sanctuary— but *without* the cheering.

Nobody loves a critic. But let's get beyond the feel-good factor. Life isn't always about feeling good. That second fellow has given me food for thought. It may not taste like ice cream, but it's probably good for me. And later on, after my bruised ego recovers, I'll find that advice not only humbling but helpful.

I'm starting to realize that rebukes are really compliments turned inside out, designed to mold and mature us in wonderful ways. Conrad Hilton established one of the greatest hotel chains on earth. In his autobiography, he tells of a time early in his career when he was practicing his public speaking, preparing to address an issue before the New Mexico state legislature. His mother walked in and listened politely, and when he finished he asked for her opinion.

"Very good for poetry. But you'll have to unlearn all this," she said bluntly, referring to his oratorical flourishes and dramatic gestures. "Connie," she continued, seeing his deflated expression, "all those trimmings are sinful. You are hiding yourself behind a lot of gestures. If you're afraid to be you, Son, you're throwing dust in God's face. He made you. If you have confidence in Him, you'll relax and be just what you are. You'd do better to pray about it than practice this."

It was a little disheartening to him at first, but by accepting her rebuke he became an influential man and a polished speaker who delighted audiences around the world.[1]

Yes, the critics can be cruel. Some advisors make the medicine taste as sour as possible, and it's true that any fool can give advice. We think of Lucy, Charlie Brown's crabby friend who has advice for everyone—often dispensed for five cents at a neighborhood psychiatric booth. But she also plays left field on the baseball team. In one of the late cartoonist Charles Schulz's strips, Lucy makes a visit to the pitcher's mound and rakes Charlie Brown over the coals, telling him his fastball is slow, his curveball is straight, and his change-up is a letdown. In conclusion, she yells, "Why don't you win one for a change?" and returns to her position. The batter hits the next pitch in the air, right to Lucy—who makes no attempt to catch it. When Charlie Brown asks her why she let it drop, she replies, "I work strictly in an advisory capacity."

But we're not here to talk about the Lucys of the world. You and I both know that caring people also work in an advisory capacity: spouses, associates, good friends. Most of us are sharp enough to sort out the malicious jabs from the wise guidance.

THE REBUKE OF THE WISE

It is better to hear the rebuke of the wise
Than for a man to hear the song of fools.
For like the crackling of thorns under a pot,
So is the laughter of the fool.
This also is vanity.

—ECCLESIASTES 7:5–6

Gordon MacDonald, in his book *Ordering Your Private World,* tells how he was corrected by one of his seminary professors—a mild rebuke that changed his life. He had prepared a paper on a controversial moral issue and was to read it to a special gathering of students and faculty. In order to finish the paper, he cut two of his regular classes during the day prior to the meeting that night. After the meeting, the professor in charge of one of the classes he had cut approached him and said, "Gordon, the paper you read tonight was a good one, but it wasn't a great one. Would you like to know why?"

Suspecting that "yes" would be painful, he nevertheless said he would.

Poking his finger into Gordon's chest, the professor said, "The paper wasn't a great one because you sacrificed the routine to write it."

Here is what Gordon MacDonald said about the rebuke:

> In pain I learned one of the most important lessons I ever needed to learn. Because my time as a Christian leader is generally my own to use as I please, it would be very easy to avoid routine, unspectacular duties, and give myself only to the exciting things that come along. But most of life is lived in the routine, and [my professor] was right: The man or woman who learns to make peace with routine responsibilities and obligations will make the greatest contributions in the long run.[2]

The specific lesson was a good one, but what counts here is his first sentence: In pain I learned one of the most important lessons I ever needed to learn. Do you think MacDonald would agree with Solomon that it is better to hear the rebuke of the wise than the song of fools? Based on his own testimony, I think he would.

Solomon likens the meaningless praise and laughter of fools to "the crackling of thorns under a pot." This was a culturally relevant comparison that we don't readily understand. Branches of a thorn bush thrown on a fire, will flame up with rapid intensity providing a short, hot burn. If you needed to heat up something quickly instead of preparing a fire for slow cooking, you would throw thorn branches on the fire. Solomon uses this illustration to say that the praise of fools is quick, hot, showy—but gone quickly. It flames up, dies out, and you need something else to stoke the fire. The rebuke of a wise man, however, can change your life forever.

Receiving rebuke and correction is a major theme in the writings of Solomon, especially in Proverbs, no doubt because it goes against human nature. Left to our own devices, we're not very teachable. It often takes us the awkward struggle of the teenage years to learn how to handle criticism—and some of us never do, even then.

We'd rather hear from the fan club. We like the schmoozing, stroking, and back-patting of those who have some motive to keep us propped. (At some point we need to ask what that motive is.) But take a look at Solomon's advice about the value of receiving correction and the folly of rejecting it:

> He who keeps instruction is in the way of life, but he who refuses correction goes astray. (Proverbs 10:17)

> Whoever loves instruction loves knowledge, but he who hates correction is stupid. (Proverbs 12:1)

> A fool despises his father's instruction, but he who receives correction is prudent. (Proverbs 15:5)

Rebuke is more effective for a wise man than a hundred blows on a fool. (Proverbs 17:10)

Like an earring of gold and an ornament of fine gold is a wise rebuker to an obedient ear. (Proverbs 25:12)

Open rebuke is better than love carefully concealed. (Proverbs 27:5)

He who is often rebuked, and hardens his neck, will suddenly be destroyed, and that without remedy. (Proverbs 29:1)

The rod and rebuke give wisdom, but a child left to himself brings shame to his mother. (Proverbs 29:15)

Famous New York Yankee Mickey Mantle tells how as a teenager playing in the minor leagues, he began playing poorly. Growing discouraged, he gave in to homesickness and self-pity, and tearfully called his father to come and take him home. But when Charles Mantle arrived, he didn't give the expected sympathy and reassurance. Instead, he looked at his son and said, "Okay, if that's all the guts you've got, you might as well come home with me right now and work in the mines."

It was a stinging slap in the face, but the young man got the message, stuck it out, and went on to make baseball history.[3]

Have you made it known to people who care about you that they are free to share a word of advice, correction, or even rebuke with you when necessary? You don't need to paint a big target on the front of your shirt, with "Hit me with your best shot" printed in the center. You also don't need to put on the false humility act when you know you've done a good job—people see right through it.

Instead, just be humble. Be open. And at the right time, tell your spouse, co-worker or friend that his or her feedback is valuable to you. Make it known that you're always interested in getting better at what you do, whether it's marriage, parenting, vocation, or hobby. The moment you open that particular door, a number of wonderful things will come through. For example:

You'll receive invaluable advice that God gives us through others.

You'll improve your relationship with the person whose advice you've invited.

You'll combat pride and enhance humility.

Don't be enamored with the praise of people who don't really care about you. Be more interested in the rebuke of a wise person who really loves you. Listen carefully to that person's instruction.

Test Yourself for Pride

The late J. Oswald Sanders wrote biblical books packed with remarkable insight and common sense. In one of them he said, "Pride is a sin of whose presence its victim is least conscious. There are, however, three tests by means of which it can soon be discovered." He went on to suggest these three tests:

The Test of Procedure: How do we react when another is selected for an assignment we expected, or the office we coveted? When another is promoted and we are overlooked? When another outshines us in gifts and accomplishments?

The Test of Sincerity: In our moments of honest self-criticism, we will say many things about ourselves and really mean them. But how do we feel when others, especially our rivals, say exactly the same things about us?

The Test of Criticism: Does criticism arouse hostility and resentment in our hearts, and cause us to fly into immediate self-justification?[4]

174

Find a friend and trust him enough to tell you when you're doing something wrong. Be humble enough to listen to the advice of your husband, wife, or parents. The next time your boss makes a suggestion, don't react defensively. Listen with a quiet prayer for wisdom and pass the "test of criticism," for the Bible tells us that rebuke is better than praise.

When he was a young pastor, Gordon MacDonald was walking down the street with a missionary friend one day when Gordon made a derogatory comment about a mutual acquaintance. The missionary immediately rebuked him with these words: "Gordon, a man of God would not say such a thing about another person."

Writing about the experience in his book *Restoring Your Spiritual Passion,* MacDonald said:

> The rebuke stung, and I lived with its pain for many days afterward. But I will always be thankful for that rebuke, painful as it was, because I hear those words every time I am about to embarrass myself with a needless comment about another person. That was a rebuke that forced me to grow. . . .
>
> Looking back, I realize that rebukes were and still are among my greatest learning moments. They set me free from things that otherwise would have destroyed my spiritual passion. They spotlighted things that were hurting me badly but that I did not understand. So I am thankful to my wife and other special friends who play the position of rebuker. I understand the proverb that says, "In the end, people appreciate frankness more than flattery." (Proverbs 28:23 TLB)[5]

Finally, if defensiveness is a problem for you, that's an issue you need to hash out with God. Some people are overly sensitive. This could come from basic insecurity or an amplified need to be admired and accepted. Some of us fly off the handle when someone criticizes us.

What happens then? Once you've snapped at someone, he or she will conclude that it doesn't pay to share certain things with you. We need to remember that for people like friends and spouses, it's more wretched to give than to receive. They know they're risking your displeasure, and possibly the relationship, by giving you unwelcomed words.

Think of the husband who will not tolerate his wife's guidance. She takes a verbal lashing every time she tries, until she stops trying. One little crack opens in the foundation of that marriage, and for every occasion when the wife grits her teeth rather than make a needed observation, the crack widens.

Or what about the account representative who has an anxiety attack whenever the boss calls her in for a performance rating? It's very unlikely she'll receive any promotions.

Not only *can* we afford to listen to advice—we *must*. Surround yourself with good people who will help you, advise you, guide you, and hold you accountable. Your life will be like a river fed by many streams. Such a river grows broader and stronger, pounding its way through rugged territory, rushing along joyfully on its way to the vast sea.

But the person who shuts off criticism is like a river fed by no streams. That one moves along neither broadening nor picking up momentum. As it hits the higher, more rugged territories, it slows to a trickle, until it finds its journey's end in some stagnant lake.

One of the glories of life is the sharing of gifts, talents, insight, love, and burdens through the community of faith. To shut ourselves off from that is a great tragedy. But as we join together with that loving assembly, the Bible tells us that something supernatural occurs. We become the very body of Christ, head to toe. We care for the things He cares about. We share in His mind, His wisdom, even His power. Then and only then, with hands joined in mutual support across the spectrum of other seekers, do we begin to see heaven on the horizon.

19

The Hard Way Made Easy

ECCLESIASTES 7:7–9

RECENTLY I SET OUT TO DRIVE to our college's basketball game at a nearby school when I happened to remember a shortcut someone had told me about, a route around the California freeways. Being in no mood for traffic, I turned down side streets and back roads. Before long I realized it was a shortcut to nowhere. After wandering around for a couple of hours in a maze of detours, bypaths, cul-de-sacs, and bridle paths, I finally arrived back home with every nerve on edge.

Have you ever taken a "shortcut" and discovered it took twice as long to get somewhere? The message of Ecclesiastes 7:7–9 is that the hard way is better than the easy way. We get what we pay for, and we reap what we sow.

Isn't that what we tell our kids? Study hard. Practice, practice, practice. Work, work, work. Keep at it. Don't give up. Don't take the easy way out. There aren't any shortcuts to success. That's the constant refrain of parents, coaches, and teachers.

THE HARD WAY IS AN INVESTMENT

Surely oppression destroys a wise man's reason,
And a bribe debases the heart.
The end of a thing is better than its beginning;

The patient in spirit is better than the proud in spirit.
Do not hasten in your spirit to be angry,
For anger rests in the bosom of fools.

—ECCLESIASTES 7:7–9

Notice how Solomon makes his point. Verse 7 says, "Surely oppression destroys a wise man's reason, and a bribe debases the heart." A bribe is nothing but a shortcut dressed in green. It's using money or some other asset to get your way without earning it. It will corrupt your integrity and destroy the purity of your heart.

One man climbs a mountain. He struggles up the path, taking frequent stops to catch his breath before continuing the slow trek to the top. He reaches the crest just as his friend steps off a helicopter. Which man enjoys the view most? The one from the helicopter says, "It's a nice view, but probably not worth the price of a 'copter ride."

His friend looks at him for a moment and says, "It's the most beautiful view I've ever seen. Every aching muscle in my body makes it look that much better."

And it's true. The hard way is an investment. If you personally work to upgrade your home, rather than hiring workers, you invest what real-estate agents call "sweat equity" in that house. The financial value increases, but not nearly as much as your sense of pride in the home. You've earned it. You've owned the betterment process. And in some cases, you may have done a better job than hired workers, because this was your own home and you cared that much more. Yes, the hard way is better. As Robert Frost said, "The best way out is always through."[1]

Imagine Jesus in the wilderness, on the very periphery of His ministry and mission to the world. There, in the most vulnerable possible zone of his life, the devil made his approach. He gave Jesus his three best pitches, and what were they? Shortcuts all.

"If you want food, just turn these stones into bread."

"If you want fame, just leap from this temple, into the arms of angels."

"If you want followers, just bow down to me."

The devil knew exactly where Jesus was going, but he suggested the wrong ways to get there.

Yes, Jesus wanted food, but He needed fasting, not fast food.

Yes, Jesus wanted fame, but through the way of the cross, not ways that were crass.

Yes, Jesus wanted followers, but through victory over sin, not by giving sin the victory.

The testing of Jesus was all about convenience versus commitment. He refused "wonder bread" for himself, but offered it to a crowd of five thousand. He refused to make an impressive spectacle at the temple, then made a shocking spectacle at the temple. He refused to accept the kingdoms of the world by bowing down to Satan, but bowed down to death so that the kingdoms of heaven and earth would bow at His name (Philippians 2:9–10).

Perhaps it came easier for someone who was the Son of God. Never think that. There was a night when Jesus prayed and wept in the Garden of Gethsemane, asking God if there might be some other way. He actually perspired in blood, which modern doctors have recognized as a legitimate symptom of profound anxiety. In the end, Jesus acknowledged that God's will was the only way, even when it was the hard way—the way of the cross. And because Jesus took the hard way, He opened heaven to those on earth.

GOD'S WAY IS THE HIGH ROAD

There is a saying "Let the devil take the high road." But in fact, the devil takes the shortcut, and wants us to do the same. He knows that if we can be persuaded to take the easy way, we have shortchanged ourselves. We have sold ourselves out in the name of convenience and opened the door to selling out everything else that is meaningful.

When you're in school, the easy way is to cheat on the big test. It's all about the grade and graduation and getting on with life, and who's going to know?

When you're in business, the easy way is to cut some corners, turn in the phony expense report, give the customer a little less than he contracted for. It's a jungle out there, and who's going to know?

When you're married, the easy way is to give in to that extramarital flirtation and have a little fling. It's all about animal drives, and who can help it? Besides, who's going to know?

And when you're a parent, the easy way is to buy your kids televisions and computers and toys rather than to spend a lot of time with them. They've never turned down the gifts, right? And what difference could it make?

Then you come to a time in life when you realize you have no moral compass. There is no inner strength, no marital closeness or family solidarity. You made the journey, took the shortcuts, and this is where they led. Who knew? *You*—and your Lord.

Solomon says the hard way is, in the end, the happy way. He says that it's better to make the right decision *now* and to be patient in spirit than to be proud. God's way may be the hard way, but it's always the high road, and if we will simply wait on Him it will lead us to higher places in life.

This thought is continued in the next verse: "The end of a thing is better than its beginning." It's true over and over in life. When you learned to ride a bicycle, the beginning was nothing but hard spills on the road and skinned knees and hurt pride. But once you got the hang of it, the end was worlds better than the beginning.

Your first year in high school—what was that like? Low man or woman on the totem pole, new standards, tougher teachers. But by the time you were a senior, you felt like you owned the place. The best way out is always through.

Joseph in Egypt found that out. The end was the Egyptian throne, but by way of slavery and the darkest prison in the country.

Job found it out. He ended up with twice as much as he had ever had. But he got there the hard way, including the collapse of his wealth and the loss of his family. God provided two blessings for every bruise.

Jesus knew it too. His road led through a trial, beatings, and the most violent and painful death we can imagine. But the destination was an empty tomb, a glorious ascension, a seat at the right hand of the Father.

The hard way will always be tough; there are no shortcuts. But it's made just a bit easier when we stop to remember that God never fails, that all His endings are happy ones, and that every bruise leads to deeper blessings.

BEGIN WITH THE END IN MIND

The second habit in Stephen Covey's popular book *Seven Habits of Highly Effective People,* says we should begin with the end in mind. Covey suggests that we isolate where we want to end up, then keep that as an image that frames the way we think and act on a daily basis.[2] He's right, but Solomon knew that all along. He made the point here in Ecclesiastes, nearly three thousand years ago.

Many people today have lost the art of thinking things through. We have so much noise around us, so many urgent demands upon us, and so little time for reflection that we make snap decisions without taking the time to mull over our choices and prayerfully work them out.

Wise people don't let that happen. In his biography of Napoleon, André Castelot wrote that sometimes the great emperor would stretch out on a settee near his fireplace, close his eyes, and appear to be asleep. But he wasn't; he was meditating, thinking through his actions:

"If I always seem to be ready for everything, to face up to anything," he told his advisors, "it is because I never undertake anything at all without first having meditated for a long time and foreseen what might happen. It is not a genie, but meditation, that suddenly reveals to me, in secret, what I must say and do under circumstances not anticipated by others."[3]

When you have to make an important decision, take a quiet walk or shut yourself in your room and pray over some questions: *Where will this lead me? What will be the result of this action? What are the possible outcomes of this particular deed?* Try to determine the end from the beginning.

In the process, remember that God saves His best for last, whereas Satan points out the shortcut. As C. S. Lewis put it, "The safest road to hell is the gradual one—the gentle slope, soft underfoot, without sudden turnings, without milestones, without signposts."[4] It all begins with the little compromises, the "so what, no big deal" moments. It's just one pornographic image, just one snort of cocaine, just one night in a hotel room somewhere. Those little access roads always take us off the King's highway—the "narrow way," as Jesus called it. We can see that highway from the access road, and we can get back on it anytime we want (or so we say). But the roads get farther apart, and the slope gets steeper, and soon it becomes very difficult to apply the brakes.

Life on the King's highway is different. As His plan for us unfolds, it becomes richer and better; we grow happier and holier as time goes by. "The path of the just," wrote Solomon in Proverbs 4:18, "is like the shining sun that shines ever brighter unto the perfect day."

Because I have participated in many weddings as a pastor, one myth I have heard over and over again is among the greatest of misconceptions. People believe that the beginning of a marriage is better than the end. Maybe our awareness of the divorce plague makes us think that. Maybe it's the abuse marriage takes on television and in the movies.

But marriage is not that way by nature. When we persevere at it, work on it, grow in it, and do it the hard way, the institution of marriage gets better and deeper and sweeter in time. When we weather the storms together like two strong oaks growing by the stream, the end is profoundly richer.

As a matter of fact, I have found through counseling that the early days of marriage are often the most tumultuous and challenging. Two distinct personalities bring their worlds together, and frequently they collide with great force. But the best part of marriage is the part that endures and mellows as the years pass and couples have smoothed off the rough edges and molded themselves together as one.

Donna and I have been married for forty-one years, and I can honestly say it gets better every year. When she happens to be away for a few days traveling or visiting our children and their families, I miss her terribly. She is the one person in the world who is committed to loving me in spite of my many imperfections. Marriage done right gets better over time, because the end of a thing is better than the beginning.

We remember Fanny Crosby as the blind hymnist who wrote such amazing gospel songs as "Blessed Assurance" and "To God Be the Glory." But there's a lesser-known Crosby hymn that underscores the truth that the end is better than the beginning. Fanny wrote this particular song during the summer of 1886 when she was staying in the home of her friend Ira Sankey in Northfield, Massachusetts. Ira, himself a noted hymnist, composed a tune. After playing it for Fanny, he suggested, "Why not write a poem for this tune tonight?" She deferred, saying she couldn't do it at present. But the next day, while her friends were out for a drive, Fanny wrote the following words:

O child of God, wait patiently when dark thy path may be,
And let thy faith lean trusting on Him Who cares for thee;
And though the clouds hang drearily upon the brow of night,
Yet in morning, joy will come, and fill thy soul with light.[5]

Our destination is heaven on earth, but to get there we will have to walk through some difficult terrain. The clouds will often cover us. The darkness will often cause us to stumble and despair of ever rising. But when the clouds break through, there is joy in the morning. The hard way is the only way, for it makes that joy even sweeter.

20

Time to Move On

Eveyone loves "the good old days"—even young people
who never lived in them. The pop music charts are filled with more song
remakes from the 1960s and '70s than ever. Kids call it "retro" and
consider it cool in the way that "futuristic" used to be. There is a fascination with the cultural remnants of certain decades, as embodied by
TV shows such as *That '70s Show* and any number of movies. Even in
professional sports, it has become fashionable for teams to have "throw-
back days" when they play their games in the caps, jerseys, helmets, and
uniforms of bygone eras.

Something within us smiles and sighs when we think about yesteryear.
Something within us insists that things were better then—music more
melodious, movies more entertaining, the news more encouraging, and
life in general more manageable. If asked for proof, we would quickly and
passionately spit out examples to prove the point. At any given time, the
best time to be alive was twenty or thirty years ago—often known as
"when I was your age."

Is it really true? Consider a few facts about "the good old days" in
America:

- From 1970 to 1992, a typical new home increased by an average
  of six hundred square feet of living area.

- Today, 45 percent of homes now have dishwashers, up from 26 percent two decades ago.

- In 1990, 75 percent of homes had clothes washers, up from 66 percent in 1970. The percentage of homes with clothes dryers jumped from 45 to 70 during the same period.

- The average home had 1.4 televisions in 1970, but 2.1 in 1990, and gained 4.5 times as much audio and video equipment, 50 percent more kitchen appliances, 30 percent more furniture, and 100 percent more equipment for sports and hobbies.

- Median real wealth rose by 2 percent per year from 1970 to 1990.

- The Dow Jones industrial average has increased sixfold since the early 1970s.

- Microwave ovens, answering machines, food processors, camcorders, home computers, home exercise equipment, cable TV, Rollerblades, fax machines, and soft contact lenses became staples of the American life in the 1990s. Multitudes of other products are better in quality and lower in price than ever before.

- A decade ago, motorists had to stop and look for a pay phone to make a call. Now, most Americans enjoy the safety and convenience of a cellular phone.

- Today's drivers go farther on a gallon of gas than ever before, and drive safer cars equipped with antilock brakes, airbags, fuel injectors, turbochargers, cruise control, and sound systems better than many home systems.

- Since 1973, workers have added the equivalent of nearly five years of waking leisure hours to their lives . . . and the list goes on.[1]

Hold it! Wait for the disclaimer! Allow me to acknowledge what's wrong with that list: most of it is about *stuff*—material things for which Solomon would have three words: *vanity, vanity, vanity!* The list doesn't mention our increasing national debt, relatively low rates of personal savings, and declining moral standards, to be sure.

But the list also neglects to drive home the truth that Americans are living longer, retiring sooner, and traveling more widely than ever before. They are reaping the benefit of radical advances in medicine, giving them more years of life and more life for their years.

Can we agree that life is better in some ways and not nearly as good in others? I hope you'll concede the point that even the most nostalgic of our elders, given the choice, would not climb into a time machine to go live fifty years in the past *without* the daily medication that helps them enjoy life. We enjoy the highest standard of living in America of any country in history.

Yesterday's Glory . . . Tomorrow's Promise

> *Do not say,*
> *"Why were the former days better than these?"*
> *For you do not inquire wisely concerning this.*
>
> —Ecclesiastes 7:10

The "good old days" is a state of mind that has no coordinates in the real world. It is just a few blocks south of the pot of gold at rainbow's end, and it's another few blocks east of that other entrancing fantasyland, "what might have been."

Your kids will someday sit back in their easy chairs, sighing over this very moment, crowning it as the new "good old days." It's hard to imagine, because today never seems like anything special to the people inhabiting it. Today is always just short of yesterday's glory, just shy of tomorrow's promise. But today is all we have. It holds all the stakes. Today is the only day we can directly make an impact, and all our hopes of a better life lie right there in the calendar box where you stand—the day marked *today.*

If you come up short on courage and decide not to live totally in the present, that's when you begin to take that detour into the land of nostalgia. But Solomon says, "You do not inquire wisely concerning this." When you talk about the past, you're not speaking from a position of careful rationality, comparing and contrasting all the micro-differences between eras (that would be impossible). You're speaking purely from emotions: feelings of fear, a sense of loss from yesterday, an insecurity about the future.

Solomon would agree that there were elements of his father's regime that were superior to his own. But his point is the same one he has made in other parts of this book: the stillborn child and the two-thousand-year-old super-senior citizen face side-by-side cemetery plots. Even a two-thousand-year life span is a vapor, here today and gone tomorrow, from the perspective of eternity—not to mention that a few feet away, in the same cemetery, we find people from the "good old days" buried right beside those from our "brave new world."

The issue in life is not your times, your trade, or your take-home pay. It's all about the question, what are you doing with today? Are you electrically charged with the prospect of all that God can do with your life in this window called Today? After all, we can do all things through Christ, and He promised we would do miracles greater than His (John 14:12). Those are not verses about the good old days or the world of the future—those are *Today* words.

The idea of heaven on earth is a Today idea. Remember how the Israelites took three steps toward the Promised Land, then two steps backward into nostalgia? Slavery never seemed so enticing. Why, those Egyptian masters actually *fed* their slaves occasionally, and there were some days when there were no whippings at all, and fifteen-minute rests between hauling those great bricks. The Israelites were anxious about the wilderness of Today, and it kept them from the promise of Tomorrow. We do much the same, forgetting that all of the great picture our life can paint will be painted on the canvas of Today.

The superiority of your yesterday is no more real than the "good old days" of slavery for the Israelites. As Paul Simon pointed out in a song, everything looks nice in Kodachrome. The only problem is that when you stare too long into your rearview mirror, you collide with the life that is coming at you.

Meanwhile, the ultimate reality in life is God, who wants to fill your life with His presence and power right here and right now. Heaven on earth has nothing of the past mixed in it, nor of what lies ahead. The heaven awaiting us, when we come face to face with our Savior, will be an eternal Now, and it stands to reason that the way to bring that heaven to earth is to live in this Now completely and consistently.

Upside Down, Inside Out

The kingdom of God always appears upside down to the human perspective. We think it's strange to die in order to live, or to give in order to receive, or to serve in order to lead. Solomon captures the perpetual enigma of our looking-glass values just as Jesus describes them in the Sermon on the Mount. He insists we should embrace sorrow over laughter, rebukes over praise, the long way instead of the short, and today instead of yesterday.

The truth is that it's not the kingdom of God that is upside down—it's the world. It's not the Word of God that turns life inside out—it's the world that has reversed all the equations that God designed for our lives. After all, we can all verify the common sense of these "upside-down" propositions—it really *is* better to give than to receive, it really does help more to embrace criticism than praise, and so on. Everyday life is a proving ground for kingdom proposition.

Arthur Bennett wrote a prayer called "The Valley of Vision" that wonderfully summarizes some of the things in this section of Ecclesiastes. He uses the language of paradox, which is really the language of the kingdom about which Solomon wrote and Jesus Christ taught—the language of truth:

Lord, high and holy, meek and lowly,
Thou hast brought me to the valley of vision,
Where I live in the depths but see thee in the heights;
Hemmed in by mountains of sin I behold thy glory.

Let me learn by paradox
That the way down is the way up
That to be low is to be high
That the broken heart is the healed heart,
That the contrite spirit is the rejoicing spirit,
That the repenting soul is the victorious soul,
That to have nothing is to possess all,
That to bear the cross is to wear the crown,
That to give is to receive,
That the valley is the place of vision.

Lord, in the daytime, stars can be seen from the deepest wells,
And the deeper the wells the brighter thy stars shine;
Let me find thy light in my darkness,
Thy life in my death,
Thy joy in my sorrow,
Thy grace in my sin,
Thy riches in my poverty,
Thy glory in my valley.[2]

THREE THINGS WE KNOW

In our quest for heaven on earth, as in any journey, the first essential is *vision*—to see where we're headed; in this case, to step out of all these upside-down worldly assumptions and see from God's perspective. But even then, it's a challenge to keep our "valley vision" of the invisible world of heaven from the visible context of earth. When I am tempted to lose focus in the midst of this life's events, to wonder if the seeming paradoxes of God are really true, I cling to three "knows" in Romans 8 that are the perfect complement to what Solomon teaches in Ecclesiastes 7.

First, I *know* that "the whole creation groans and labors with birth pangs together until now" (Romans 8:22). That is, I know that the way things are now is not the way they were supposed to be, nor the way they will be. Troubling things happen in this world for a multitude of reasons, all of which are rooted in sin. When bad things happen, the frailty of my flesh is tempted to yield to the pressure of those events, because I am fallen. But this is all unnatural, not the way God designed it. So I don't get discouraged or deceived by something that I know is temporary. I cling to the image of heaven on earth, that which I know is eternal.

Second, I *don't know* what I should pray for as I ought, but "the Spirit Himself makes intercession for me with groanings which cannot be uttered" (Romans 8:26). This means that I am not alone in the battle. When I become tempted to do things the world's way—the way of laughter and flattery and the good old days—I fall to my knees and depend on the Holy Spirit to pray through me when I can't find the words. When I am tempted to take the short and easy way instead of the long and difficult way, I cry out to God for strength with the Spirit's help. He is there for me at every turn, for every challenge. He is my Comforter and Counselor and Guide, the deposit of God that ensures what He has begun in me will be completed in the day of Christ Jesus. Even when I don't know what to pray, I know the Spirit does.

And third, I *know* that "all things work together for good to those who love God, to those who are called according to His purpose" (Romans 8:28). As one of those who love Him, I can latch onto the prospect that every single event is part of an equation with a positive solution. There is power, incredible power, in grasping that paradigm.

This world seems out of control, and I have to depend on the Spirit to help me through. But ultimately I know that God is in control of everything. Nothing that happens in my life falls outside the bounds of His reach. He corrals every seemingly random and stray event and brings them together for good in my life because I love Him and have been called according to His purpose. That means that I am free to live paradoxically in this world, free to embrace the truths of God's kingdom in the face of every contrary teaching of the majority. Free to be a contrarian for Christ and His kingdom!

Ecclesiastes helps us see that God's plan is good and clear but sometimes mysterious. When we know what we know, it doesn't matter, because to God it is not a mystery. He is the Author of the Book of Life, and He knew the ending before He set the beginning in place. Therefore, it is okay for Him to know and for us *not* to know, because He is God and we are not. And we choose to let Him be God in our lives.

I encourage you to embrace sorrow when it comes, a rebuke when you feel its sting, the hard way when it is the right way, and especially the power of Today—*carpe diem!* Seize the day He has given you. This is the day He made, so rejoice and be glad in it. Heaven is at hand, not in the rearview mirror nor in the unknown future. It is within your grasp. Take hold, take counsel, and take advantage!

21

The Perspective of Wisdom

ECCLESIASTES 7:11–18

A WISE OLD CHINESE WOODCUTTER lived on the troubled Mongolian border. One day his favorite horse, a beautiful white mare, jumped the fence and was seized on the other side by the enemy. His friends came to comfort him. "We're so sorry about your horse," they said. "That's bad news."

"How do you know it's bad news?" he asked. "It might be good news."

A week later, the man looked out his window to see his mare returning at breakneck speed—beside a beautiful stallion. He put both horses into the enclosure, and his friends came to admire the new addition. "What a beautiful horse," they said. "That's good news."

"How do you know it's good news?" replied the man. "It might be bad news."

The next day, the man's only son decided to try the stallion. It threw him, and he landed painfully, breaking his leg. The friends made another visit, all of them sympathetic, saying, "We're so sorry about this. It's such bad news."

"How do you know it's bad news?" replied the man. "It might be good news."

Within a month, war erupted between China and Mongolia. Chinese recruiters came through the area, pressing all the young men into the army. All of them perished, except for the woodcutter's son, who couldn't go off to war because of his broken leg.

"You see," said the gentleman. "The things you considered good were actually bad, and the things that seemed bad were actually good."[1]

This wise woodcutter expresses the heart of Solomon's words in Ecclesiastes 7. We've already learned that mourning is better than laughing, funerals are better than weddings, a dying day is more important than a birthday, rebuke is better than praise, the long way is better than the shortcut, and "the good old days" are highly overrated.

Life is a paradox, and we're not always sure which end is up. Forrest Gump says life is like a box of chocolates because you never know what you'll get; Solomon would add that even after you take a bite, you can't be certain how it's going to digest!

We have to rely on our Lord, who knows the end from the beginning. His values are often different, and that's the underlying theme of Ecclesiastes 7.

Solomon teaches us that wisdom is knowing we can't know; it's realizing how small is the single puzzle piece we hold—that only God controls the final picture. We see through hazy glass, but His vision is perfect and all-encompassing; we know little, but His wisdom is perfect and all-knowing. Our perseverance is weak, but God plays every issue for the long haul.

Our response to all this should be Thanksgiving with a capital *T*.

THANK GOD FOR THE PERSPECTIVE OF WISDOM

American Olympic speed skater Dan Jansen suffered a series of devastating defeats and setbacks in his career until 1994, when he finally took the gold in a thrilling 1,000-meter race in Lillehammer, Norway. As a young skater he learned to keep defeat in perspective. Competing in the youth national skating championships in Minnesota at the age of nine, he was positioned to capture the title when he tripped on a lane marker coming around a turn.

That mistake cost him the victory. He was so distraught that he cried through the awards ceremony and the entire six-hour drive home. His father didn't say anything about the loss until they pulled into their driveway, but what he said then has stuck with Jansen ever since: "You know, Dan, there's more to life than skating around in a circle."

That might strike you as an insensitive remark from a father to a heartbroken son, but it is true. It arises from the father's enhanced perspective, which indeed renders the pain smaller and less significant. Dan Jansen, being a veteran competitor even at age nine, needed that greater perspective. It helped him pursue his Olympic dream while remembering the true place of victory and defeat.

Wisdom may not solve all our problems or smooth out all the bumps in the road, but it gives the mind the right information for controlling the emotions.

A few years ago there was a popular style of picture featuring an optical illusion. At first glance, the picture only seemed to be a pattern of swirling blue or green lines. Then, as you placed your focus on the dot in the middle and slowly stepped backward from the picture, an image would emerge. The effect was startling. The work of God's perspective is similar. We look at the scene and see only random swirls of events until we fix our gaze on Christ, who is at the center of creation and holds all things together (Ephesians 1:10). As we step slowly back, we see the picture through new eyes.

Perspective is seeing things in their true size and significance, in their proper relationship to each other. Children's art is notable for a lack of perspective. Everything is on one flat plane. There is no distance, no horizon. A good artist can suggest a distance of several miles on a single canvas—such as a country road narrowing until it vanishes into the sunrise. God's wisdom allows us to take the long view and to see how all roads lead back to Him in the end.

Wisdom gives us depth, relationship, meaning—the long view of things. There are three ways wisdom increases our perspective on the events of life.

WISDOM TO DEAL WITH PROSPERITY

Wisdom is good with an inheritance,
And profitable to those who see the sun.
For wisdom is a defense as money is a defense,
But the excellence of knowledge is that wisdom gives life
to those who have it.

—ECCLESIASTES 7:11–12

The world's brand of wisdom fluctuates like a roller-coaster week on Wall Street. *Newsweek* runs a column each week called "Conventional Wisdom Watch" to chart the "up and down arrows" of fleeting popularity. One week a president or a pop singer might receive an "up arrow" for some positive publicity event; the next week the arrow may be pointing dead south. But the wisdom of God holds consistent and unchanging now and forever.

Solomon tells us that wisdom and wealth make good companions. *The Living Bible* says, "To be wise is as good as being rich; in fact, it is better. You can get anything by either wisdom or money, but being wise has many advantages" (Ecclesiastes 7:11–12).

Solomon wrote something similar in Proverbs: "For whoever finds [wisdom] finds life, and obtains favor from the LORD" (8:35). Rich people who lack wisdom end up miserable; their wealth becomes a curse instead of a blessing. Wisdom gives perspective to prosperity. Wisdom keeps wealth in perspective.

Worldwatch Institute, an environmental/economic think tank in Washington, D.C., recently issued a surprising report showing increasing numbers of people in the world are "fat, rich, and unhappy." Private consumption expenditures, (the amount spent on goods and services at the household level), have increased fourfold in the world since 1960, topping more than $20 trillion in 2002. In America, where consumption has skyrocketed, there are more private vehicles on the road than people licensed to drive them. The average size of refrigerators in U.S. homes increased by 10 percent between 1972 and 2002, and new homes in America are 38 percent larger than those built in 1975, despite having fewer people in each household. Yet increased consumption has not brought Americans happiness, said the report. "Only about a third of Americans report being very happy, the same as in 1957 when Americans were only half as wealthy."[2]

Wealth we have; wisdom we need. We can only thank God that while wealth is hard to come by, wisdom is actually freely available through God. A lifetime supply is available in this book of Ecclesiastes.

WISDOM TO DEAL WITH PROVIDENCE

Consider the work of God;
For who can make straight what He has made crooked?
In the day of prosperity be joyful,
But in the day of adversity consider:
Surely God has appointed the one as well as the other,
So that man can find out nothing that will come after him.

—ECCLESIASTES 7:13–14

As we have seen, providence is God's supervision of all creation, ensuring that all His plans work out. It means that things will come to pass in our lives that only He understands. You may be trying to fill in a certain picture with your life, such as the picture of yourself as an entrepreneur who owns his own business; or yourself as courting and marrying a certain candidate. God may be (and usually is) filling in a completely different picture, a vaster and more comprehensive one involving any number of people and having implications that might be played out in coming centuries.

So you might not understand why God didn't allow you to start your own business or marry that specific person, but He has His reasons. And they are always reasons we would heartily approve if we were only wise enough.

"See the way God does things and fall into line" reads The *Living Bible.* "Enjoy prosperity whenever you can, and when hard times strike, realize that God gives one as well as the other.."

Affliction, that crooked thing we can't fix, is the appointment of God. I wrote a book called *A Bend in the Road,* in which I affirmed God's presence with His children in the difficulties of life. But if you're like me, you'd rather not have a bend in the road to begin with, or at least you'd like a bend you could straighten on your own. But wisdom says there is something deeper to be learned in the bends than in the straight lanes of life.

As I studied Solomon's words, I thought of Job, a man blessed by God with incredible wealth before suddenly losing it all. The only thing left was his wife, and she gave him the most offensive advice we can imagine: "curse God and die" (Job 2:9).

Job replied, "You speak as one of the foolish women speaks. Shall we indeed accept good from God, and shall we not accept adversity?" (v. 10).

When good things happen, we never ask why God allowed them. Apparently we figure we have them coming! But when bad things happen, that's when we talk theology. Wise people know that God is in all of it; that He is never closer than in our affliction. Pity those who have never known the comforting presence of God in the eye of the storm.

Bible teacher and author Warren Wiersbe puts it this way:

> God balances our lives by giving us enough blessings to keep us happy and enough burdens to keep us humble. If all we had were blessings in our hands, we would fall right over, so the Lord balances the blessings in our hands with burdens on our backs. That helps keep us steady, and as we yield to Him, we can even turn burdens into blessings.[3]

Blessings in the hand plus burden on the back equals balance in the spiritual life—a formula for contentment and maturity.

Wisdom to Deal with the Puzzles of Life

A longstanding holiday tradition in the Jeremiah household is the annual jigsaw puzzle. We get a new one each year, one with a gazillion pieces, and work on it during the Christmas holiday season. All the pieces are spread out on a table that is reserved solely for the holiday puzzle. Various Jeremiahs will stop and try a few more pieces until the picture is finally completed. (I won't reveal what percentage of these puzzles have been completed over the years.)

It's a great diversion when friends and family are gathered and a good opportunity to exercise our puzzle-solving skills. We always get the sides completed so that we have a nice frame that needs a picture inside. Corners and straight edges are simple. It's what's inside that gives us trouble.

In the puzzles of life, we are often able to work out the borders of things—the places where life is straight, where its corners meet neatly. But to solve the big picture, we need wisdom, persistence, and perhaps the help of loved ones. There are two puzzles in particular.

The Puzzle of Reversed Rewards

I have seen everything in my days of vanity:
There is a just man who perishes in his righteousness,
And there is a wicked man who prolongs life in his wickedness.

—Ecclesiastes 7:15

Once again, we come to the question everyone asks (you and I included). Why do good people suffer and bad people prosper?

I once worried over the hazy areas of my faith, like those spots on a sparkling car window that simply won't come clean. Now the hazy areas tell me that our God is real, dynamic, and too great for our conception. His ways are higher than mine. If there were no hazy areas, the whole thing would be too neat, too trite. If I could fully understand His thoughts, He would be no more God than I am.

We hear those who approach this puzzle with an ultimatum: solve it or God is not real. This is like approaching a ten-thousand-piece jigsaw puzzle and saying, "If I can't assemble this in five minutes, I will deny that it's a picture."

That's unfair, isn't it? It's also irrational. Our inability to work out an answer reflects only on our limitation, not God's.

God is both loving and powerful, but He allows the rewards to be reversed—success for the evil, suffering for the good—for reasons relating to His eternal plan, and because it is the consequence of a fallen world in which we ourselves have invited such chaos. And remember the wisdom of the woodcutter. We see only a fragment of life at a time, but God sees the whole.

The Puzzle of Righteous Rhetoric

Do not be overly righteous,
Nor be overly wise:
Why should you destroy yourself?
Do not be overly wicked,
Nor be foolish:
Why should you die before your time?
It is good that you grasp this,
And also not remove your hand from the other;
For he who fears God will escape them all.

—Ecclesiastes 7:16–18

Some liberal-leaning Bible scholars love this passage (Ecclesiastes 7:16–17) because it seems to suggest that a middle-of-the-road approach to the spiritual life is acceptable: "Do not be overly righteous, nor be overly wise. . . . Do not be overly wicked, nor be foolish."

In other words, be "sorta righteous," but don't let this thing get out of hand by trying to make the world a better place. This is the basic posture of those who say, when asked if they know where they'll spend eternity, "Well, I'm not as good as some, but not as bad as most. I'm hoping that's good enough to get me there!"

Let me state emphatically that there is no "sorta holy" any more than there is a "kinda pregnant." "Sorta holy" is the way to "sorta hell." Partial obedience to God is total disobedience.

Let's clarify what Solomon does mean. He *isn't* telling us to be moderately godly; he *is* telling us not to exalt our godliness before others. You've seen people with Christian bumper stickers who get more than their share of honks when they do inconsiderate things in traffic.

The fact is that self-righteousness isn't good for the self, and it isn't righteous. It arises from sin, and it is the central reigning sin. Solomon counsels staying in the middle of the road, which is described in verse 18: "It is good that you grasp this, and also not remove your hand from the other; for he who fears God will escape them all."

A man was caught in adultery, but he confessed and repented. He began to spend all his time in church activities until he became very self-righteous. Pretty soon he was giving the pastor preaching advice. The pastor told him, "I liked you better as an adulterer. At least you were humble."

Better to avoid both adultery *and* self-righteousness. Those who live by the world's wisdom will never be content in their quest for heaven on earth. But the perspective of God's wisdom helps us see a better road and a more blessed destination.

22

The Power of Wisdom

O NE WORD FOR WISDOM in Hebrew is *hokmah*. It occurs more than three hundred times in the Old Testament. While *hokmah* (and its derivatives) are usually translated "to be wise," "wise," and "wisdom," the root meaning of the word is *skill*—skill of all sorts.

For example, *hokmah* describes the high priest's tailors (Exodus 28:3) and the tabernacle's engravers (Exodus 35:35). Jonadab, a skillful man, has *hokmah* (2 Samuel 13:3), as does a good snake charmer (Psalm 58:5). Ants, badgers, locusts, and spiders have their own *hokmah* skill (Proverbs 30:24–28), as do idol makers (Isaiah 40:20) and navigators (Ezekiel 27:8).

The skillful are those who bring order out of chaos, who take raw materials and turn them into something useful or beautiful, and who have the ability to navigate chaotic situations such as storms at sea or to turn a chaotic situation to one's advantage. The ultimate image of *hokmah*, of course, is God creating an awesomely beautiful and complex earth from the chaos described in Genesis 1:2. The earth was without form and void before God applied His skill.

When we apply *hokmah* to the everyday course of human events, we could be said to possess the skill of living. We would be those who know how to bring order out of a sometimes chaotic life, who can gather up life's random bits and pieces and shape them into something that bears fruit, and who can keep from crashing on the shallows and shoals of life and make it safely to port.

Solomon cherishes that wisdom manifest in a godly perspective and godly power, wisdom to deal with whatever life brings our way.

Perspective on life is good. But power makes life a lot more exciting. Wisdom can help in understanding prosperity, providence, and puzzles in life, but it doesn't promise to provide perspective on everything. Nor does perspective exist alone. Perspective and power are like the two wings on a bird, the two blades of a pair of scissors, or the two sides of a coin. The whole of wisdom doesn't exist without both perspective and power.

Solomon notes four different areas of life in which wisdom can provide power.

WISDOM TO DEAL WITH THE PROBLEMS WE ENCOUNTER

Wisdom strengthens the wise
More than ten rulers of the city.
For there is not a just man on earth who does good
And does not sin.

—ECCLESIASTES 7:19–20

"Wisdom," wrote Solomon, "strengthens the wise." Wisdom leads to strength and mastery. When we have aligned ourselves with the right Lord, we become more courageous. Ten city rulers hold no terror for us.

I think of Shadrach, Meshach, and Abednego in the book of Daniel. When they were told they would be thrown into a fiery furnace if they didn't worship the king's statue, they shrugged and said:

O Nebuchadnezzar, we have no need to answer you in this matter. If that is the case, our God whom we serve is able to deliver us from the burning fiery furnace, and He will deliver us from your hand, O king. But if not, let it be known to you, O king, that we do not serve your gods, nor will we worship the gold image which you have set up. (Daniel 3:16–18)

These three young men were not afraid of the problem they faced. Wisdom told them that God's plan, not Nebuchadnezzar's, would ultimately prevail.

Wisdom to Deal with the People We Employ

Also do not take to heart everything people say,
Lest you hear your servant cursing you.
For many times, also, your own heart has known
That even you have cursed others.

—Ecclesiastes 7:21–22

People who study the corporate workplace say that interpersonal problems are far more time-consuming than technical problems. Psychologists tell us that one's "emotional quotient" (EQ) is more critical to life success than one's "intelligence quotient" (IQ). It is only by wisdom that employers can effectively manage those who work for them.

Solomon's advice to the wise is not to listen to the gossip people say about you, because you know in your heart you have said unkind things about others as well.

I stopped reading negative, critical notes from people a long time ago. My secretary reads them first, and if they're constructive and written in a spirit of love rather than antagonism, then she passes the notes to me. When they're carnal or unhelpful, she throws them away.

Listening to meanspirited input isn't wise since it only serves to cause internal agitation when we hear it. So avoid it. One man said, "I never worry about people who say evil things about me because I know a lot more stuff about me than they do, and it's worse than what they are saying."

What Solomon means by his counsel is this: "Let's be honest. If we get upset when people talk about us, we are holding them to a higher standard than we hold ourselves to, because we are prone to do the same thing."

WISDOM TO DEAL WITH THE PERPLEXITIES WE EXPERIENCE

All this I have proved by wisdom.
I said, "I will be wise";
But it was far from me.
As for that which is far off and exceedingly deep,
Who can find it out?
I applied my heart to know,
To search and seek out wisdom and the reason of things,
To know the wickedness of folly,
Even of foolishness and madness.

—ECCLESIASTES 7:23–25

Wisdom gives you power to live with what you don't understand. Solomon's experience is typical—we exercise our minds to try to find "the reason of things," but we can't. Those things that are "far off" and "exceedingly deep" may remain that way for the duration of our time on earth. The power that wisdom provides is to release such things into the hands of God lest our obsession with finding out ruin us.

When I was growing up I would often hear this statement: "I don't know about the future, but I know who holds the future." That is more than a euphemism to quiet the quest of a curious mind. It is biblical truth. You have learned already in these pages that God's plan is good and His purpose is clear, but His program is mysterious. Wisdom gives us the power to live our lives in the realm of the first two and leave the third to God. There is power in not being a slave to knowing why everything in life happens as it does, a power that comes from freedom. Many a martyr's body has been shackled into submission while his spirit remained free. That is true power, and it comes from the wisdom of God.

Wisdom to Deal with the Pitfalls We Escape

And I find more bitter than death
The woman whose heart is snares and nets,
Whose hands are fetters.
He who pleases God shall escape from her,
But the sinner shall be trapped by her.
"Here is what I have found," says the Preacher,
"Adding one thing to the other to find out the reason,
Which my soul still seeks but I cannot find:
One man among a thousand I have found,
But a woman among all these I have not found.
Truly, this only I have found:
That God made man upright,
But they have sought out many schemes."

—ECCLESIASTES 7:26–29

Wisdom can give us the power to steer clear of illicit relationships. The *Living Bible* brings this out clearly: "A prostitute is more bitter than death. May it please God that you escape from her, but sinners don't evade her snares" (Ecclesiastes 7:26).

A marital affair leaves incredible destruction in its wake—emotional destruction both in the marriage and in the illicit relationship.

An affair is not real—it is only an illusion of real love. It's a sham—a pitiful misrepresentation of what God designed marriage to be. In this illusion, lovers can only imitate marital intimacy, because the beauty of the commitment of one man to one woman is lost. The delight of ongoing discovery between two people totally dedicated to one another cannot be attained, because one or both unmarried partners are painfully aware of the third person, who is being damaged by their affair. The end result is emotional confusion in the hearts and lives of all concerned.

Solomon addresses the issue of wisdom and immorality extensively in the book of Proverbs. In Proverbs 2:1–10 he talks about acquiring wisdom by listening to instruction, asking for it, searching for it like buried treasure. Then, when wisdom enters your heart, "discretion will preserve you; understanding will keep you" (Proverbs 2:11). Preserve and keep you from what?

> From the immoral woman,
> From the seductress who flatters with her words,
> Who forsakes the companion of her youth,
> And forgets the covenant of her God.
> For her house leads down to death,
> And her paths to the dead;
> None who go to her return,
> Nor do they regain the paths of life. (Proverbs 2:16–19)

To put it plainly, wisdom gives us the power to resist sexual immorality, as Solomon himself should know. Ray Stedman writes:

> Solomon was trapped by sexual seductions. He went looking for love and thought he would find it in a relationship with a woman. He went looking for that which would support him, strengthen, and make him feel life was worth the living. But what he found was nothing but a fleeting sexual thrill. He found

himself involved with a woman who did not give what he was looking for at all; he still felt the same empty loneliness as before.[1]

Solomon made his choices, suffered heartbreak, paid the price, and lived to tell the tale. He wants that tale to serve as our warning. "Think!" he exhorts us. "Don't get caught up in the 'greener grass' myth. All that you need, all that can give you joy, is on your side of the fence. Follow the wisdom from above."

That wisdom from above, as James tells us in the New Testament, is "first pure, then peaceable, gentle, willing to yield, full of mercy and good fruits, without partiality and without hypocrisy" (James 3:17). In other words, wisdom flows from a rich, daily walk with God. It is like a cool stream emerging from the heights of a mountain, plunging delightfully to earth, where people come from many villages to enjoy its richness and beauty. As a wise believer, you will have that same effect on people. Who wouldn't be attracted to the person James describes?

George Washington Carver, born in slavery, became a famous agricultural chemist and scientist. He is especially known for his work with the peanut. Once he was invited to testify before a senate committee, and there he was asked, "Dr. Carver, how did you learn all these things?"

"From an old Book," he replied.

"What book?"

"The Bible."

"Does the Bible talk about peanuts?" asked the senator.

"No, Mr. Senator," replied the great scientist, "but it tells me about God who made the peanut. I asked Him to show me what to do with the peanut and He did."[2]

"In [Christ] are hidden all the treasures of wisdom and knowledge" (Colossians 2:3). When you're facing difficult issues and you don't know what to do, remember that you know Jesus Christ, the wisdom of God. The particulars of your daily decision may not be found in God's Word, but Christ will always be found abiding there. And He will give you what you need through His Holy Spirit, who brings God's Word and our hearts together. The least of the saints has more wisdom in Christ than the most ingenious scientist possesses without Christ.

How, indeed, does that scientist or anyone else make it through a day without the hand of God on his shoulder and the voice of the Spirit in his soul? Imagine taking a walk through the world's greatest and largest technology facility with the president of that company. He gives you an orderly tour, pointing out all the intriguing processes and principles and people involved in the busy work of the factory. Now imagine walking through those vast corridors without the president. You would be lost and confused. I need God to walk with me. So do you.

One of Christianity's oldest hymns comes from the sixth century, written in Latin by an unknown believer. The title is "O Boundless Wisdom, God Most High."

> Oh boundless Wisdom, God most high,
> O Maker of the earth and sky,
> Who bid'st the parted waters flow
> In heaven above, on earth below.
>
> The streams on earth, the clouds in heaven,
> By Thee their ordered bounds were given,
> Lest 'neath the untempered fires of day
> The parched soil should waste away.
>
> Even so on us who seek Thy face,
> Pour forth the waters of Thy grace:
> Renew the fount of life within,
> And quench the wasting fires of sin.

Grant us wisdom, O Lord. Grant us courage. As we seek to find what really matters in life, we need wisdom. And the more of it we have, the smaller we feel and the more wisdom we realize we need. Someday, when we feel the smallest and need your wisdom the most desperately, we will find the great object of our quest—and we will know You are there, walking joyfully inside us, eager to share the intricacies of Your wondrous kingdom.

23

Hard to Be Humble

Ecclesiastes 8:1–17

⁓

R AGS TO RICHES, back to rags, riches again, rags—that's the short answer if you ask quarterback Kurt Warner about his career.

Warner was an all-state high school football player from Iowa who tried out for the Green Bay Packers in 1994, but he was summarily cut. There were no more options for him, athletically speaking, so he took a job in Cedar Falls stocking grocery-store shelves.

Warner's attitude and ambition might have gone south at that point; instead, he grew in humility and redoubled his ambition to make it in football. It wasn't long before he found a niche in the Arena Football League, calling signals for the Iowa Barnstormers. It was fun, but no NFL scouts came calling. So Warner headed for Europe, where he played in Amsterdam. An outstanding season made the St. Louis Rams take notice, and he earned a contract backing up Trent Green for the Rams.

Green went down with a knee injury before the 1999 season, and Rams fans were in misery; all they had in reserve was a former grocery-store stocker. Surely the team would finish in last place. The rest, as they say, is history.

Warner set eight team records, won the NFL's Most Valuable Player award, and led the Rams to their first world championship as the Super Bowl MVP.

Warner climbed the mountain, but he still hadn't reached the top.

In 2001, Warner led the NFL in multiple categories on the way back to the Super Bowl, and he was league MVP for the second time in two years. *That* was the mountaintop. He had written his name across the NFL record book, as well as in the hearts of the fans.

But in 2002, Warner started down the other side of the mountain. A broken finger and broken hand cramped his style. His record for the first six starts: 0–6. Then came backup quarterback Marc Bulger, who went 6–0.

The 2003 season looked like a potential comeback year for Warner, but his disappointing performance in the opening game relegated him to the bench. Here came Bulger again, leading the Rams to a 12–4 record and the NFC West title.

A *Sports Illustrated* piece focused on Warner at the mountaintop. His game was unsurpassed, he won a Super Bowl, he was a talk-show staple, he nailed down the highest passing rating in NFL history, he wrote a book, and he enjoyed life immensely. Then he was sliding back down that steep slope toward obscurity.[1]

How would you have handled such a life?

In one game, when Bulger was struggling as a starter, the coach called for Warner. Here was his chance. But Warner advised the coach to give the kid a chance to fight through his problems. Bulger came back to win that game.

When asked in the locker room about supporting his competitor, Warner shrugged and said he wouldn't have liked to have been pulled, and he cited the golden rule. He treated Bulger as he himself would have wanted to be treated.

The mountaintop is our destination, but it is on the downward slopes that life takes its measure of us. Tom Selleck said, "Whenever I get full of myself, I remember that nice couple who approached me with a camera on a street in Honolulu one day. When I struck a pose for them, the man said, 'No, no. We want you to take a picture of us.'"

Humility puts us in our proper place; it strips away the coat of pride that collects on our surface as we travel through life's more successful moments.

Most of us are like former secretary of state Dean Acheson, a brilliant man who didn't like being humbled in the presence of his boss, President Franklin D. Roosevelt. Acheson once bitterly complained to his friend, Clark Clifford, "Roosevelt made you feel like one of the peasants being called in by the lord of the castle."

Clifford related that conversation and added, "It was ironic that Acheson felt this way about Roosevelt, since so many people felt something similar when in the presence of Dean Acheson."[2]

The eighth chapter of Ecclesiastes defines humility in five ways: knowing how much you don't know, living with what you don't like, accepting what you can't change, enjoying what you can't explain, and discovering what you can't discover.

HUMILITY IS KNOWING HOW MUCH YOU DON'T KNOW

Who is like a wise man?
And who knows the interpretation of a thing?
A man's wisdom makes his face shine,
And the sternness of his face is changed.

—ECCLESIASTES 8:1

Proverbs warns us consistently about being wise in our own eyes (Proverbs 3:7; 12:15; 26:5, 12; 28:11). The prophet Isaiah also writes, "Woe to those who are wise in their own eyes, and prudent in their own sight!" (Isaiah 5:21). Solomon, the author of both Proverbs and Ecclesiastes, speaks to the way true wisdom impacts a man. A man who is truly wise is changed by the wisdom of God; even his countenance reflects his humility. He knows how much he doesn't know because he knows Who he does know. He has access to God's wisdom, and that is enough.

215

Paul wrote these words to the Corinthian believers: "And if anyone thinks that he knows anything, he knows nothing yet as he ought to know" (1 Corinthians 8:2). Researchers tell us that the world's knowledge base is replaced every thirty-eight years. More and more quickly, we upgrade or replace what we know, and any good scientist will tell you how often the scientific community has discovered that everything they thought they knew was wrong!

Solomon tells us that a wise man knows his own boundaries of knowledge. This kind of humility, he writes, makes a person's face shine and removes the harsh edges of sternness from his countenance. Perhaps you need to spend less time with cosmetics and more time making your face shine through God's wisdom. William L. Stridger said, "A person's face is the signature of his soul."

It was said about missionary Henry Martyn:

> His features were not regular; but the expression was so luminous, so intellectual, so affectionate, so beaming with Divine charity, that no one could have looked at his features and thought of their shape or form—the outbeaming of his soul would absorb the attention of every observer.[3]

Just as Moses came down from the mountain with a shining face, you and I will glow with supernatural beauty from walking down the slope with the Master of our wisdom.

HUMILITY IS LIVING WITH WHAT YOU DON'T LIKE

I say, "Keep the king's commandment for the sake of your oath to God. "Do not be hasty to go from his presence. Do not take your stand for an evil thing, for he does whatever pleases him."

*Where the word of a king is, there is power;
And who may say to him, "What are you doing?"*

He who keeps his command will experience nothing harmful;
And a wise man's heart discerns both time and judgment,
Because for every matter there is a time and judgment,
Though the misery of man increases greatly.
For he does not know what will happen;
So who can tell him when it will occur?

—ECCLESIASTES 8:2–7

What about our feeling of being out of control? In verses 2–7, Solomon uses the illustration of a king whose authority no one would dare question: "And who may say to him, 'What are you doing?'" (verse 4). Solomon has an answer for the person who is forced to live contrary to his desires: "Keep the king's commandment for the sake of your oath to God" (verse 2). Humility is knowing when to submit and obey, even in circumstances where you lack understanding.

We must submit to bosses we don't always respect. We must study textbooks whose assumptions we question. The church may make a decision or two that doesn't sit well with us. At what point do we quit the job or leave the church? It's hard to know; we feel humbled and we move closer to God for guidance. There is much we can't change and simply trust to Him.

HUMILITY IS ACCEPTING WHAT YOU CAN'T CHANGE

Are you a control freak? Maybe you've been in a place where someone else was in control, and it drove you crazy! Or perhaps you lost your control of a work, health, or family situation. Some people are deserted by their spouse or have divorce forced upon them, and the prevailing sense is an outrage at having no control over something so personal and profound.

Impotent anger fills us when others control our lives. But in situations we can't change, the only healthy response is humility. Though it

217

may sound trite or ineffectual, we must leave it all to God, knowing He will care for us.

I recently read a very telling headline: "Controlled Burn Goes Out of Control." It was about forestry experts whose carefully planned brush fires got away from them. Have you ever experienced that feeling of helplessness? In Ecclesiastes 8:8–14, Solomon suggests four categories we can't control.

1. Death

> *No one has power over the spirit to retain the spirit.*
> *And no one has power in the day of death.*
> *There is no release from that war,*
> *And wickedness will not deliver those who are given to it.*
>
> —ECCLESIASTES 8:8

The day of your death is out of your hands. Comedian Redd Foxx once said, "Health nuts are going to feel stupid someday, lying in a hospital dying of nothing." There are health-conscious people who work out daily, eat a disciplined diet, take their vitamins, and then suffer a heart attack while jogging. We can and should care for our bodies, but there's nothing we can do to be in total control. It's particularly difficult for those in our modern culture to grasp that there could be anything at all out of their control, even death. We are a country of control freaks. The whole message of our society is to be independent, to take control of everything, to be your own boss. But God didn't design us that way.

During her lifetime, Queen Elizabeth I was considered the most powerful woman on earth. But as she was dying, she said, "Oh my God! It is over. I have come to the end of it—the end, the end. To have only one life, and to have done with it! To have lived, and loved, and triumphed; and now to know it is over! One may defy everything else but this."[4]

We have to accept this. Perhaps you've lost loved ones recently, and you have mourned deeply. But after a period of mourning, we have to go on with our lives; for Solomon told us that true humility is realizing that "no one has power over the spirit to retain the spirit, and no one has power in the day of death." For Christians, of course, that's not such a bad thing after all, for to die is gain; it is better by far (Philippians 1:21, 23).

2. Distress

All this I have seen, and applied my heart to every work that is done under the sun: There is a time in which one man rules over another to his own hurt.

—ECCLESIASTES 8:9

Solomon says that everyone under the sun gets hurt. That's life. But it's hard to accept the pain that is imposed on us. We want to do something, whether it's strike back, hurt someone "smaller," or simply sit around and feel sorry for ourselves. We cannot live in a world filled with people without some of them stepping on our feet.

As we think of all the things that worry us, we must ask, "Which of these things can I change?" If you can change some of them, do so; but if you can't, accept them, trust God with them, and don't let them ruin your life. Jesus said, "Which of you by worrying can add one cubit to his stature?" (Matthew 6:27).

Ruth Bell Graham wrote extensively along these lines. After her two sons had spent a frightening season in the "far country," she wrote a book for worried parents. In *Prodigals and Those Who Love Them*, Ruth writes:

> We mothers must take care of the possible and trust God for the impossible. We are to love, affirm, encourage, teach, listen to and care for the physical needs of the family. We cannot convict

of sin, create hunger and thirst after God, or convert. These are miracles, and miracles are not in our department.[5]

That's a good rule for all of life. We must trust God with what we can't control. That includes those who want to hurt or distress us—along with all the other unavoidable, unalterable troubles of life.

3. Deception

> *Then I saw the wicked buried, who had come and gone from the place of holiness, and they were forgotten in the city where they had so done. This also is vanity.*
>
> —ECCLESIASTES 8:10

Warren Wiersbe paints this picture:

> In verse 10, Solomon reports on a funeral he had attended. The deceased was a man who had frequented the temple ("the place of the holy") and had received much praise from the people, but he had not lived a godly life. Yet he was given a magnificent funeral, and an eloquent eulogy, while the truly godly people of the city were ignored and forgotten.[6]

Oh, how we see the same phenomenon. Television shows us a godless celebrity whose death is mourned by the entire world. A successful millionaire is ushered to his grave with great fanfare. But the simple, humble, godly man or woman isn't even afforded an inch on the obituary page. The memory of all their deeds of love and kindness appears to be swiftly forgotten, blown away like the particles of the wind.

This is one more item on which God doesn't ask our advice. It just happens, fair or not. We reflect that if *we* were in control, we would make things fair—but to be sure, we would make a huge mess in trying. God has a perfect plan, and if people get more praise than they deserve, let them, for it's little enough reward in the big picture, and they still have to stand before God. If you see someone receiving too little praise, take the initiative and call a celebration. But know that this one, too, will stand before God and receive his or her crown of glory.

4. Defiance

Because the sentence against an evil work is not executed speedily, therefore the heart of the sons of men is fully set in them to do evil. Though a sinner does evil a hundred times, and his days are prolonged, yet I surely know that it will be well with those who fear God, who fear before Him. But it will not be well with the wicked; nor will he prolong his days, which are as a shadow, because he does not fear before God.

There is a vanity which occurs on earth, that there are just men to whom it happens according to the work of the wicked; again, there are wicked men to whom it happens according to the work of the righteous. I said that this also is vanity.

—ECCLESIASTES 8:11–14

In his book *Can Man Live without God?* Ravi Zacharias relates a conversation he had with British journalist Malcolm Muggeridge. Svetlana Stalin, daughter of the evil Soviet dictator Josef Stalin, spent some time in the Muggeridge home. According to Svetlana, as Stalin lay dying, plagued with terrifying hallucinations, he suddenly sat halfway up in bed, clenched his fist toward heaven, and fell back on his pillow, dead.[7]

Defiance! Would you shake your fist at God? Many do so, even if figuratively. "I've done it my way," they boast. "Nothing's happened to me yet, and nothing is going to happen to me. I am the master of my soul, the captain of my fate, and the lord of my life." We live in a generation that wants to go its own way, thinking it knows better than the ancient wisdom of God and His people. We think money, popularity, pleasure, and many of Solomon's "vanities" have suddenly become wise choices.

But the Bible says, "For what profit is it to a man if he gains the whole world, and loses his own soul? Or what will a man give in exchange for his soul? For the Son of Man will come in the glory of His Father with His angels, and then He will reward each according to his works" (Matthew 16:26–27).

We don't see God sending the lightning rod upon the neighborhood hedonist, so we assume He's asleep at the wheel. He is not. There will be a reckoning for all who have strayed between the cradle and the crypt.

HUMILITY IS ENJOYING WHAT YOU CAN'T EXPLAIN

So I commended enjoyment, because a man has nothing better under the sun than to eat, drink, and be merry; for this will remain with him in his labor all the days of his life which God gives him under the sun.

—ECCLESIASTES 8:15

My great surprise in Ecclesiastes is the number of times Solomon tells us to enjoy life. He reminds us that we can't control death, distress, defiance, and deception—and then he tells us to go out and have a good time?

Yes, that's exactly the point! If you can accept that which is unacceptable—not be ignorant of it, but know it and acknowledge it and simply trust everything to God—you will not be ruled by misery or anxiety. You will have the power to enjoy life.

This life is difficult but abundant. Goodness and mercy will follow us all our days, but we'll often be walking through the valley of the shadow of death when they follow us. The secret of life, the power of finding heaven on earth, is embracing heaven while accepting earth. We change what we can, we accept what we can't, and we walk on with the joy of God's companionship. Yes, that job is difficult—but God is with me, teaching me humility and competence and patience. Yes, that marriage has been on the rocks—but God is teaching us so much about Himself as it heals and strengthens in His grace.

Every mountain has an uphill and a downhill, and they're the same! It depends upon which way you're facing.

Humility Is Discovering What You Can't Discover

When I applied my heart to know wisdom and to see the business that is done on earth, even though one sees no sleep day or night, then I saw all the work of God, that a man cannot find out the work that is done under the sun. For though a man labors to discover it, yet he will not find it; moreover, though a wise man attempts to know it, he will not be able to find it.

—Ecclesiastes 8:16–17

We upgrade our knowledge base every year, yet there is so much we will never discover. The pursuit for knowledge will never reach its goal. French philosopher Blaise Pascal wrote this in his famous *Pensées* (#446):

If there were no obscurity, man would not feel his corruption; if there were no light, man could not hope for a cure. Thus it is not only right but useful for us that God should be partly concealed and partly revealed, since it is equally dangerous for man to know God without knowing his own wretchedness as to know his wretchedness without knowing God.

God didn't forget to tell us anything important. There are things too great for our comprehension and others too dangerous for our grasp. Perhaps we will discover the cure for cancer. Perhaps we will invent a spaceship capable of taking us to other galaxies. But we will only ever know what God permits us to know. As the guardian of all knowledge, He holds every secret. Our response is to bow in humility then to look up toward the peak of the mountain and get on with the journey.

24

Dropping the "D" Word

ECCLESIASTES 9:1–10

⸺❧⸺

THE GAMBLER DID EVERYTHING WITH STYLE—and I mean everything. One day, with all his friends gathered around, he sat at the steering wheel of a brand-new, custom-equipped Cadillac Seville, loaded with luxuries. He wore a hot pink suit and had five hundred-dollar bills clutched between his thumb and forefinger. He looked so natural—almost alive.

Yes, he happened to be embalmed at that time. He was ready to be lowered into the ground, buried in the manner of his choosing. He appeared ready to cruise to the pearly gates on brand-new wheels. (That may have been his biggest gamble!)

A friend walked around the car, studying the silver spokes, the vanity plate, and all the other fine custom details. "Man," he whispered. "That's *living!*"

Funerals come in many flavors. The possibilities are nearly endless if you have enough money to spend. There is only one requirement: all the living must be over.

Death is one of those subjects we don't like to discuss. That's why it's the subject of so many euphemisms. Instead of using the word *dead,* we say, "passed away," "gone to a better place," "sleeping in Jesus," "returned home," or "went to be with the Lord." At least, we use those terms around the sanctuary and the funeral home. In less guarded moments, the same people speak of "kicking the bucket," "buying the farm," "cashing in chips," "biting the dust," or the ever-popular "croaked."

Whether we lean to the reverent right or the flippant left, we shy away from speaking directly of the ultimate enemy.

In his poem "Graveyards," Sir John Betjeman, the late poet laureate of England, wrote:

> Oh, why do people waste their breath
> Inventing dainty names for death?[1]

Solomon was facing his own mortality when he wrote the book of Ecclesiastes during his final years. He tackled the subject head-on, discussing its reality and our responses.

The Reality of Death

For I considered all this in my heart, so that I could declare it all: that the righteous and the wise and their works are in the hand of God. People know neither love nor hatred by anything they see before them. All things come alike to all:

One event happens to the righteous and the wicked;
To the good, the clean, and the unclean;
To him who sacrifices and him who does not sacrifice.
As is the good, so is the sinner;
He who takes an oath as he who fears an oath.

—Ecclesiastes 9:1–2

On February 1, 2003, the space shuttle *Columbia* broke up over Texas just minutes before its scheduled landing in Florida. What a terrible moment in our collective memory. The seven-member crew was returning home after a successful sixteen-day mission. The burning capsule streaked across the sky of the southern United States, dropping flaming debris and burning reminders of the suddenness of death. We wondered silently, *What would it be like to take that final ride, knowing the end was imminent?*

But for all of us who ride on spaceship Earth, the end is imminent. Every human being lives out a death sentence—the important matter is what we do with the *lives out* part of that phrase. Nineteenth-century Anglican bishop J. C. Ryle wrote:

> Death is the mighty leveler. He spares no one. He will not tarry till you are ready. He will not be kept out by moats, and doors, and bars, and bolts. The Englishman boasts that his home is his castle, but with all his boasting, he cannot exclude death. An Austrian nobleman forbade death and the smallpox to be named in his presence. But, named or not named, it matters little, in God's appointed hour death will come.[2]

You play the board game Monopoly. You buy railroads and place hotels on Park Place and Boardwalk. You pass "Go" and collect two hundred dollars. Everyone has fun. Then the game ends, and all the hotels, all the colorful tokens, and all the funny money go back into the box. Solomon, who held an empire much less plastic, would tell us that whether you build in plastic or gold it's all the same. Build a temple, extend a dynasty, even write three God-inspired books—in the end, it all goes back in the box.

Even the righteous and the wicked, Solomon tells us, are cemetery neighbors. Many things set them apart and determine their eternal standing—but in the end, they all die. As Hebrews 9:27 puts it: "It is appointed for men to die once, but after this the judgment." When relatives are on their way, you prepare a room. Death is the cousin everyone shares and no one has met; we only know he will get around to see every relative sooner or later. Are you squirming yet? Stay with me—it's not morbid to discuss what is so inevitable, so universal, and so profoundly important to the soul.

The late pastor Ray Stedman wrote:

> I have noticed that some people . . . are very uncomfortable at funerals. They are nervous and edgy; they want to get it over quickly and get back to their local bar, their comfortable living room, or whatever. In observing that phenomenon, I have asked myself what it is about funerals that makes them so nervous. The answer I came to is that a funeral is one event where one can no longer escape ultimate reality. A funeral is proof that we are not in control of our own lives. This is what makes people uncomfortable and anxious to get back to the comfortable illusions of life.[3]

THE RESPONSES TO DEATH

Even as a young seminary student, I dealt daily with death as a hospital chaplain. As I watched the family members and friends of the deceased, I saw some fall into absolute despair. Others grieved, but not as those having no hope.

In *None of These Diseases,* Dr. David E. Stern relates some of his experiences as a medical doctor who dealt with dying patients. He told of Matt, who wouldn't see a pastor and even discarded his room's Gideon Bible. In his case there was no physical pain, but he suddenly sat up in bed, eyes blazing, and screamed, "No! No!" Then he expired. His wife suffered grief-driven trauma for many months.

Yet the same week, Dr. Stern also sat with a woman dying of breast cancer. In her case there was terrible physical pain, but she passed away whispering to her husband, "I love you, John. See you soon." He kissed her cheek as the pastor read the words of Psalm 23, and one could almost feel the presence of angels coming to bear away a heavenly traveler.

The good doctor never forgot the contrast of the two rooms: "One, a terrified man dropping into the unknown. The other, a restful soul passing through heaven's gate."[4]

How, then, shall we face death?

Don't Deny It

This is an evil in all that is done under the sun: that one thing happens to all. Truly the hearts of the sons of men are full of evil; madness is in their hearts while they live, and after that they go to the dead.

—ECCLESIASTES 9:3

I have always liked the legend of the merchant in Baghdad who sent his servant to the market. When the servant returned he was as white as a sheet, trembling all over. He told his master, "When I was at the market I was bumped by someone in the crowd. When I turned around, I saw it was Death who jostled me and made a threatening gesture toward me. Master, please, lend me your horse so I may flee to Samarra and hide where Death cannot find me."

The merchant lent him his horse and the servant galloped off in great haste. Later that day, the merchant himself was at the market and saw Death standing in the crowd. He approached her and asked, "Why did you threaten my servant this morning?"

"I did not threaten him," Death replied. "I was only surprised to see him in the market in Baghdad, for I have an appointment tonight to see him in Samarra."[5]

We can run from death, but we cannot hide from it. "It is appointed for men to die once, but after this the judgment" (Hebrews 9:27). David, the psalmist, wrote that our days were written in God's book before we were even born (Psalm 139:16).

As a young pastor in Fort Wayne, Indiana, I was asked to conduct the funeral of someone I'd never met. I was told only that he had been a godly individual. As I was returning to my car after the service, a young woman came running across the parking lot toward me, screaming at the top of her lungs. She cursed me in words I'd not heard in a long time. She was furious that I had mentioned her sister's name in the service without mentioning hers as well.

The family was unfamiliar to me, and I hadn't purposefully omitted her name. But there was her dad, lying in a casket, and she turned her wrath to something smaller, more trivial, more manageable to the emotions. It was her way of denying death and deflecting the intensity of what was inside her. Unprepared to grieve, she vented toward me.

DON'T IGNORE IT

But for him who is joined to all the living there is hope, for a living dog is better than a dead lion.
For the living know that they will die;
But the dead know nothing,
And they have no more reward,
For the memory of them is forgotten.
Also their love, their hatred, and their envy have now perished;
Nevermore will they have a share
In anything done under the sun.

—ECCLESIASTES 9:4–6

Unbelievers live sad half-lives. In a sense, they are already dead. There is no reward, no motivation, no future, no genuine love or even hate. When the end comes, they finish their time under the sun and face only a darkness. Believers, however, can live now in the fullest sense. We can do good things, enjoy life, and embrace hope under the sun.

Recently Ted Koppel interviewed David Letterman about his heart bypass surgery. Koppel asked, "Do you think about death a lot? I mean, is death something that bothers you?"

Listen to Letterman's response:

> No, no. I mean, always before, I knew I was going to drop dead of a heart attack. I just knew it. You know, I've seen it in my family. I had the genetic tendency. My cholesterol—it didn't make any difference what I was doing—was always sky high. I could eat pocket lint and it would be 800. But after the surgery, no, I don't think about it anymore.[6]

Letterman seems to think that since he has had heart surgery, he isn't going to die. At least, not soon. So he isn't going to think about it. With his heart repaired, he thinks he can ignore death.

But who knows?

Have you heard the phrase, "Where there's life there's hope?" It comes from Ecclesiastes 9:4: "But to him who is joined to all the living there is hope." Solomon said that it's better to be a living dog (a despised animal in biblical times) than a dead lion (the king of the jungle).

Solomon was warning us that we can't successfully deal with death by whistling past the graveyard. It's not enough to shrug and say, "Hey, I'm still standing. As long as there's life there's hope."

Hope is only valid when it's reality based—and our hope is based on the ultimate reality. We are citizens of heaven, ambassadors from a better country whose joys make the pale pleasures of earth look sad indeed. We can therefore keep heaven on earth—in our hearts.

LIFE, AS IF!

Solomon's message is, if you like ice cream, have a second helping while you can. If you enjoy travel, see the world as soon as possible. You know the number of minutes in an hour and the number of hours in a day, but you do not know the number of days in a lifetime. There could be seven more, or seven thousand.

Solomon does *not* say, "Eat, drink, and be merry for we're going to die." But he does give some advice for life.

1. Eat Every Meal As If at a Banquet

> *Go, eat your bread with joy,*
> *And drink your wine with a merry heart;*
> *For God has already accepted your works.*
>
> —ECCLESIASTES 9:7

We're surprised to see how many verses in the Bible tell us to simply enjoy our meals. In the Jewish culture, the meal was a very important time. In Solomon's day, the evening meal occurred after a grueling day of work. It was a time of joy. Today we rarely eat a meal together. We share a meal with the television or eat on the run as we drive. We've lost the ancient art and pleasure of a shared meal.

Most cultures have recognized something sacred in the idea of a meal shared in fellowship. In warring cultures, peace is often made when the chieftains sit down and eat together. Food is strength, and while we have the strength to live on this earth, we celebrate the gardens and pastures and rivers, seas, and skies all filled with good things to eat, furnished by our Lord for our enjoyment.

2. Celebrate Every Day As If at a Party

> *Let your garments always be white,*
> *And let your head lack no oil.*
>
> —ECCLESIASTES 9:8

Births, weddings, and harvest festivals were special occasions in Solomon's day. He tells us to dress every day as if we're on the way to a celebration of life.

Paul joins the chorus: "Rejoice in the Lord always. Again I will say, rejoice!" (Philippians 4:4). And "rejoice always" (1 Thessalonians 5:16).

Some would say, "What do I have to rejoice about? I could die anytime."

Exactly! That's a great reason to let every waking moment be a celebration of God's gift of life. Get dressed. Eat out with a friend. Why? Because you can! And because God enjoys your enjoyment.

3. Enjoy Marriage As If on Your Honeymoon

> *Live joyfully with the wife whom you love all the days of your vain life which He has given you under the sun, all your days of vanity; for that is your portion in life, and in the labor which you perform under the sun.*
>
> —ECCLESIASTES 9:9

Solomon had many honeys and many honeymoons—to the debasement of his kingdom. He treated himself to hundreds of wives and concubines. Now, at the end of his life, he wishes he had lavished all his love on the wife of his youth. A man who had hundreds of wives now speaks in the singular rather than the plural. One partner, one heart.

Your husband or wife should be looked upon as a treasure from heaven, prepared for your joy, to serve and to be served. There are moments of irritation and seasons of discontent, but remember those are days and seasons we have but once. Why not let each day be as joyful as your honeymoon? Marital fulfillment is a choice, so choose to live and love joyfully.

4. Work As If It Were Your Final Workday

> *Whatever your hand finds to do, do it with your might; for there is no work or device or knowledge or wisdom in the grave where you are going.*

—ECCLESIASTES 9:10

I've read that a man or woman of fifty, having worked consistently since school, will have put in fifty-six thousand hours of work. Imagine, if you will, fifty-six thousand hours of boredom and resentment. Who would come through such an ordeal with a sound mind? Yet a poor attitude toward one's job creates that environment.

Now imagine someone rising in the morning to say, "Thank You, Lord! Another day to use the gifts and the strength and the mind You have given me—to apply them to fruitful enterprise. What a gift You have given me, that I may work and serve." That mind-set will add years to your life and life to your years. It will also bring you success, promotions, and glory for God.

Note the change in the world view of prize-winning Irish poet Evangeline Paterson: "I was brought up in a Christian environment where, because God had to be given preeminence, nothing else was allowed to be important. I have broken through to the position that because God exists, everything is important." [7]

Work, therefore, as if today were your final workday, for it may be; work as if God is inspecting your work, for He is. "For he will not dwell unduly on the days of his life, because God keeps him busy with the joy of his heart" (Ecclesiastes 5:20).

Why worry about the span of your life? I'd rather be like Solomon and stay busy with the joy of my heart. Once again, this is heaven on earth, paradise in our hands, delivery from dread and drudgery—for this is the day the Lord has made, and we can rejoice and be glad in it.

25

Life Cheats!

ECCLESIASTES 9:11–18

ECCLESIASTES 9 covers the ground of life and death—a pretty nice section of intellectual acreage to plow in one chapter. Solomon's short answer would read something like this: "Death plays to win; life plays unfairly."

The long answer? Well, you have to read the chapter. We've already moved through the first ten verses, and we've seen how death wins. It comes for the just and the unjust, the rich and the poor, the child and the ancient.

But *life?* Now things get complicated.

THE BEST MAN ISN'T ALWAYS REWARDED

I returned and saw under the sun that—

The race is not to the swift,
Nor the battle to the strong,
Nor bread to the wise,
Nor riches to men of understanding,
Nor favor to men of skill;
But time and chance happen to them all.
For man also does not know his time:

Like fish taken in a cruel net,
Like birds caught in a snare,
So the sons of men are snared in an evil time,
When it falls suddenly upon them.

—ECCLESIASTES 9:11–12

Life is unfair. Being the best isn't the same as winning the contest.

Olympic swimmer Ian Thorpe knows it's true. Widely hailed as the world's fastest swimmer, Thorpe was expected to be the 2004 Olympic champion in the 400-meter freestyle, his best event. Then, at the trials in Sydney, he was getting into starting position just before the race when a terrible thing happened: he tumbled off the blocks into the pool.

Thorpe was disqualified. That's the way it works; the rules are written very clearly. The distraught swimmer appealed his case, but a referee and a three-person competition jury refused the hearing. Ian Thorpe, Australia's certain gold medal winner, wouldn't even be in the water for his best event. An uproar ensued, and Australians were furious with the judges. No one likes cruel technicalities, but rules are rules.

Ian Thorpe, the world's fastest swimmer, calmed his nation by saying, "I accepted it, and now everyone else has to as well. Although it doesn't seem fair, and in a lot of cases life isn't fair, you just have to deal with it. I'm not unlucky or unfortunate."[1]

The young man has more wisdom in his grasp than he knows. It's not a matter of "luck" or "fortune," whatever dubious providential philosophy those terms may signify.

We've seen this particular little drama played out many times before. A young athlete spends a lifetime preparing for this golden moment in time. The athlete makes every sacrifice imaginable, sacrificing a normal life and many of the joys of a more ordinary childhood and adolescence for this one chance to be the best in the world.

Then something happens: a twisted ankle, an inopportune tumble, even a political crisis such as the United States pulling out of the Olympics in 1980—and the former Soviet Union doing the same in 1984.

Just like that, our stomachs turn upside down as we see the tears of some young man or woman who has given up so much to come away with so little—other than one more lesson in the proposition that *life isn't fair.* The race isn't always to the swift.

But this doesn't sit well with us. Things are *supposed* to be fair, aren't they? Everyone would agree that life—and the people in it—should play by the rules. As C. S. Lewis points out in *Mere Christianity,* every human being appeals to a common law of fair play: "That's my seat—I was there first," or "Give me a bite of that orange; I gave you a bite of mine." Fairness is a kind of natural instinct we carry inside. Lewis shows that no one ever questions that standard of basic fairness; it seems to be implanted within us at birth.

Why? Animals don't live by standards of fairness and justice. Earthquakes and bolts of lightning certainly are impartial when they pick their victims. But regardless of 100 percent of our history and personal experience, we humans can't get beyond this idea of the way things are *supposed* to run.

Why do we have that idea? Why are we so transfixed by the book of Job, in which the worst happens to the best? It is so because we have our Father's eyes. We are made in the image of a God of justice, created for a heaven of pure rightness. As Solomon has already told us, we have eternity stamped upon our hearts. We are made for heaven, where life is fair; but we must settle for earth, where life deals from the bottom of the deck.

Solomon expands on this idea to tell us that hardly anything on this upside-down planet comes out the way it seems it should. This is why the race isn't to the swift. Who was the toughest? Goliath, but he was defeated by a flimsy shepherd. Who was the wisest? Solomon, who was brought down by the foolishness of love. Who was the most handsome? Absalom, who was brought down by ugly behavior. And oddly enough, who was the man after God's own heart? It was the covetous, lying, murdering adulterer David. Life is complicated; so is godliness.

When our youngest son, Daniel, played college football, he competed for starting quarterback. Even allowing for a proud dad's bias, I will say that nearly everyone thought my son had won the job. Daniel had worked hard during the off-season, hustled during spring practice and fall camp, and had done all that he could to ensure the job. All the same, it went to someone else.

That disappointment was hard on Daniel; it may have been even harder on that proud dad. But my son and I talked about the fact that here it was, case in point: *Life isn't fair.* The race isn't always to the swift, nor the quarterback position to the best arm. "Learn it now when you're young," I told him, "lest you learn it much more painfully down the road."

As we've seen over and over again, this is an amazing book before us. Solomon gives us every reason under the sun to be gloomy. He tells us that death always wins, and life always cheats. He tells us that the best effort we can put forth guarantees exactly nothing. Then, as always, he tells us to be joyful!

Solomon's message is not to candy-coat life, but to tell us that life doesn't need candy-coating. Life is unfair and death is unstoppable, but we have what we have, and it happens to be this day before us—a gift from God, filled with pleasures, beauty, the satisfying enterprise of work, and the precious presence of God overseeing it all.

Life is smelly, noisy, cruel, and uncaring. How much more glorious is the God who can be seen through the darkness, felt in the cold, and embraced in the valley of the shadow of death! He triumphs over the gloomiest observations you or Solomon could dish out. How shall we then live? Joyfully!

The Good Man Isn't Always Remembered

This wisdom I have also seen under the sun, and it seemed great to me: There was a little city with few men in it; and a great king came against it, besieged it, and built great snares around it. Now there was found in it a poor wise man, and he by his wisdom delivered the city. Yet no one remembered that same poor man. Then I said:

"Wisdom is better than strength.
Nevertheless the poor man's wisdom is despised,
And his words are not heard.
Words of the wise, spoken quietly, should be heard
Rather than the shout of a ruler of fools.
Wisdom is better than weapons of war;
But one sinner destroys much good."

—ECCLESIASTES 9:13–18

Another paradox: wise words are often ignored even as foolishness is given the blue ribbon. Solomon shares a little parable—almost a fairy tale—to make his point.

Once upon a time, he tells us, a great army was smashing its way through the countryside. It found in its path a small, unassuming town. The town wasn't even worth taking a detour around; burning through it would be child's play. The general surrounded the town, placed it under siege, deployed all his heavy artillery, and sent in his messenger to demand surrender and the spoils of war.

The terrified little village was in need of a few good men, but this was a single-stoplight-and-convenience-store kind of town. There wasn't any army, but there was a single pauper who rose to the occasion. Yes, he was just a beggar by the street side, someone everyone had seen and no one had noticed. But he had some spark of hidden genius just waiting for its special moment. The pauper showed up in the war room with an outside-the-box idea that saved the day. What that idea was is a story for another day. Suffice it to say that his clever stroke ended the siege and relegated the attackers to Plan B, the detour.

Now, Solomon asks, wouldn't you expect that little man to have a few books written about him? A few songs sung in his honor? You'd think the town would place his statue out in front of city hall and that he'd never go hungry again.

But somehow, in the midst of the weeklong celebration, all the medals are handed out to the clueless characters who carried out the plan, while the pauper is overlooked. Next week he's back on the sidewalk, begging for bread as the "heroes" walk by, followed by worshipful girls. They don't even stop to throw a nickel in his cup.

Life is unfair, and people have short memories. The people who do the most heavy lifting on church committees get the least credit. We say we have no heroes, but we have a million unsung ones like the little man in the town. In the end, we don't value wisdom very highly. We don't appreciate the people who deserve the credit. We've all experienced this painful truth.

But Solomon says, "Get used to it. Life takes what you have to give, forgets all about you, and moves on." You may try to have a biblical perspective on death by being realistic and responding to it by focusing on life—and then life sticks it to you!

So what is the solution? What are we supposed to do, given the unfairness of life? The secret is to remember that this life is just a preparation for the real life that is to come. We are foolish if we think we will ever find heaven on earth.

Remember what Jesus told His disciples on the eve of the most unfair several days in the history of the world:

> Let not your heart be troubled; you believe in God, believe also in Me. In My Father's house are many mansions; if it were not so, I would have told you. I go to prepare a place for you. And if I go and prepare a place for you, I will come again and receive you to Myself; that where I am, there you may be also. (John 14:1–3)

Jesus's Crucifixion—the Ultimate Unfairness

The unfairness of life reached its wretched culmination in the life of Jesus Christ. Here was a man who never hurt anyone, went about doing good, was gentle and humble, and had every reason to be received and accepted for what He was trying to accomplish; a man who is today considered the centerpiece of human history, more influential than all the governments and armies that have tried to hold sway over mankind. Yet Jesus and His disciples after Him were attacked and treated as criminals. Jesus was beaten, scourged, crucified, and killed after a mockery of a trial on trumped-up charges. And each of His disciples was put to death in a similarly unjust way, except John, who died of natural causes while in exile at Patmos.

Jesus understood the unfairness of life. On the night before His arrest, He told His disciples not to put their hope or trust in this world. Though we may keep seeking heaven on earth, our true home is with Him, and He will return for us and take us there someday.

The unfairness of this world, along with death itself, will be swallowed up in the great victory of Jesus Christ over death and this world (1 Corinthians 15:54). And when we know that, when we claim the victory that we cannot see with our eyes but can feel with our hearts, then we can do something remarkable and unexpected and wonderful—something therefore miraculous. We can create those "heaven-on-earth" moments that occur when, against all odds, people let themselves become channels for the searing, white-hot grace and love of God in a world cold and darkened by evil. In those grace moments, we reveal our true birthright as creatures of another world, a world where life is infinitely better than simply "fair."

We can be like Elisabeth Elliot and Steve Saint, two family members left behind by martyred missionaries. Jim Elliot, Nate Saint, and four other men committed their very lives to bringing the gospel to the Auca Indians of Ecuador—and they gave their lives in so doing. They would fly in food, gifts, and supplies to their primitive friends, preparing to tell the news of the much greater gift that is Jesus.

But on January 8, 1956, as the missionaries landed their plane, they were unaccountably met by rage rather than friendly welcome. The spears of the Aucas killed every one of them.

The widows and orphans of the martyred men grieved for a time. For decades, no one understood why the attack had happened. I'm certain it crossed the families' minds more than once that not only is life unfair, but it is savagely and viciously cruel to those who are the least deserving.

Yet they also knew that Jesus said, "Blessed are you when they revile and persecute you, and say all kinds of evil against you falsely for My sake. Rejoice and be exceedingly glad, for great is your reward in heaven, for so they persecuted the prophets who were before you" (Matthew 5:11–12).

After a time, the widows went to the jungle to finish the job their husbands had begun. They worked patiently among the Aucas until a great many of them became followers of Jesus Christ. Their message: death always wins; life plays unfairly; *love conquers all.*

Years later, Steve Saint came across a few Aucas (now known as Huaorani) who had been present at the massacre by the stream in 1956. All his life he had wondered what that horrible moment was like. How did his father greet death? Why did this senseless mass murder happen? Now he would find some answers.

The story of the tragedy unfolded from the accounts of Indians who had been eyewitnesses. One man in the tribe had committed some sexual misdeed. His life was on the line, so to divert the anger of the people, he said all manner of evil against the missionaries. He claimed that the six white men were planning to eat the Aucas. This was why the ambush occurred. But there was more to the story.

Dawa, a young woman, hid in the brush during the tragedy. From the bushes by the pool of water where the men died, she heard the whole event. But as the men were killed, she and others who were present heard an odd kind of music peculiar to their ears. They looked up and saw *cowodi* (foreign visitors) singing above the treetops in flashes of bright color.

Only later, when Dawa heard choral music on phonograph records for the first time did she identify the treetop music as being very similar to what was on the record.[2]

Could it be that angels ushered the martyrs to the reward that awaited them? The story is compelling, but there is no way for us to know for sure. We can only be certain that heaven is very close during such moments. When God's heartbreaking goodness intersects with human barbarity, the lights of heaven break through the trees. For just a moment, the intense darkness flees in the presence of that eternal light. All the unfairness and injustice is momentarily forgotten in the face of the obvious truth that our God is near, He is in control, and He will make all things right.

Then we can shrug away the insistence of death and the injustice of life, and stand to sing a chorus with yet another missionary. Amy Carmichael, Christ's servant in India, prayed she might bring the light of heaven to the earth—the greatest goal life offers us, the ultimate joy, the Rosetta stone that deciphers every one of life's imponderables.

Here is Amy's prayer:

> Before the winds that blow do cease,
> Teach me to dwell within Thy calm;
> Before the pain has passed in peace,
> Give me, my God, to sing a psalm.
> Let me not lose the chance to prove
> The fullness of enabling love,
> O love of God, do this for me:
> Maintain a constant victory.
> Before I leave the desert land
> For meadow of immortal flower,
> Lead me where streams at thy command
> Flow by the borders of the hours,
> That when the thirsty come, I may
> Shew them the fountains in the way.
> O love of God, do this for me:
> Maintain a constant victory.[3]

26

Foolishness in Little Things

ECCLESIASTES 10:1–3

LIFE ROLLS ALONG. It's another slow news day, and we each grind through our own daily rituals—work, eat, sleep, play—with reassuring predictability. We nod and smile at familiar faces on the street. We see neighbors at the grocery store and pause for a moment of superficial chatter. The world turns one more revolution, the sun retreats, the moon rises, and all is calm on the western front.

Then, abruptly, something jars us awake from the trance of regularity. News of a terrorist attack, a misfortune in some relative's life, a scandal at church, a lost job, a broken leg, a tearful child. That's when we find out about people.

Exhibit A: the series of devastating wildfires that broke out in California in 2003. Our community responded in a variety of ways, all revealing. Here I was, typing away, immersed in the ancient wisdom of Solomon—and just like that, his observations are played out before me in the reactions of the community.

Two dozen people tragically lost their lives. Many of our friends lost their homes. The flames spread faster than people could flee. Many folks complained about lack of warning. Sgt. Conrad Grayson commented, "We're begging people to leave, and they don't take us seriously. They want to pack some clothes, or fight it in the backyard with a garden hose. They don't seem to understand that this is unlike any fire we've seen. If people don't move fast, they're going to become charcoal briquettes."

Jon Smalldridge sounded the alarm like Paul Revere only to be received like Chicken Little. People either ignored him or took things casually—you know, the California way. They spent time unhooking their home theater systems, computers, and other equipment as the fires raged ever closer. "They looked like they were packing for a trip," said Smalldridge. "The ones who listened to me and left the area, lived. The ones who didn't, died."[1]

A fool is traditionally a comic figure, but foolishness can be as serious as wildfire.

WISDOM AND FOLLY

Dead flies putrefy the perfumer's ointment,
And cause it to give off a foul odor;
So does a little folly to one respected for wisdom and honor.
A wise man's heart is at his right hand,
But a fool's heart at his left.
Even when a fool walks along the way,
He lacks wisdom,
And he shows everyone that he is a fool.

—ECCLESIASTES 10:1–3

Solomon spent a lifetime dealing in wisdom—accepting it, nurturing it, exercising it, brooding upon it, and eventually betraying it. Wisdom was the one shining gift he asked of God, when any gift in the world could have been his. Solomon knew that God's wisdom was his in a way that no other man or woman would ever be able to claim. He wrote a section of the Bible—Proverbs, Song of Solomon, Ecclesiastes—that we refer to now as the Books of Wisdom. So this king had a keen eye for the wise stroke, and therefore the foolish joke as well.

If wisdom is your highest reference point, then you see foolishness as the bane of existence. Solomon saw it everywhere, and it galled him. In his three books he uses the words *fool, fools, foolish,* and *folly* a staggering total of 128 times. In Ecclesiastes 10, he uses these words nine times. The word *fool* occurs in verses 2, 3, 12, 13, 14, and 15.

A sharp dividing line is drawn between the ways of the wise and the follies of the foolish. Not surprisingly, criminals often turn up on the wrong side of that line. The often hilarious misdeeds of the world's most inept crooks have been documented in books and on Web sites. We find that, unlike the suave, ingenious criminal masterminds of the movies, real-life hoodlums are often little more than common fools. And for the chronically inept, a life of crime can be highly stressful.

Rafiq Abdul Mortland simply wasn't cut out for a life of crime. The thirty-eight-year-old found that robbery made him a nervous wreck. Mortland committed a string of robberies in Hennepin County, Minnesota. Eventually he was taken into custody and received a sentence of eight to ten years in prison for holding up eight local businesses.

Mortland was known in law enforcement as "The Rolaids Robber." Apparently his signature calling card was demanding antacid tablets from store clerks while the crimes were in progress. He explained that the job was too stressful; robbery gave him a bad case of indigestion.[2]

It's true, of course. Crime and foolishness are known causes of both heartburn and heartache. Wisdom, on the other hand, is healthy, has no ill side effects, and is recommended by 100 percent of doctors.

Solomon knows there is more than a dividing line between wisdom and folly—there is a canyon! He warns us to stay away from the edge. He seeks to provide us with mile markers and signposts that help us stay on the safe side of life. Ecclesiastes 10, like a lost chapter of Proverbs, dispenses short nuggets of wisdom to keep us on the wise side. He warns us about foolishness in four prominent areas of life: in little things, in leadership, in labor, and in language.

A FLY IN THE OINTMENT

To illustrate his point that little things can create big problems, Solomon uses a rather unusual illustration about perfume. The wealthy king had access to the rarest and costliest perfumes of his day. In Proverbs 7:17 he speaks of the seductive power of perfume in the arsenal of the prostitute. In Proverbs 27:9, he notes the legitimate power of perfume and ointment to delight the heart. Twice in Song of Solomon, he mentions perfume's power to enhance a married couple's relationship. But without question, his strangest reference to perfume is this one: "Dead flies putrefy the perfumer's ointment, and cause it to give off a foul odor; so does a little folly to one respected for wisdom and honor" (Ecclesiastes 10:1).

Suppose you purchased a small vial of expensive perfume, took it home, and put it in a safe spot. Sometime later, you opened the vial and discovered a dead horsefly floating on top. The insect, now partially decayed, had putrefied the precious perfume. This is the source of the well-known phrase, *a fly in the ointment*. It's Solomon's vivid way of illustrating how a tiny bit of foolishness can destroy the powerful fragrance of a person's dignity and reputation.

They say the devil is in the details, and that can be very true. On the big days and big events of life, we're more likely to be on our guard. It's the details that trip us up. We witness the downfall of this politician or that well-known Christian and wonder how such a little thing, something so avoidable, brought down a big man.

Think of the enormous impact of little things in the realm of politics. All it took was the perspiration on Richard Nixon's lip to ruin his televised debate with John F. Kennedy. All it took to make a difference was a few tears in the eyes of Edmund Muskie, Michael Dukakis riding in a tank, Al Gore sighing and moaning during his debate with George

W. Bush, Jimmy Carter talking about malaise, Howard Dean screaming into a microphone.

Over and over, giants are slain by the details. In 1 Corinthians 5:6 we read that "a little leaven leavens the whole lump." If you've ever baked homemade rolls, you know it doesn't take much yeast to have an impact on dough.

Song of Solomon 2:15 warns about the "little foxes that spoil the vines." James 3:5 warns that although the tongue is a small part of the body, it can produce a spark that kindles a forest fire.

"Little sins are not like an inch of candle which soon expires," said a seventeenth-century British clergyman named William Secker, "but they resemble a trail of powder, which takes the fire until at last the barrels burst asunder."

In 1859, Charles Haddon Spurgeon (at the time only twenty-four years old) preached a sermon entitled "Little Sins." Here's part of what he said:

> The best of men have always been afraid of little sins. . . . Men, with their eyes well opened by divine grace, have seen a whole hell slumbering in the [smallest] sin. Gifted with a microscopic power, their eyes have seen a world of iniquity hidden in a single act, or thought, or imagination of sin; and hence they have avoided it with horror—have passed by and would have nothing to do with it. . . . Little sins lead to great ones . . . . Nay, stand back! Little though the temptation be, I dread thee, for thy little temptation leads to something greater, and thy small sin makes way for something worse.

> Years ago there was not a single thistle in the whole of Australia. Some Scotsman who very much admired thistles—rather more than I do—thought it was a pity that a great island like Australia should be without that marvelous and glorious symbol of his great nation. He, therefore, collected a packet of thistle-seeds,

and sent it over to one of his friends in Australia. Well, when it was landed, the officers might have said, "Oh, let it in; is it not a little one? Here is but a handful of thistle-down, oh, let it come in; it will be but sown in a garden—the Scotch will grow it in their gardens; they think it a fine flower, no doubt—let them have it, it is but meant for their amusement." Ah, yes, it was but a little one; but now whole districts of country are covered with it and it has become the farmer's pest and plague. It was a little one; but all the worse for that, it multiplied and grew. If it had been a great evil, all men would have set to work to crush it. . . . Take heed of the thistle-seed, little sins are like it. Take care they are not admitted into your heart.[3]

Thistle seeds are all over the place, everywhere we go. They are like the little burrs that stick to your socks as you walk through a meadow. As Spurgeon points out, the whole town rallies to fight the barbarian at the gate, so the enemy is more likely to send a spy who can more easily penetrate the castle walls.

No big deal, we think, *It's just a little thing.* A "little" relationship, a "little" flirtation at the office," a "little" edge in the tone of voice, a "little" padding on the expense account, a "little" experimentation in the wrong area—*just a little thing.*

OBEDIENCE IN LITTLE THINGS

French priest Jean Nicolas Grou, who died in 1803, said:

Little things come daily, hourly, within our reach, and they are not less calculated to set forward our growth in holiness, than are the greater occasions which occur but rarely. Moreover, fidelity in trifles, and an earnest seeking to please God in little matters, is a real test of devotion and love. Let your aim be to please our dear Lord perfectly in little things.[4]

Solomon adds an interesting thought to his reasoning: "A wise man's heart is at his right hand, but a fool's heart at his left" (Ecclesiastes 10:2). Now, this has nothing to do with being right-handed or left-handed. In biblical times, a person's right hand was perceived to be the place of power. The adviser who stood or sat to the king's right was his most trusted official.

Obedience in little things implies that we're standing in a place of wisdom and power. When we keep slipping up in little things, it indicates we're standing in a place of foolishness, and our power and influence are diluted.

On January 12, 1997, Swiss men Bertrand Piccard and William Verstraeten set out on a venture to be the first to circle the earth in a hot-air balloon. Their aircraft, the *Breitling Orbiter,* was a picture of high-tech perfection, complete with solar panels for power and a pressurized cabin allowing them to fly at high altitudes. Their plan was to float high enough to enter the jet stream, which would carry them around the globe at two hundred miles per hour. The price tag for their venture was a lofty $1.5 million.

Not long after takeoff, however, disaster struck. Inside their sealed and pressurized cabin, the two men noticed a strong kerosene smell—and it got worse by the minute. They tried tightening all the connections on the lines carrying the kerosene fuel, to no avail. They e-mailed their support crew of technicians on the ground seeking advice and, hopefully, a solution. They were told to descend to an altitude at which it would be safe to depressurize the cabin so they could get fresh air, and try to hold on until they reached the northern coast of Africa. However, the fumes proved to be overwhelming, and they were forced to ditch their craft in the Mediterranean Sea.

Upon inspection, they discovered what ended the $1.5 million epic voyage: a defective hose clamp, like those that secure an automobile radiator hose. Cost of the clamp? $1.16. A small, seemingly insignificant defect can ruin an otherwise noble venture.[5]

SMALL DECISIONS AFFECT BIG OUTCOMES

I'm certain you're familiar with this old saying:

> For want of a nail, the shoe was lost;
> For want of the shoe, the horse was lost;
> For want of the horse, the rider was lost;
> For want of the rider, the battle was lost;
> For want of the battle, the kingdom was lost;
> And all for the want of a horseshoe nail.

Think about that. For want of a nail, a kingdom was lost. You'd think that would be impossible, but every detail of life sets in motion a chain of events we cannot predict. We've talked about that desert sojourn when Jesus prepared for the ministry upon which all of human history would turn. The devil's very first suggestion involved no more than a crust of bread. Jesus was hungry; He was fasting so that His spiritual perception and unity with the Father would be fully optimized.

"If You are the Son of God, why not just command these stones to become bread?" the devil asked. Why not indeed? It was no big deal, just a little thing. Here is how "little":

> For want of abstaining from a crust of bread, a fast would be lost.
> For want of a fast, a prayer would be lost.
> For want of a prayer, a vision would be lost.
> For want of a vision, a mission would be lost.
> For want of a mission, a sacrifice would be lost.
> For want of a sacrifice, an eternal kingdom would be lost.

If Jesus had yielded to the lure of the little thing at that moment, all that followed would have been impossible. The spotless Lamb could not have been slain, the atonement could not have been achieved, the sin could not have been forgiven; and you and I would be without any hope for this life or the one to come.

What about your life? What are the little horseshoe nails, the little crusts of bread, the tiny temptations that affect the direction of your life? According to Solomon, the one who pays the terrible price for the tiny bait is the fool.

Saintly Scottish preacher Horatius Bonar wrote:

> A holy life is made up of a multitude of small things. It is the little things of the hour and not the great things of the age that fill up a life like that of the apostles Paul or John, David Brainerd, or Henry Martyn. Little words, not eloquent speeches or sermons; little deeds, not miracles or battles, or one great heroic effort or martyrdom, make up the true holy life.[6]

Another new day faces you. Ask God, through the loving grace and overcoming power of His Holy Spirit, to afford you the wisdom to choose light at every turn. I believe that as you connect the dots of wise choices, a great haze will drop away from your vision. A dark cloud may have followed you for so long that you've ceased to be aware of it. But that haze is a barrier that can keep you from seeing the City of God that lies ahead. It can make an eleven-day journey turn into thirty-eight years of wandering in the wilderness. It can make you stop believing in your God or yourself after a while. It's just the kind of cloud the enemy wants to keep you wrapped up in, all the better to deliver you to the destiny of his choosing.

But as you make wise choices, live the godly way, and keep the vision of Christ before you—the light will begin to disperse the darkness. You will see the very image of heaven on earth. And that sight, my friend, is *not* a little thing.

27

Foolishness in Leadership

ECCLESIASTES 10:4–7, 16–19

Among those who enjoy the activity of rock climbing, *Trail* magazine is a popular periodical. The February 2004 issue provided directions for climbers descending Britain's highest peak, Ben Nevis. The summit is 4,409 feet high, and coming down in bad weather can be tricky. *Trail* offered detailed instructions for the descent—but the instructions were wrong.

Roger Wild of the Mountaineering Council of Scotland caught the error and immediately contacted the magazine to point it out. *Trail* admitted that a crucial step in the instructions was somehow left out.

It's a good thing nobody had followed the plan. In poor visibility, climbers would have walked off the edge of a cliff into Gardyloo Gully. The one-thousand-foot drop is one of the longest in Britain.

Guy Procter, editor of *Trail,* apologized for the missing sentence that made the potentially tragic difference. He pointed out that *Trail* advises all climbers to use an ordnance survey map and a good compass.[1]

A deleted sentence is a "little" thing with large consequences. So is the issue of leadership. What if we find out, all too late, that it's all been a case of the blind leading the blind? We have to be careful who we follow, because it's a long way to the bottom. Solomon now turns to the topic of foolish leadership, providing sound advice for all of us who lead in church, in business, in government, and at home (Ecclesiastes 10:4–7, 16–19).

In tough times, we look to our leaders. Families, churches, businesses, cities, states, and nations all need strong leadership, or the future will be bleak for those who follow. Just look at the sons and successors of Solomon, the kings who followed in his wake on the throne of Judah. The books of 1 and 2 Kings are studies in wise and foolish leadership. When the king was a morally upright man and a wise manager, the nation prospered. When the king was careless, heartless, ruthless, and godless, the entire nation slid toward abysmal ruin.

In a 1954 speech, Winston Churchill reflected on his leadership during World War II when he rallied the British Isles to withstand the Nazi threat. He said, "I have never accepted what many people have kindly said, namely, that I inspired the nation. It was the nation and the race dwelling around the globe that had the lion heart. I had the luck to be called upon to give the roar."

EGO-DRIVEN LEADERS

If the spirit of the ruler rises against you,
Do not leave your post;
For conciliation pacifies great offenses.

—ECCLESIASTES 10:4

This is a picture of a leader who shouts and screams at everyone around him. This leader verbally abuses those who want to serve him. He thinks he's above everyone else, giving him the right to oppress them with cruel language.

Woodrow Wilson once wrote that every man who takes office in Washington either grows or swells. He said, "When I give a man an office, I watch him carefully to see whether he is swelling or growing."

The ego-driven leader swells, and he often bursts out in anger. Sound like your boss?

Solomon has ideas for dealing with the ego-driven leader. He says, "If the spirit of the ruler rises against you, do not leave your post; for conciliation pacifies great offenses."

When we see a boss or a leader of any kind abuse power, our first impulse is to just walk away. At least, it's a better strategy than staying and doing something foolish. But Solomon says there's a better way still. Don't panic, don't quit your job, and don't leave your post. Don't over-react to an overreaction. Just hang in there and deal with the person.

In the book of Proverbs, Solomon gives similar advice:

> As messengers of death is the king's wrath,
> But a wise man will appease it. (Proverbs 16:14)

> By long forbearance a ruler is persuaded,
> And a gentle tongue breaks a bone. (Proverbs 25:15)

> A soft answer turns away wrath,
> But a harsh word stirs up anger. (Proverbs 15:1)

The apostle Paul says much the same thing in Romans 12:18: "If it is possible, as much as depends on you, live peaceably with all men." (With all women too!)

King Solomon is saying that we may find ourselves in the workplace dealing with obnoxious, temperamental, ego-driven leaders. Stay calm in the face of their tirades. Follow the Scripture. Try underreacting. Remember that a soft answer turns away wrath. We're often surprised at what happens when we try that.

In his book *At Ease: Stories I Tell to Friends,* President Dwight Eisenhower tells how he learned this lesson. When he was ten, he became so angry at someone that he beat his fists into an old apple tree until his knuckles were bleeding. That night his mother came into his bedroom. He was sobbing into the pillow, and she sat in the rocking chair by the bed and said nothing for a long time. Then she began to talk about anger, quoting Proverbs 16:32: "He who is slow to anger is better than the mighty, and he who rules his spirit than he who takes a city."

There was little to be gained in hating another person, she told him as she put salve on his injured hands. We only hurt ourselves.

Eisenhower considered that conversation one of the most valuable moments of his life, and it led to his developing a curious habit as an adult. Whenever someone angered him, he would write the person's name on a piece of scrap paper, drop it into the lowest drawer in his desk, and say to himself, "That finishes the incident."[2]

In other words, there's a time to stay at our post with unruffled spirits even when others are ranting and raving around us. As Rudyard Kipling said, "If you can keep your head when all about you are losing theirs and blaming it on you. . . . you'll be a man, my son."[3] That's true, even when facing egomaniacal tyrants and swaggering rulers.

Missionary-author Isobel Kuhn discovered this at a critical moment. She was serving in China with her husband, John, and their little son, Danny, who was six. John was in a distant location, so Isobel found herself virtually alone and in horrible danger. Dreaded bands of local thugs, the Lo-zi-lo-pa, had been bribed by the Communists to terrorize the area in advance of a full-fledged invasion.

Friends and national Christians encouraged Isobel to flee with her little son, because her status as a foreign Christian would put her at special risk. Isobel was paralyzed with uncertainty. She had no way of sending word to John, that she was fleeing, and he might well lose his life trying to get to her. In addition, escaping from China across the rugged Pienma Pass would involve grave danger and hardship.

In her fascinating book, *In the Arena*, she wrote:

> I use a Scripture calendar and the verse that morning was, "Do not leave your post!" (Ecclesiastes 10:4). Very appropriate. Just like an answer. . . . On this occasion, with the threat of the ruth-

less Lo-zi-lo-pa descending on us, I felt the verse was from Him. And after deciding not to flee I had perfect peace—another sign it was His voice. . . . And so it proved. Day after day passed with quietness.[4]

Conditions improved just long enough for Isobel's husband John to reach his family, and they were able to begin planning a safer evacuation from the area.

Robert Greenleaf coined the term *servant-leader* to refer to leaders who choose, as their highest priority, to serve those under them. Here is how he describes the servant-leader:

> The servant-leader is servant first. . . . It begins with the natural feeling that one wants to serve, to serve first. Then conscious choice brings one to aspire to lead. He or she is sharply different from the person who is leader first, perhaps because of the need to assuage an unusual power drive or to acquire material possessions. For such it will be a later choice to serve—after leadership is established. The leader-first and the servant-first are two extreme types. Between them there are shadings and blends that are part of the infinite variety of human nature.
>
> The difference manifests itself in the care taken by the servant-first to make sure that other people's highest priority needs are being served. The best test, and difficult to administer, is: Do those served grow as persons? Do they, while being served, become healthier, wiser, freer, more autonomous, more likely themselves to become servants? And, what is the effect on the least privileged in society? Will they benefit, or, at least, will they not be further deprived?"[5]

Greenleaf says servant-leaders may or may not be in formal positions of leadership. That means anyone can be a servant-leader. I believe Solomon would say there is wisdom in being a servant-leader when you are being abused by an ego-driven leader. By using conciliation, servant-leaders may well change the hearts of the abusive leaders over them.

EASYGOING LEADERS

There is an evil I have seen under the sun,
As an error proceeding from the ruler:
Folly is set in great dignity,
While the rich sit in a lowly place.
I have seen servants on horses,
While princes walk on the ground like servants.

—ECCLESIASTES 10:5–7

Solomon next warns against easygoing leaders. Easygoing leaders put unqualified people in office while ignoring those who should be serving under them. Often, strong leaders put strong people around them, but weak leaders surround themselves with weak people. Often these so-called leaders are insecure; sometimes they're just lazy. In any event, they aren't effective.

It happens all the time in our society that seasoned veterans—those who have served for years with loyalty—are passed over. Has it happened to you? Have you been in an environment where the most qualified people were replaced or sidelined, while unqualified people assumed the reigns? You could see disaster in the making, yet there was little you could do about it.

Leaders without strength are not leaders but mere puppets. James Truslow Adams, in his book *The Adams Family*, describes what set many of America's colonial leaders apart:

As we look over the list of the early leaders of the republic,
Washington, John Adams, Hamilton, and others, we discern that

they were all men who insisted upon being themselves and who refused to truckle to the people. With each succeeding generation, the growing demand of the people that its elective officials shall not lead but merely register the popular will has steadily undermined the independence of those who derive their power from popular election. The persistent refusal of the Adamses to sacrifice the integrity of their own intellectual and moral standards and values for the sake of winning public office or popular favor is another of the measuring rods by which we may measure the divergence of American life from its starting point.[6]

Winston Churchill was beside himself in the years leading up to World War II because England's easygoing, peace-at-any-cost leaders were naive about the rising Nazi threat on the Continent. To Churchill's exasperation, Britain's ruling class continued to maintain a relaxed schedule, adhering to antiquated customs of leisurely weekends in country estates away from London. Churchill bitterly complained that Parliament "takes its weekends in the country while Hitler takes his countries in the weekends."

One of America's foremost leadership gurus, Peter Drucker, once observed there is little correlation between a leader's effectiveness and his or her intelligence, imagination, or knowledge. Brilliant people are often strikingly ineffectual, he said. "They never have learned that insights become effectiveness only through hard systematic work."[7]

THE ENGINEERED LEADER

Woe to you, O land, when your king is a child,
And your princes feast in the morning!
Blessed are you, O land, when your king is the son of nobles,
And your princes feast at the proper time—
For strength and not for drunkenness!

—ECCLESIASTES 10:16–17

I love the way *The Message* paraphrases Ecclesiastes 10:16–17: "Unlucky the land whose king is a young pup, and whose princes party all night. Lucky the land whose king is mature, where the princes behave themselves and don't drink themselves silly" (MSG).

Solomon speaks of inexperienced leaders who acquire office by the help of family and friends. Their leadership is orchestrated, arranged, or negotiated. They often haven't a clue as to what they're doing; consequently, they do little at all. In the morning, when they should be caring for the matters of work, home, state, or government, they're feasting and drinking, enjoying the perks of their roles without investing the passion or perseverance needed for success. Woe to you when your king is childish, wrote Solomon, and when your leader is immature.

Childish leaders are a terrible problem today. We seem to have plenty of them in the sports world. They should be role models, but instead they're moral disasters. Ditto for many of our politicians, entertainers, and business and financial leaders.

Do you know how to identify mature leaders? They're the ones who take the blame when things go wrong but share the credit when things go well. In his book on leadership, *The Winner Within,* Coach Pat Riley tells of pulling Magic Johnson aside one afternoon during the summer of 1980 and telling him that in more than twenty years of playing and coaching basketball, he'd never seen such a complete package—great skills combined with great attitude. Riley asked Magic point-blank to explain his success.

Magic Johnson said that when he was a little boy, playing youth league basketball in East Lansing, Michigan, his coach had told him, "You're the biggest. You're our best player. You should shoot the ball all the time."

Magic did as he was told, but it wasn't satisfying to him. Even though he scored the most points and his team won consistently, the other players seemed miserable. They felt like nobodies. Magic didn't like it that way, especially because it was driving a wedge between him and his friends. So he changed his style. Instead of scoring all the points, he would draw the defenders then pass to whoever was open. His unselfishness enhanced others' skills, and his team began to experience the same kind of enthusiasm that he enjoyed.[8]

The engineered leader, however, never understands that. He thinks it's all about him.

The Evil Leader

Because of laziness the building decays,
And through idleness of hands the house leaks.
A feast is made for laughter,
And wine makes merry;
But money answers everything.

—Ecclesiastes 10:18–19

Picture a guy sitting at home with a bottle of beer in his hand, watching television. He's supposed to be doing work, taking care of things, providing for those for whom he is responsible. He's supposed to be a steward of the tasks entrusted to him. But the house is falling down. The roof is leaking. The bills are stacking up. The beer belly's growing larger.

Solomon offers no excuses for such a person. He's just an evil man who cares nothing about his responsibilities. Through his laziness, his leadership is dissipated and his kingdom is destroyed.

Solomon has strong views on this subject—and remember that this book of Ecclesiastes was inspired by the Holy Spirit, so it reflects God's views. How does God view laziness? Take your Bible sometime and read through Proverbs, underlining the verses that talk about being slothful, lazy, diligent, or hardworking. You'll come away with a whole new perspective on ambition and energy in your life.

If we want to be wise leaders, what should we do? How should we live? The following is from the private diary of William E. Sangster, a great Methodist leader who helped London endure the Battle of Britain during World War II. After his death, this journal entry was found in which Sangster expressed his growing conviction that he should take a more active part in the leadership of the Methodist church in England. His attitude is a shining example of what we'll find inside a true leader:

> This is the will of God for me. I did not choose it. I sought to escape it. But it has come. Something else has come too. A sense of certainty that God does not want me only for a preacher. He wants me also for a leader. . . . I feel a commissioning to work for God for the revival of this branch of His church—careless of my own reputation, indifferent to the comments of older and jealous men. I am thirty-six. If I am to serve God in this way, I must no longer shrink from the task, but do it.[9]

In what field of life are you a leader? In the home? At work? In a Sunday school class? If you're wise, you'll realize that you never stand alone before God; with you stand the souls of those you lead. Your stewardship of these souls is an issue with eternal consequences—a heaven-on-earth issue. Remember that a good leader walks ahead of his people, to point the way; beside his people, to share in their journey; and behind his people, to protect them and cover their mistakes. In other words, he leads in the same way Christ leads us. So as Christ covers us, and we cover those we lead, we make our way forward in wisdom and eagerness for all that God has in store.

28

Labor, Language, and Lunacy

Ecclesiastes 10:8–15, 20

~~~~~~

I T HASN'T BEEN LONG since the book *Working Smart* by Michael Leboeuf was all the rage in management circles. The author demonstrated that the key to better production isn't longer hours but more effective ones. And we all know the truth of that proposition. There's no substitute for putting in the time, but it doesn't mean much if you're not working as wisely as possible. It pays to work smart.

This chapter in Ecclesiastes might be called "Working Dumb." Solomon paints a slightly amusing picture of the ignorant and ineffective laborer. He gives us five illustrations of the errors we make on the job.

Foolishness in Labor

He who digs a pit will fall into it,
And whoever breaks through a wall will be bitten by a serpent.
He who quarries stones may be hurt by them,
And he who splits wood may be endangered by it.
If the ax is dull,
And one does not sharpen the edge,
Then he must use more strength;
But wisdom brings success.

—Ecclesiastes 10:8–10

It's the weekend, and you're out in the backyard digging a pit. You've decided to put in a swimming pool, so you make the hole nice and deep. You're really sweating, and the shovel is putting calluses on your hands. But you start thinking about a nice, cool swim—and in the midst of your reverie, you're swimming in loose dirt! You've fallen into your own hole. Calling for help, you know you'll *never* live this one down.

This kind of thing actually happens, and in even worse settings. My friend the mortician once told me of the time people were walking to put a casket down and one of the pall bearers fell into the grave. It was a double hole where two people are buried, one on top of the other. The poor man fell all the way down and landed with a thump on the casket that was already there.

It's important to watch where you're walking and to make sure the hole you're digging isn't your own grave!

While Solomon is in outdoor-project mode, he moves to a second example: knocking out a section of wall. The worker forgets that snakes love to live in the cold caverns of walls, and when he reaches into the wall he just breached, he is bitten by a snake. Serpents of one sort or another are always lurking nearby, and the wise laborer keeps an eye out for them.

A third man labors in a stone quarry. He becomes careless and brings a great stone down on himself. I'm certain Solomon was thinking of a specific case here, because he had eighty thousand men who quarried stone in the mountains for the great public-works projects he initiated.

> And the king commanded them to quarry large stones, costly stones, and hewn stones, to lay the foundation of the temple. So Solomon's builders, Hiram's builders, and the Gebalites quarried them; and they prepared timber and stones to build the temple. (1 Kings 5:17–18)

There weren't any construction firms that specialized in world-class temples, so Solomon must have been exposed to his share of foolish laborers. One of the eighty thousand was a careless soul, and the sad news came to the throne. We can imagine the supervisor reporting to the king. "We lost another one down in the quarry," he says. Solomon wants to know how. "Just some stupid mistake. The guy dug out a small stone that turned out to be the only thing keeping a five-ton one from rolling out."

Our fourth witless worker is splitting wood. He, too, becomes careless, and someone is hurt. Moses had anticipated this kind of thing, for we read in Deuteronomy 19:5:

> When a man goes to the woods with his neighbor to cut timber, and his hand swings a stroke with the ax to cut down a tree, and the head slips from the handle and strikes his neighbor so that he dies—he shall flee to one of these cities [of refuge] and live.

Numbskull number five is another one who failed Woodshop 101 in high school—or at least he was out sick on the day when tool maintenance was covered. This fellow doesn't stop to sharpen his ax, so he works twice as hard, twice as long, and sees half the results. If he were wise, he'd take time to sharpen his ax and thus save himself a lot of time and energy. As it is, he's working harder when he should be working smarter.

The world is filled with ineffective workers. For example, did you read about the fellow who was killed when a Coke machine toppled on him as he was attempting to tip a soda out of it?

Or the Toronto lawyer named Garry Hoy who was demonstrating the safety of windows in a downtown Toronto skyscraper? He crashed through a pane with his shoulder and plunged twenty-four floors into the courtyard of the Toronto Dominion Bank Tower. He had been explaining the strength of the building's windows to visiting law students. Peter Lauwers, managing partner of the firm Holden Day

Wilson, told a Toronto newspaper that Hoy was "one of the best and brightest" members of the two-hundred-man association.

Ken Charles Barger accidentally shot himself to death in Newton, North Carolina. He was in bed when the phone rang, and when he reached for it he grabbed instead a Smith & Wesson .38, which discharged when he drew it to his ear.

A news report recently told of six people who drowned while trying to rescue a chicken that had fallen into a well in southern Egypt. An eighteen-year-old farmer was the first to descend into the sixty-foot well. He drowned, apparently after an undercurrent in the water pulled him down. His sister and two brothers, none of whom could swim well, went in one by one to help him, but they also drowned. Two elderly farmers then came to help, but they apparently were pulled by the same undercurrent. The bodies of the six were later pulled out of a well in the village of Nazlat Imara, south of Cairo. The chicken was also pulled out. It survived.[1]

All of which makes Solomon's point. When you're using your hands, use your head. The best power tool you have is the one whirring away between your ears. We need to learn to use that wonderful thing called "common sense," although it seems more and more uncommon to find people with good sense. Work in wisdom.

FOOLISHNESS IN LANGUAGE

Poet Robert Frost once gave this commentary about the tongue: "Half the world is composed of people who have something to say and can't, and the other half who have nothing to say and keep on saying it."

Another writer quipped, "Nothing is more frequently opened by mistake than the human mouth."

FOOLISHNESS AND THE TONGUE

How appropriate for Solomon to conclude Ecclesiastes 10 with a discussion about the tongue. I've observed, in studying the wisdom literature of Scripture, that there's seldom a discussion about foolishness without some reference to a person's use of the tongue.

Jesus says, "A good man out of the good treasure of his heart brings forth good things, and an evil man out of the evil treasure brings forth evil things" (Matthew 12:35).

If there's one place where we can spot foolishness, it's in the way people use their tongues. Solomon shows us five ways misuse of the tongue reveals a foolish heart.

1. The Untamed Tongue

> *A serpent may bite when it is not charmed;*
> *The babbler is no different.*
>
> —ECCLESIASTES 10:11

In Solomon's colorful court, there were charmers purported to hypnotize snakes. Many of these snakes were cobras, with their flickering tongues and beady eyes. The snake would rise and sway to the plaintive tones of the charmer's flute. People would marvel at the obedience of such a sly and powerful creature—until the cobra showed he was even slyer than they thought!

The charmer, it seemed, wasn't quite charming enough. It works just the same way with the "babbler"—the person with the gift of gab. Solomon points out that this person's tongue is much less charming than expected, and at the least predictable moment—it *bites*. We've all been victims of biting comments, and we recognize the universality of this principle. Solomon does well in comparing the tongue to a cobra.

In Ecclesiastes 3, Solomon says there is a time to speak and a time to be silent. Babblers forget the latter part of that advice. They always have an opinion or an answer. The tongue is the rudder with which they navigate their way through life (an analogy James uses in the New

Testament), and it's a far less trustworthy implement than they think.

Occasionally I'll find myself determined to say something when I know in my heart I should be silent. *Jeremiah, just keep your big mouth shut. Don't say anything,* whispers the Spirit. I'm always wise when I listen to that counsel, and never wise when I ignore it. Whatever you do, don't be a babbler because you might get hurt in the process.

This is the question no one wants to answer, so take a deep breath. Just between you and me, do you have a tendency to talk too much? Have you seen it in people's eyes during your conversations? A young man known for his incessant talking once approached Socrates for speech lessons. The great orator agreed but warned, "I will have to charge you double my usual fee. I can show you how to use your tongue, but first you must learn how to hold it."

The ancient philosopher Zeno said, "We have two ears and one mouth; therefore we should listen twice as much as we talk." A good rule of tongue.

2. The Unkind Tongue

> *The words of a wise man's mouth are gracious,*
> *But the lips of a fool shall swallow him up.*
>
> —ECCLESIASTES 10:12

Compare Ecclesiastes 10:12 with Proverbs 10:32, which says, "The lips of the righteous know what is acceptable, but the mouth of the wicked what is perverse."

I'm sure you'll agree that some of the worst problems of your life have been instigated by your tongue—or someone else's. Ill-chosen words are like the evil spirits released from Pandora's box. Once loose, they never again can be contained. You can't "unsay" something you've said any more than you can "unring" a bell. James says you can control a horse or rudder a ship more easily than you can guide the weapon that lurks behind your teeth.

What's fascinating about the tongue is that as evil as it can be, it is capable of amazing goodness as well. Solomon says the words of the wise are filled with grace. Robert Webber grew up on the mission field, where his parents served with Africa Inland Mission. Once, on furlough, the family settled in Montgomery, Pennsylvania, in a small home near a farm. Robert was nine, and he loved blackberries. One day he grabbed a bucket and started picking from the nearby bushes. Without thinking, he strayed onto the neighbor's property and started picking the farmer's crop.

Suddenly, the neighbor burst out the front door, waving his fist. "Get out of my field!" he shouted. "And don't let me catch you on my property ever again! Do you understand me?"

Robert was terrified, and he quickly ran to tell his father. Mr. Webber said, "Give me that pail of blackberries. We're going next-door to talk to that man."

The two marched across the yard, Robert thinking to himself, *Good! My dad will show him a thing or two!*

"Mr. Farmer," said Robert's dad, "I'm sorry my son was on your property. Here, I want you to have these blackberries."

The neighbor was completely disarmed. "Hey," he said, "I'm sorry I yelled at the boy. I don't want the blackberries. I don't even like blackberries. You keep them. And you can pick all the berries you want from my field."[2]

"The words of a wise man's mouth are gracious," says Solomon, "but the lips of a fool shall swallow him up" (Ecclesiastes 10:12).

3. The Unwise Tongue

> *The words of his mouth begin with foolishness,*
> *And the end of his talk is raving madness.*
> *A fool also multiplies words.*
>
> —ECCLESIASTES 10:13–14

273

Some people are simply enamored with the sound of their own voices. I'm certain you know someone like this. There may be nothing in the world to say, but these people say it anyway; then they say it again. Few things in the world test our patience more grievously. Proverbs 10:19 tells us, "In the multitude of words sin is not lacking, but he who restrains his lips is wise."

Students who talk excessively are one of the biggest disciplinary challenges schoolteachers face now, and entire seminars are devoted to managing children who are incessant talkers. When it's an adult, it's even more vexing.

Roxanne Lulofs labels an undisciplined talker as "HARM," for Hit-and-Run Mouth. She says that people with hit-and-run-mouths, for whatever reason, feel compelled to tell you just what they think of you and your actions, regardless of how well they know you. Their desire is to be heard without hearing, to be known without knowing. They don't care about getting their facts straight. They want attention.

Here is the epitaph of a hit-and-run mouth.

> Beneath this stone, a lump of clay,
> Lies Arrabella Young,
> Who on the 24th of May
> Began to hold her tongue.

4. An Unreasonable Tongue

> *No man knows what is to be;*
> *Who can tell him what will be after him?*
> *The labor of fools wearies them,*
> *For they do not even know how to go to the city!*
>
> —Ecclesiastes 10:14–15

Solomon tells us about the man who is always forecasting what roads lie ahead then gets lost on his way to the office. Here are people with little sense of direction in life, yet they're always talking about what they're planning to do in the future, how the future is going to be played out, and what they intend to accomplish. Solomon refers to this phenomenon several other times in Ecclesiastes:

> For who can bring him to see what will happen after him? (3:22)

> Who can tell a man what will happen after him under the sun? (6:12)

> For he does not know what will happen; so who can tell him when it will occur? (8:7)

The same point comes up in Solomon's book of Proverbs: "Do not boast about tomorrow, for you do not know what a day may bring forth" (27:1).

In the evening of his life, Solomon must have wondered about the future of the kingdom he had built. Due to the king's unfaithfulness, God had determined that Israel would become a house divided against itself. Solomon knew that the judgment had to come and that he bore primary responsibility. This lends a touch of poignancy to Solomon's fascination with a future no one knew—except for the ill forebodings in his heart.

5. An Unfaithful Tongue

> *Do not curse the king, even in your thought;*
> *Do not curse the rich, even in your bedroom;*
> *For a bird of the air may carry your voice,*

275

And a bird in flight may tell the matter.

—ECCLESIASTES 10:20

This is the origin of the little expression: "A little bird told me." Birds don't talk, of course, but Solomon is reminding us with this illustration that a wise person doesn't say something in private that he wouldn't want someone to hear in public.

Zig Ziglar was playing golf with a young associate. At the beginning of the game, he looked at the youth with amusement. The young man was about six foot three and weighed about 220 pounds. He was uncomfortable as he approached the tee in an unorthodox way. He picked up his club, wiggled it a few times, laid it down, then repeated the whole process. Zig whispered to someone nearby, "That young man is obviously not a golfer." A moment later, the young man drove the ball about 240 yards right down the middle of the fairway. So much for Ziglar's opinion!

After the fellow hit the ball, he walked over to Zig, looked him in the eye, and said, "Mr. Ziglar, I heard what you said."

Zig wanted to disappear. He wished he could evaporate into thin air. But the young man continued, "I heard what you said when you spoke in my hometown three years ago, and it completely changed my life. I want you to know, Mr. Ziglar, that it is an honor for me to even be on the same golf course with you."

Writing in his book *Top Performance,* Ziglar said that he breathed a sigh of relief and made a new resolution that day to be far more careful in uttering his comments—especially negative ones—about another person.[3]

So we must guard our own tongues, not allowing them to be untamed, unkind, unwise, unreasonable, or unfaithful. Our language, like our labor, is part of the "little things" that guide the well-being of our lives.

Perhaps the best way to end this chapter is to give you an assignment. Before going to the next chapter, take a few moments to memorize a verse of Scripture that will be of constant help to you in all areas of life.

Here it is—the greatest treasure I could give you: "If any of you lacks wisdom, let him ask of God, who gives to all liberally and without reproach, and it will be given to him" (James 1:5).

That verse has meant a great deal in my life. I make it my "Solomon prayer" every morning as I ask God for His wisdom, just as the young king did. I record the request in my prayer journal like this: "My Lord and my God, I am a rudderless ship without You. I cannot work; I cannot speak; I cannot live or love as I should, unless Your wisdom lights my path. Protect me from my own foolishness and teach me Thy way."

> Teach me Thy way, O Lord, teach me Thy way!
> Thy guiding grace afford, teach me Thy way!
> Help me to walk aright, more by faith, less by sight;
> Lead me with heav'nly light, teach me Thy way![4]

29

Life Is Uncertain: Embrace It!

Ecclesiastes 11:1–6

Newspaper columnist rosemary smith recently wrote about where she finds her daily encouragement. "When I need cheering up," she writes, "I read my paper towels." Her favorite brand comes imprinted with sayings, jokes, and proverbs. One day, on the verge of tears, she tore off a sheet to wipe up some coffee and read, "When the chips are down, switch to popcorn." Something about that gave her a needed uplift.

When paper towels fail her, Smith looks for encouraging words on church signs. Sometimes she finds inspiration from bumper stickers or billboards or even on the sides of trucks. If all else fails, she keeps an assortment of little books full of pithy advice. One of her favorite sayings is "Life is uncertain. Eat dessert first."[1]

That saying actually comes from the title of a book published several years ago, based on the story of a lady who loved dessert but who, one day, put off eating her favorite treat until later that evening. The problem was that she was aboard the *Titanic.*

The Bible is a far better source of inspiration than paper towels or church signs, but as Solomon ends his book of Ecclesiastes, his message is one the columnist would embrace—life is uncertain.

Solomon began this journal of Ecclesiastes by giving us a conclusion about life: all is vanity. Arriving at the end of the book he returns to the same conclusion: "Vanity of vanities," says the Preacher, "all is vanity."

In his vast wisdom, Solomon understands that life under the sun, without God, is a meaningless experience. It's life on the treadmill—you get your exercise, but you don't go anywhere.

Solomon employs many metaphors to describe the vanity of life. Chasing the breeze. A puff of smoke. Dust in the wind. The laughter of fools or a forgotten memory. Life without God, as Solomon has demonstrated in many ways, is utterly meaningless.

Now, toward the end, Solomon resolves all the questions he has raised, and he gives us his ultimate conclusion. In preparing for this climactic finish, Solomon articulates some overarching principles on which we should base our lives. These are his final admonitions—four of them:

1. Life is uncertain: embrace it! (Ecclesiastes 11:1–6)
2. Life is short: enjoy it! (11:7–12:8)
3. Life is mysterious: examine it! (12:9–12)
4. Life is obedience: express it! (12:13–14)

Have You Hugged Your Life Today?

Solomon's first point about life is that it's uncertain; therefore, it is to be embraced. Have you hugged your life today?

A few years ago, the newspaper of Camden, Maine, the *Herald,* ran two photos on the same page. The first was a picture of Camden's board of selectmen and town manager huddled around a table, hard at work. The second photograph showed a healthy flock of sheep.

As often happens in the hurried world of newspaper deadlines, someone reversed the captions. The caption under the picture of the sheep identified them left to right as town officials. The first picture, however, had a caption that read, "The Sheep Fold—naive and vulnerable, they huddle for security against the uncertainties of the outside world."[2]

Who is to say whether both pictures might not have wound up with more informative captions than were originally intended?

After all, we often feel like those selectmen are purported to feel: naive and vulnerable, huddled together against the uncertainties of the outside world. That's exactly the problem Solomon addresses in these verses. We are like helpless sheep in a dangerous world, given all that we don't know about the way the world works. Four times in Ecclesiastes 11:1–6, Solomon reminds us of what we do not and cannot know:

- You do not know what evil will be on the earth.
- You do not know what is the way of the winds.
- You do not know the works of God.
- You do not know which will prosper.

Consider the variables. Because men are evil, we do not know what will happen. We must not leave our houses unlocked. We must not trust a stranger on the phone with our credit card numbers. We must not leave our wallets and pocketbooks unattended in public. People are evil, and that invites uncertainty into the world.

Because the winds are unaccountable, we do not know what will happen. We will say more about this later, but the earth itself reflects the fallen state of humanity. A tornado never announces its schedule in advance. A wildfire may come along and destroy neighborhoods. The wind blows where it will, and that invites uncertainty into the world.

Because God's plans are hidden, we do not know what will happen. We trust Him, we love Him, and we obey Him; but we do not know His timetables. He may call us home at any instant—or He may send us on some new earthly mission. God moves in mysterious ways, and that invites uncertainty into the world.

Because we cannot foretell the future, we do not know what will happen. We work hard and seek prosperity, but the economy and the company and even our ability to work are all intangibles. We do not know what the future holds, and that, too, invites uncertainty into the world.

Solomon doesn't tell us to eat dessert first, but he gives us two much more practical, much more useful scraps of advice.

BE DIVERSIFIED IN YOUR INVESTMENTS

Cast your bread upon the waters,
For you will find it after many days.
Give a serving to seven, and also to eight,
For you do not know what evil will be on the earth.

—ECCLESIASTES 11:1–2

Did you read that heading right? The last thing you expected from Solomon was advice about a diversified investment portfolio. Had I been Solomon, I would have advised, "Since life is so uncertain, make sure your spiritual foundation is strong. Make sure your hope of heaven is secure. Make sure your faith is in Christ, the unchanging Rock."

Solomon will come to such considerations in due time. But part of the charm and uniqueness of Ecclesiastes is that it's so surprisingly grounded in everyday life on planet Earth. And who can deny that finance is a considerable part of that everyday life? Not only that, but economic issues are as uncertain as everything else in life. If you've ever followed the Dow Jones industrial average, you understand perfectly.

Actually, Paul wasn't above a little investment tip himself. In 1 Timothy 6:17 he warns, "Command those who are rich in this present age not to be haughty, nor to trust in uncertain riches." Guard your investments with humility.

Solomon was one of the richest men in history, and his legendary wisdom encompassed money management. To this day, some of the best financial advice ever written is contained in the book of Proverbs. And here, in this passage in Ecclesiastes, we see the invention and advancement of the widely lauded strategy of financial diversification.

Notice verse 1: "Cast your bread upon the waters, for you will find it after many days." This is one of the most quoted verses in Ecclesiastes, but what does it mean?

As it happens, Solomon had quite a fleet of ships. "King Solomon also built a fleet of ships at Ezion Geber, which is near Elath on the shore of the Red Sea, in the land of Edom" (1 Kings 9:26).

The next chapter talks about ships transporting gold, precious stones, and expensive woods (1 Kings 10:11). We read of his traveling merchants, his income from international trade, and of yet more ships bringing in the wealth of the world, including "gold, silver, ivory, apes, and monkeys" (verses 15, 22).

Then as now, one of the main trade commodities was grain. The merchants of Solomon's day would load their grain ships and send them off. The Israelites were "casting [their] bread upon the water." But notice that with Solomon, the word is plural: "cast your bread on the *waters.*" In other words, don't put all your grain in one ship. Put your wheat in several ships, and send it out in a diversified way so that if one of the ships should sink, you'll not be ruined.

Grandma called this not putting all your eggs in one basket; we call it diversifying our portfolio. Solomon is telling us that since life is so uncertain, we should spread out our investments. In fact, he goes so far as to recommend that we diversify using seven or eight different places. Look at Ecclesiastes 11:2: "Give a serving to seven, and also to eight, for you do not know what evil will be on the earth."

That is God's counsel regarding our financial investments. Spread them out because life is uncertain.

BE DILIGENT IN YOUR INVOLVEMENT

If the clouds are full of rain,
They empty themselves upon the earth;
And if a tree falls to the south or the north,
In the place where the tree falls, there it shall lie.
He who observes the wind will not sow,
And he who regards the clouds will not reap.

As you do not know what is the way of the wind,
Or how the bones grow in the womb of her who is with child,
So you do not know the works of God who makes everything.
In the morning sow your seed,
And in the evening do not withhold your hand;
For you do not know which will prosper,
Either this or that,
Or whether both alike will be good.

—ECCLESIASTES 11:3–6

Some people are paralyzed by uncertainty. Like a soldier who suddenly becomes aware that he's run into the middle of a minefield, every step is uncertain, and you tend to freeze. When the Allied troops landed on the beach at Normandy on June 6, 1944, they found the shore well fortified by German machine guns. Many of the men crouched behind the great wood-and-iron mines, shaped as crosses and protruding from the water. Those who hunkered down in fear inevitably died; those who kept moving, even into the cascade of gunfire, had much greater hopes of surviving.

Solomon's advice is to keep moving forward; the more uncertainty, the more determined we should be. When he heard people say, "Life is uncertain, so let's give up," he replied, "Life is uncertain, so let's roll up our sleeves."

Prepare for the worst, and work for the best. Over and over, the Bible tells us to work, to be faithful, to be diligent, to be strong, and to use our gifts and resources wisely. "[Redeem] the time," says Ephesians 5:16, "because the days are evil."

After all, the king asserts, we are surrounded by intangibles and variables. Solomon stands in the field between the sky and the dust and the waters, and he knows that greater forces surround him. Overpowering natural forces were not given to our control. No one under the sun can know when the rain will fall, yet it holds within its capricious course the future of all that we grow, all that we eat.

Solomon rests upon a fallen tree and observes that this solid wood, at least, is no mystery; it is tangible, sturdy, and we know its seasons of bloom and decay. But the rain, the clouds, and their inscrutable time-tables—these are beyond our mastery.

The king feels the breeze in his hair and broadens his observation. He comments that the wind, too, is a furtive stranger among us. It moves and ceases moving without regard to the affairs of God's children. It respects no kings, neither does it hold contempt for peasants. It glides among them all, heralding its presence by the tossing of leaves and the rippling of wheat, before moving on to some destination we cannot know.

That wind carries the distant laughter of a child to Solomon's ears, and again he reflects on the mystery of the world—not just around us, but within us. Greatest of all riddles, perhaps, is the living, breathing one that lies within the mother's womb. From the tiniest seed springs all the complexity of the human spirit.

Solomon smiles faintly, and the years show themselves around the corners of his eyes. With all his godly and world-renowned wisdom, with all his years and experience and authority and international relations—he still doesn't possess the tiniest mustard seed of comprehension of this miracle. All Solomon can do is look beyond the sky—there is the One who harnesses the wind, who dispenses the rain, who hand-forms the child.

Solomon rises from the fallen tree and offers his response. To the wisest man in the world—fully as much as to the most outrageous fool—the world is like the wind, uncertain and inscrutable. The only One who knows is the only One who controls, and that is a hopeful thought. It remains for us to sow our seeds vigorously and trust in the rain even if it isn't trustworthy, to count on the wind whether it tosses the hair or topples the barn, to embrace the newborn child for what he is: a creation of and gift from God.

The world is a mystery and life but a vapor, Solomon tells us; but hard work, wise living, and joyful countenance are not. They are the best chance for those who would make the most of earth on their way to heaven. Life is uncertain—embrace it with joy.

More than two hundred years ago, the Connecticut House of Representatives was in session on a bright, sunny springtime day. Suddenly, the sky grew dark and ominous shadows flooded across the chamber. The representatives grew alarmed as they looked out the windows in puzzlement. This was an age that lacked the science to foretell solar eclipses. No one could have expected or understood the sudden blanket of darkness.

A clamor arose among the representatives. *Adjourn! Let us hurry from this House to get our own houses in order!* was the consensus. Some legislators believed the second coming of Christ was surely at hand.

But the Speaker of the House, a devout believer himself, rose to speak. He gently acknowledged that the House was upset by the darkness and that some were afraid. "But the Day of the Lord is either approaching or it is not," he said. "If it is not, there is no cause for adjournment. And if the Lord is returning, I, for one, choose to be found doing my duty. I therefore ask that candles be brought."[3]

In these days of uncertainty, we can ask for no better course. Even as the darkness falls, the light is certain to overcome it. So bring the candles. Lift them aloft to spread their light for as long as the wax holds out, for as long as our strength holds out. The Lord could come today, or He could come in a thousand years. In either case, let us be about our Father's business.

Let us seize the day, raise His flag, and set our thoughts on things eternal.

> Tomorrow, Lord, is Thine
> Lodged in Thy sovereign hand;
> And if its sun arise and shine,
> It shines by Thy command.

Life is Uncertain: Embrace It!

The present moment flies,
And bears our life away;
O make Thy servants truly wise,
That they may live today.[4]

30

Life Is Short: Enjoy It!

Ecclesiastes 11:7–12:8

D<small>R. BENJAMIN ELIJAH MAYS</small>, a great Christian educator and president of Morehouse College, wrote a classic poem that's worth memorizing. It's entitled "Life Is Just a Minute."

> Life is just a minute—only sixty seconds in it.
> Forced upon you—can't refuse it.
> Didn't seek it—didn't choose it.
> But it's up to you to use it.
> You must suffer if you lose it.
> Give an account if you abuse it.
> Just a tiny, little minute,
> But eternity is in it![1]

Dr. Mays must have been reading Ecclesiastes when he wrote that, for it captures the theme of the last two chapters. Life is uncertain, so we should embrace it. Life is short, so we should enjoy it.

How do we enjoy life? Solomon is going to suggest four specific ways for our consideration.

EXPERIENCE EACH DAY TOTALLY

Truly the light is sweet,
And it is pleasant for the eyes to behold the sun;
But if a man lives many years
And rejoices in them all,
Yet let him remember the days of darkness,
For they will be many.
All that is coming is vanity.

—ECCLESIASTES 11:7–8

We don't know how long we have to live, so we should live every day with gusto. Listen to these same verses in *The Message:*

> Oh, how sweet the light of day,
> And how wonderful to live in the sunshine!
> Even if you live a long time, don't take a single day for
>   granted.
> Take delight in each light-filled hour,
> Remembering that there will also be many dark days
> And that most of what comes your way is smoke.

That opening sentence resonates with my spirit. I love the sunshine. I love to see the sun peeking through the window when I get up in the morning. The psalmist said, "From the rising of the sun to its going down the LORD's name is to be praised" (Psalm 113:3).

That's the theme behind the anonymous hymn "When Morning Gilds the Skies." There are many, many stanzas—far more than I can quote here. But here are a few:

> When morning gilds the skies my heart awaking cries:

May Jesus Christ be praised!
Alike at work and prayer, to Jesus I repair:
May Jesus Christ be praised!

When you begin the day, O never fail to say,
May Jesus Christ be praised!
And at your work rejoice, to sing with heart and voice,
May Jesus Christ be praised!

Sing, suns and stars of space, sing, ye that see His face,
Sing, Jesus Christ be praised!
God's whole creation o'er, for aye and evermore
Shall Jesus Christ be praised![2]

We praise God because it is right, because it is appropriate, and because it is commanded. But praising God also has a radical effect on us. I dare you to begin the next seven days with intense, heartfelt praise and worship. Read a praise psalm each day, and reflect on a thoughtful hymn like the one above. Praise Him for the sunshine or the rain—whichever blessing comes that day. Exalt Him for the sheer goodness of a life that features His presence. Sit at His feet for just a few moments, and then watch the effect on your day.

Sigmund Freud suffered from a horrible cancer in his mouth. In 1926, he also developed heart trouble and spent time in a sanitarium. He returned to Vienna with a yearning for morning drives, and for the first time he experienced the glories of springtime in Vienna. "What a pity," he wrote, "that one has to grow old and ill before making this discovery."

Keith LeClair was one of America's youngest and brightest baseball stars. As a twenty-five-year-old head coach, he took Western Carolina University to within one game of the College World Series. LeClair was named the Southern Conference coach of the year three times before leaving to take over the East Carolina program in 1998. He continued his success with the Pirates and turned the program into a perennial contender. Suddenly, his career came to a dramatic stop when he was diagnosed with ALS, amyotrophic lateral sclerosis, more commonly called Lou Gehrig's disease.

"Not long ago, baseball absorbed my life 365 days a year," LeClair said. "I gave the profession of coaching everything I had until after the 2002 season, [when] a doctor said, 'I'm sorry, but you have ALS and there is nothing I can do to help.' All of a sudden, baseball seemed to not matter a whole lot to me anymore. Instead, my thoughts were focused on God and my family."

LeClair now begins each day in the Scriptures, and he has gained a new appreciation for the beauties of each morning. "It astounds me to think of all the help God has provided for our family, and that keeps me going to see another day," LeClair said in a recent article.[3]

I'm glad I can make this discovery anew every morning. Were you to peek inside my journal, you'd find that almost every entry says in one way or another: "Thank You, Lord, for this day, for a good night's rest, and for the privilege of being alive one more day on this earth to serve You."

Robert Louis Stevenson said, "The person who has stopped being thankful has fallen asleep in life." Develop the attitude of totally experiencing each day.

ENJOY YOUR YOUTH THOROUGHLY

Rejoice, O young man, in your youth,
And let your heart cheer you in the days of your youth;
Walk in the ways of your heart,
And in the sight of your eyes;
But know that for all these
God will bring you into judgment.
Therefore remove sorrow from your heart,
And put away evil from your flesh,
For childhood and youth are vanity.

—ECCLESIASTES 11:9–10

Life Is Short: Enjoy It!

By now, you've realized that Solomon has a favorite string on his violin, and it's *the enjoyment of life*. Here, he tells young people to live it up. He encourages those who are young to live with adventure and excitement, because these are some of their best days.

As I've watched the young people in my church and community, it seems that they're always eager to be older. Sixteen-year-olds want to be eighteen, and eighteen-year-olds can't wait to be twenty-one.

Somewhere along the way that process starts to reverse itself!

We ought to be telling our kids to enjoy themselves. Youth has many advantages: less responsibility, lots of energy, many good friends, and boatloads of opportunity. I have watched my own children and grandchildren over the years. One day, after football practice, my sons and I were talking about how much fun it was to play football in college, yet we all agreed it was even *more* fun in high school. College football is a pressure-packed business, but in high school there's camaraderie, school spirit, family, friends, and the brisk aura of Friday nights on the field.

While young people face many challenges and difficulties today, it's also true that life tends to become harder and heavier as we grow older. Solomon counsels us to rejoice in our youth.

But there's a warning. Sow joyfully, but sow healthy seeds and not wild oats. Youth is no excuse for exploits that don't honor Him.

If I were a young person, I would look at my life as a bowl of premium chocolate ice cream. I would savor every bite. It would be foolish to hurry through it when there's only so much in the bowl. I would take a moment to thank God before digging in, and be grateful that He designed this treat to melt so delightfully on the tongue. He would be ever in my grateful thoughts. Youth is to be enjoyed, and dedicated to the One who planned it for us.

If I were a new parent, I would let my kids be kids. I wouldn't want them to grow up too quickly, and when they stumble along the learning path, I would gently help them up and show them how to walk upright. Kids have lots of energy and crazy imagination, but I would see God's joy in that rather than shushing them and imposing unnatural restraint on their natural vitality.

EXPRESS YOUR FAITH THOUGHTFULLY

Remember now your Creator in the days of your youth,
Before the difficult days come,
And the years draw near when you say,
"I have no pleasure in them":
While the sun and the light,
The moon and the stars,
Are not darkened,
And the clouds do not return after the rain.

—ECCLESIASTES 12:1–2

I think of Solomon, sitting in the courtyard of the palace and watching the children romp beneath the trees. With all the weight of the empire on his shoulders, the presence of children must have made him feel young again.

A teenager sits at the king's feet. Perhaps it is a grandchild, a pretty young girl. Solomon is struck by how fast she is growing up. He smiles and begins telling her why she should take care not to lose God in all the commotion of adolescence. The king knows how easy it is for young people to say, "I've got a lot of living to do; the whole world is out there waiting for me! And the Lord will always be there for me later."

He can already see the patronizing look in the eyes of this young girl before him. He says, "Really, hear me out! *Now* is the very time to draw near to your God. The longer you wait, the less you will desire Him, and the more elusive He will prove to be. *Now* is the time when you will make the pivotal decisions on which your whole future will turn. Please don't make them without your Lord."

"Remember" is about memories for us. But as Solomon uses the word—remember your Creator—the term signifies commitment and involvement. *Get with God.* Get with Him daily as you spend time together. Get with Him through His Word. Get with Him in service and with His other children. Get with Him and honor Him.

It's traditional for kids to be criticized by ex-kids. Grumpy old former kid Martin Luther said about the teens of his day: "The young people of today are utterly dissolute and disorderly."

Plato, philosopher and past child, agreed. "The youth are rebellious, pleasure-seeking, and irresponsible," he wrote.

"They have no respect for their elders," sniped Socrates, a one-time juvenile. "Children now love luxury. They have bad manners, contempt for authority. They show disrespect for elders and love chatter."

There is also the Egyptian from six thousand years ago—anonymous but presumably a previous youngster—who carved this inscription on a tomb: "We live in a decadent age. Young people no longer respect their parents. They are rude and impatient. They inhabit taverns and have no self-control."

Well, the next time you think the modern generation is going from bad to worse, remember that God always has a rich handful of teenage heroes ready to change the world. In the Bible, we read of Joseph the dreamer, Daniel in Babylon, David the giant killer, and the virgin Mary (likely still a teen when she gave birth to Jesus).

As a teenager, Charles Spurgeon preached to great crowds, but when they referred to his youthfulness, he replied, "Never mind my age. Think of the Lord Jesus Christ and His preciousness."

In our own day, we've been deeply moved by young people like seventeen-year-old Cassie Bernall of Littleton, Colorado, who was gunned down for her faith during the Columbine tragedy.

Let's encourage our young people and pray for them. God's going to use them to change the world, and they need a head start. They need to remember their Creator in the days of their youth.

Embrace Your Aging Thankfully

In the day when the keepers of the house tremble,
And the strong men bow down;
When the grinders cease because they are few,
And those that look through the windows grow dim;
When the doors are shut in the streets,
And the sound of grinding is low;
When one rises up at the sound of a bird,
And all the daughters of music are brought low;
Also they are afraid of height,
And of terrors in the way;
When the almond tree blossoms,
The grasshopper is a burden,
And desire fails.
For man goes to his eternal home,
And the mourners go about the streets.
Remember your Creator before the silver cord is loosed,
Or the golden bowl is broken,
Or the pitcher shattered at the fountain,
Or the wheel broken at the well.
Then the dust will return to the earth as it was,
And the spirit will return to God who gave it.
"Vanity of Vanities," says the Preacher,
"All is vanity."

—ECCLESIASTES 12:3–8

Life can only be enjoyed day by day, bite by bite. We enjoy our youth thoroughly, express our faith thoughtfully, and finally we learn to embrace the aging process thankfully.

Notice how wonderfully clever God is as He inspires Solomon to write these pages. He knows our smiles might fade a bit as He brings up this particular subject. But Solomon keeps a heavy subject light—and downright funny. Isn't that just what we need when we fret about fresh wrinkles? We need to take ourselves a little less seriously. We need a good laugh.

Solomon gives us a poetic picture of getting older. Let's work our way through this passage looking at the phrases he chooses:

The day when the keepers of the house tremble. Those are your arms and hands. As we get older, they begin to shake and tremble more.

And the strong men bow down. Knees and shoulders grow weaker, more frail as we age, bending and bowing and slumping.

When the grinders cease because they are few. What are "grinders"? Your teeth, of course! We can be thankful for improved dental care, but we still lose a tooth every now and then.

And those that look through the windows grow dim. Are you getting the idea? Our eyes, the windows of mind and body. No one had spectacles in Solomon's time; they had to live with blurry vision.

When the doors are shut in the streets, and the sound of the grinding is low. Our ears and our hearing begin to fail. We can't hear the old street sounds or the mills grinding away.

When one rises up at the sound of a bird. Teenagers can sleep until noon, but that's a skill we lose as we age. We old-timers are up with the chickens. My parents used to stay at our house. No matter what time I got up in the morning, my dad was sitting at the kitchen table. I'd ask him, "Dad, did you go to bed last night?" Sure—he just liked those early hours.

And all the daughters of music are brought low. Your voice starts to quiver and weaken. You don't sing as loudly or clearly as you once did.

Also they are afraid of height, and of terrors in the way. We become much less eager to climb ladders and stairways as we grow older. We don't even like a high curb.

When the almond tree blossoms. What tree blossoms as you grow older? Your hair puts forth white shoots! Rather than informing your spouse you've spotted another gray hair, why not say, "Nice almond tree, honey!"

The grasshopper is a burden. By summer's end, grasshoppers lose their hop. They're more like "grasslimpers."

And desire fails. You can work this one out for yourself. Hint: there's a whole new line of pharmaceuticals to help.

For man goes to his eternal home, and the mourners go about the streets. This is referring to the unavoidable funeral and funeral procession.

This description of aging in the Bible reminds me of the couple in Florida who wanted to get married. Jacob was ninety-two and Rebecca was eighty-nine. As they discussed their wedding, they passed a drugstore, and Jacob suggested they go in. Addressing the man behind the counter, Jacob said, "We're getting married. Do you sell heart medication?"

"Yes, of course we do," said the pharmacist.

"How about medicine for circulation?"

"All kinds."

"Medicine for rheumatism, scoliosis?"

"Definitely."

"Medicine for memory problems, arthritis, jaundice?"

"Yes, a large variety," said the pharmacist. "Whatever the doctor orders."

"What about vitamins, sleeping pills, Geritol?"

"Absolutely."

"And wheelchairs and walkers?"

"All speeds and sizes."

"Great!" said Jacob, "We'd like to use this store as our bridal registry!"

Live long enough and, upon hearing that one, you won't laugh but say, "Hmm, good idea." Regardless of whether you've recently been hatched or you're soon to be dispatched, why not enjoy life to the fullest?

Solomon goes on in verse 6 to give us four images of what it's like to die.

- It's like a silver cord that loosens and falls away.
- It's like a golden bowl that plummets to the floor and crashes.
- It's like a pitcher shattered at the fountain.
- It's like a wheel broken at the well.

Fallen. Crashed. Shattered. Broken. These are all images of lost beauty. Together their picture is heartbreaking.

Then again, Art Linkletter once said that it's better to be over the hill than under it. Whatever life is for us, wherever we find ourselves in age or stage, every moment is a gift of God—brightly wrapped, waiting to be opened, admired, and delighted in. The bittersweet nature of loss makes the present more precious; knowing that the silver cord will one day slip away, we cherish it all the more while it is in our hands.

We mustn't spend too much time brooding over life's transience, for that defeats the very purpose. The time is to be used, to be invested in joy and meaning.

That includes *today.* Go ye therefore and have fun!

31

Life Is Mysterious: Examine It!

ECCLESIASTES 12:9–12

$\sim$

So you finish the course. What happens? Final exam!

There's King Solomon at the front of the classroom, passing everyone a copy of the exam. "Let's test your wisdom," he intones. "Use a number two pencil, and keep your eyes on your own scroll."

The test is going to cover all twelve chapters of Ecclesiastes. You'll be asked about life, death, pleasure, suffering, food, work, money, poverty, wisdom, foolishness—pretty much everything under the sun.

"That's a lot of material!" you whisper in panic to the fellow in the next seat. "What if I don't have a clue?"

"Whenever you don't know one, the probable answer is 'vanity,'" your friend whispers back. "Works every time. When I'm stumped I just write, 'Life is filled with such questions that can't be answered. This too is vanity.' Teacher likes that one."

You mutter, "I hope he was serious when he said that true wisdom is realizing how much we *don't* know. If he sticks to that one, I'll get an A."

Solomon comes to the exam in these final verses, but characteristically, he reverses the formula. For Solomon it's exam first, lessons later. It's a bit like the scene in Lewis Carroll's *Alice in Wonderland* when the king asks the jury to consider its verdict. "No, no," objects the queen. "Sentence first, verdict afterward."

In school, we study and then take an exam. Solomon claims that in the real world we face the exam, and *then* we study. He tells us that wisdom comes through instruction, through insight, and through inspiration.

This world desperately needs wise people. In the late 1700s in France, a young man named Jean-Baptiste Vianney who wanted to become a preacher. His family was very poor, and his studies were hindered by lack of funds. When he finally came up with a way to attend school, his studies were interrupted by the terrors of the French Revolution, then by the wars of Napoleon.

As it turned out, Jean-Baptiste was not a particularly bright student, and when he was finally ordained at age twenty-nine, he was described by his superiors as being academically underqualified. He was sent to the small, obscure village of Ars-en-Dombes, where, to everyone's surprise, he became a powerful preacher whose sermons forcefully impacted the everyday lives of his parishioners.

Jean-Baptiste was especially skilled in individual counseling, and he seemed to be blessed with extraordinary psychological insight. He possessed a knack for helping people know how to apply the Word of God to their daily lives so as to find freedom for real living. Some people became convinced he was a mind reader; and as his fame spread, people came from hundreds of miles to hear him preach and to seek his counsel. During the last year of his life, one hundred thousand people traveled from all over Europe to hear him. He was a kind of eighteenth-century Solomon.[1]

Couldn't we use a few people like him today? If you agree, then why not volunteer? You can be a Solomon. You can be wise. You can acquire the biblical, spiritual, and mental skills to help people.

WISDOM COMES THROUGH INSTRUCTION

And moreover, because the Preacher was wise, he still taught the people knowledge; yes, he pondered and sought out and set in order many proverbs.

—ECCLESIASTES 12:9

Solomon taught the people knowledge through the use of proverbs. A proverb is an earthly saying containing heavenly truth. It's the wisdom of God wrapped in a pretty package. It's distilled wisdom, a practical word for a complicated world. Proverbs are God's "sound bites."

The preamble to Solomon's book of Proverbs says:

> The purpose of these proverbs is to teach people wisdom and discipline, and to help them understand wise sayings. Through these proverbs, people will receive instruction in discipline, good conduct, and doing what is right, just, and fair. These proverbs will make the simpleminded clever. They will give knowledge and purpose to young people.
>
> Let those who are wise listen to these proverbs and become even wiser. And let those who understand receive guidance by exploring the depth of meaning in these proverbs, parables, wise sayings, and riddles. (Proverbs 1:2–6 NLT)

Some define wisdom as "seeing life from God's point of view." I prefer to say that wisdom is the ability to apply biblical truth to real-life situations.

Without the Bible, no one can be wise, for wisdom is the ability to see more than things as they are "under the sun." It's the ability to perceive how the God of heaven sees a situation and to apply His divine wisdom to it.

As we study the proverbs of Solomon, we'll grow in wisdom. And sometimes a simple sentence of truth—one Spirit-inspired sentence—can change a person's whole attitude and life.

WISDOM COMES THROUGH INSIGHT

The Preacher sought to find acceptable words; and what was written was upright—words of truth.

—ECCLESIASTES 12:10

Solomon's teaching was like that of Jesus, who (being God incarnate) possessed an infinite magnification of the wisdom of Solomon. Christ's words were acceptable, full of grace and truth.

Do you ever struggle to find just the right words to say to someone? Well, remember God's offer in James 1:5: "If any of you lacks wisdom, let him ask of God, who gives to all liberally and without reproach, and it will be given to him."

How often I have been in a crisis or tense situation and claimed this truth! I've been with my children, my parishioners, or with someone needing my help, and I've whispered a prayer to God: "Lord, give me wisdom!" If you've been abiding in the Scriptures, it's amazing and inspiring how just the right word rolls off your tongue. You may have little or no education, but you have access to the greatest wisdom of the universe.

Alexander Grigolia immigrated to America from Soviet Georgia, learned English, earned three doctoral degrees, and became a successful professor at the University of Pennsylvania. But despite his freedom and achievements, there was a deep shadow in his heart—a misery he couldn't remove.

One day, while getting a shoeshine, he noticed that the bootblack went about his work with a sense of joy, scrubbing and buffing and smiling and talking. Finally Dr. Grigolia could stand it no longer. With his Russian accent he asked, "Why are you so happy?"

Looking up, the bootblack paused and replied, "Jesus. *He loves me.* He died so God could forgive my badness. He makes me happy."

The professor snapped his newspaper back in front of his face, and the bootblack went back to work. But Dr. Grigolia never escaped those words, and they brought him eventually to the Savior. He later became a professor of anthropology at Wheaton College, where he taught a young student named Billy Graham. An accomplished professor had to bow to the wisdom of a simple, unlearned bootblack.[2]

WISDOM COMES THROUGH INSPIRATION

The words of the wise are like goads, and the words of scholars are like well-driven nails, given by one Shepherd. And further, my son, be admonished by these. Of making many books there is no end, and much study is wearisome to the flesh.

—ECCLESIASTES 12:11–12

Wisdom comes through instruction, insight, and inspiration. The best, deepest, finest, and most lasting wisdom is that which comes from "one Shepherd." Notice the word *Shepherd* is capitalized. That Shepherd is God. The wisdom He gives is like nails that drive truth into the walls of our hearts by the Holy Spirit. Elsewhere the Word of God is likened to a sharp, two-edged sword and is like a hammer that breaks rocks to pieces.

In verse 12, Solomon warns us against studying too many books to the exclusion of the Bible. "Of making many books there is no end, and much study is wearisome to the flesh." That's a favorite verse for college students, but Solomon isn't telling us not to love and appreciate books. He is warning us that we shouldn't study other books to the exclusion of Holy Scripture. Other books were given for our information, but the Bible was given for our transformation. Ruth Bell Graham was once asked the best way to become wise. Her reply, "Read, read, read—but use the Bible as home base."[2] She's right!

In one of his remarkable sermons, Charles Spurgeon thundered:

> Ah! You know more about your ledgers than your Bible; you
> know more about your daybooks than what God has written;
> many of you will read a novel from beginning to end, and what
> have you got? A mouthful of froth when you have done. But
> you cannot read the Bible; that solid, lasting, substantial, and
> satisfying food goes uneaten, locked up in the cupboard of
> neglect.[3]

The Bible is an every-single-day book for me. It has been for many
years, and it will be until the day I die. To go through a day without
immersing myself in its freshness would be like going through a day
without bathing—or breathing, for that matter. As D. L. Moody said,
"Those who read the Bible most find it ever new." The Bible that is
falling apart, it has been said, usually belongs to someone who isn't!

I try to read the Bible every day, but I also read whatever assists me
in grasping it. I read newspapers, journals, and sometimes bestsellers. I
try to read the classics of the ages. But I use the Shepherd's words as the
grid on which I chart all other information, since I believe that the Bible
gives us the final answers to life. What Solomon is saying, I believe, is
that our faith is not primarily about searching; it's about finding. It's not
about questions; it's about answers.

In C. S. Lewis's *The Great Divorce,* there's a scene in which the main
characters are on the borders of heaven, and a lifelong searcher outside
of heaven is being told to come in. The person called the White Spirit
meets him at the borders and says, "The only thing I can give you when
you come in is forgiveness for having perverted all of your values and all
of your brain and all of your intelligence. There is no atmosphere in this
place called Heaven for inquiry. I am going to bring you to the land, not
of questions, but of answers, and you will see the face of God."

The man answers, "Ah, but we must interpret those beautiful words
in our own way!"

The White Spirit replies, "Once you were a child. Once you knew what inquiry was for. There was a time when you asked questions because you wanted answers, and you were glad when you had found them. Become that child again, even now."

"Ah," said the inquirer, "but when I became a man I put away childish things."

The encounter ends when the inquirer mentions he has an appointment, and he makes his apologies, leaving the borders of heaven and hurrying off to his discussion group in hell. Here was a character exposed to the answer, but because he thought reality was in the quest, he wouldn't accept the fact that *answers are available.*[4]

We often wonder whether those in the no-absolutes camp—who claim one person's "truth" is as good as another's—really *want* to find the final Truth. If they could stand on the very borders of heaven, would they embrace the final answers, or would they turn and walk away to keep playing the game of unending speculation?

There is one truth from one Shepherd. Jesus said, "Your Word is truth." We mustn't get so caught up in postmodern inquiry as to forget that questions are for answers, and the answers are available in God's Word.

Conclusion

Life Is Obedience: Express It!

ECCLESIASTES 12:13–14

LET US HEAR THE CONCLUSION of the whole matter:

> *Fear God and keep His commandments,*
> *For this is man's all.*
> *For God will bring every work into judgment,*
> *Including every secret thing,*
> *Whether good or evil.*

(ECCLESIASTES 12:13–14)

Old Solomon sits in his private chamber—the place where he studies and thinks the deep thoughts; the place where his path intersects with the path of the Shepherd who has herded him for so many years of obedience, grazing, growing, and wandering—and not a few wolf bites.

As Solomon ponders "the conclusion of the whole matter," he thinks not simply of the end of a book, nor the end of a king's life, but the beginning of wisdom in life before the King. All of it comes together here. Solomon thinks of childhood at the elbow of his beloved father, King David. He thinks of that evening when he made his great request of God, the years of building and conquest and prosperity, the advisors, the too-many wives—all of it blurs together and he feels smaller than ever before the God of his fathers.

Having held the world's greatest jewels, built the world's greatest temple, and led the world's greatest nation, Solomon has sought the final treasure—no less than the meaning of life itself. He has hungered for the image of heaven on earth, the foretaste of heaven divine.

So much flashes before him: the world's great libraries, wise men from around the world, priests and princes and prophets, ships from exotic lands previously unknown. And all of it comes down to . . . *nothing.*

Never was there the brief hint of heaven on earth. But there was something Solomon's father taught him, something known to Abraham and Isaac and Jacob, to Joseph and all the brothers and their tribes, some simple little thing you might hear on the tongue of the poorest peddler down in the street. And somehow this brief word trumps all the wisdom and learning of the world.

And the word is this:

> Fear God, and keep His commandments, for this is man's all. (Ecclesiastes 12:13)

All indeed.

> For God will bring every work into judgment, including every secret thing, whether good or evil. (12:14)

You could have no riches, no power, no glory, none of life's ordinary pleasure, and if you knew that *one thing*—simple enough for any child—you would have the map to finding heaven on earth. Eternity is fixed in our hearts; light calls to light; deep calls to deep. Therefore we must travel or be forever wretched, miserable creatures.

Fear God: that's the point of departure. *Keep His commandments*: that's the path. Travel it seriously, eyes fixed ahead as you walk the narrow way, and you will indeed see glimpses of the Eternal City.

And thus Solomon comes to journey's end, a rest for his soul. It is as if the final installment of that gift he requested so many years ago has just been made. Surely this is the end point of all wisdom.

A single tear wells up in the eye of the world's wealthiest, wisest, and most powerful man. In his journal, he scribbles in blunt letters, jagged with a hand trembling from age and emotion: "FEAR GOD." To fear God means to be struck with awe in His all-consuming, holy presence; to stand always and forever in breathless exaltation of who He is and what He has done and how vastly and infinitely His greatness overshadows our brief, vaporous existence.

Just beneath that, Solomon scrawls, "KEEP HIS COMMANDMENTS!" Yes, Solomon nods, it is the only way. Find out what God wants done, and *go do it* regardless of the cost. All the rest is vanity, heartache, wandering blind.

In 1866, D. L. Moody was conducting a series of evangelistic meetings in Brockton, Massachusetts. Daniel B. Towner, director of the music department at Moody Bible Institute in Chicago, was leading the music for those meetings.

A young man rose to give his testimony of following Christ, and he included in his remarks these words: "I am not quite sure—but I am going to trust, and I am going to obey."

Mr. Towner was so touched by these words that he jotted them down and sent them to the Reverend J. H. Sammis, a Presbyterian minister and later a teacher at Moody Institute. Reverend Sammis expanded those words into the stanzas and chorus of the beloved hymn, "Trust and Obey." We could inscribe those words right beneath the ones Solomon has written:

> When we walk with the Lord in the light of His Word
> What a glory He sheds on our way!
> While we do His good will, He abides with us still,
> And with all who will trust and obey.

Trust and obey for there's no other way

To be happy in Jesus, but to trust and obey.[1]

God created you with a place in your heart that only He can fill. He has set eternity in your heart. Life for you and for me is like a trip to the mall on Christmas Eve. There is color and music and mingled fragrances everywhere, all sensuous, all seductive, all competing for our attention—all the vanities and pursuits that come up empty. Solomon tried every one of them.

Then, in the back corner, we see the narrow door. It is quiet, plain, unmarked, and largely ignored as people rush by. But we know that our Savior has left this door ajar for us and that it leads us to the place where we will find all that our hearts have desired.

The door is open just a crack, as if in invitation, and we see a brilliant light trying to break through. We know instantly it is the light of another world. It is the light of heaven on earth.

The Good Shepherd said, "I have come that you might have life, and that you might have it more abundantly" (John 10:10). The door may be plain, but the world behind it is rich indeed. Rich and joyful, filled with pleasures. As a matter of fact, all the vain things that charmed us most in this earthly life—the pleasures and pursuits that felt and tasted so empty—are now as wonderful as they always should have been. The Shepherd makes the very sunshine itself feel brighter.

My friend, open that door. Begin the adventure that will be the greatest of your life and the joy that will be the richest. If you don't know my Lord Jesus Christ, I ask you to meet Him this very moment by praying:

Lord, I realize now that my whole life has been a search for heaven on earth. I long to know, to taste, to feel the truth that is true, the love that is genuine, the Master who will never let me down. You died for me so many years ago on a painful cross, and I realize now that You took the payment for all my sins—every one of them. How I long to be relieved of their burden! Just as You rose from the dead, conquering death forever, I choose right now to accept eternal life— to know that death will have no hold on me. And I will pursue You down that path toward the Eternal City with every breath I breathe for the rest of this life until the day You and I meet face to face. Amen.

Notes

Preface

1. *Celebrity Skin*, written by Courtney Love, Copyright © 1998, Mother May I Music. BMI.

Introduction

1. *Christianity Today*, April 1, 1977, 25–26.
2. Carl Jung, *Modern Man in Search of a Soul* (Harvest Books, 1955), 70.
3. Victor E. Frankl, *Man's Search for Meaning* (New York: Washington Square Press, 1984), 128.
4. Rick Warren, *The Purpose-Driven Life* (Grand Rapids: Zondervan, 2002), 19–20.
5. Abba Eban, *Abba Eban: An Autobiography* (New York: Random House, 1977), 609.
6. Jon Krakauer, *Into Thin Air* (New York: Doubleday/Anchor Books, 1997) 3–4.

Chapter 1

1. Thomas Toivi Blatt, *From the Ashes of Sobibor* (Evanston, IL: Northwestern Univ. Press, 1997).
2. Bertrand Russel, *Autobiography* (London, Routledge, 2000), 237.
3. Harold Kushner, *When All You've Wanted Isn't Enough,* (Random House, 1988), 20.
4. Douglas Caffey, *Brevity of Life*. Copyright © 2002. All rights reserved. Used by permission.
5. "Dust in the Wind," words and music by Kerry Livgren, Copyright © 1977. EMI.
6. James S. Hewett, *Illustrations Unlimited* (Wheaton: Tyndale House Publishers, 1988), 291–292.

Chapter 2

1. Paula Guran, *OMNI Online,* Jan. 1998 http://www.darkecho.com/darkecho/archives/ koja.html
2. Michael Crichton, *Timeline* (New York: Ballantine Books, 1999), 443.
3. Victor Frankl. *Man's Search for Meaning* (Boston: Beacon Press, 1000), 169–170.
4. Clifton Fadiman and Andre Bernard, eds., *Bartlett's Book of Anecdotes* (Boston, MA: Little, Brown & Co., 2000), 146.
5. Rudyard Kipling, *The Years Between.* "The Holy War 1917," (London: Methuen, 1919).
6. Chris Ross, *The Jacksonville Daily Progress.* Saturday, November 2, 2003.
7. "Higher Ground," words by Johnson Oatman, Jr., 1898, music by Charles H. Gabriel, 1892.
8. Howard Mumma, "Conversations with Camus," *Christian Century* 117, No. 18: 644.
9. Information on Pascal taken from: www.gospelcom.net; Emile Caillet and John C. Blankenagel, trans., *Great Shorter Works of Pascal* (Philadelphia: Westminster Press, 1948); and www.apologetics.org/articles/pascal.html

Chapter 3

1. Lawrence Taylor, Steve Serby, *LT: Over the Edge* (New York:HarperCollins, 2003).
2. Jim Sami, "L.T. Comments Rile TV Analysts," *Smith Florida Sun-Sentinel,* December 1, 2003.
3. James Dobson, monthly newsletter, May 1996.
4. T.S. Elliot,. "Choruses from The Rock," 1934.
5. *The Star,* Johannesburg, South Africa (Dec. 13, 2003), 1.
6. Vance Havner, *The Secret of Christian Joy* (Old Tappan, NJ: Fleming H. Revell, 1938), 40.
7. David W. Henderson, *Culture Shift: Communicating God's Truth to Our Changing World* (Grand Rapids, MI: Baker, 1998), 186.
8. David Kidner, *A Time to Mourn, and a Time to Dance* (Downers Grove, IL: InterVarsity Press, 1976), 35.
9. CNN.com Report, "Nigeria No. 1 in Happiness, U.S. Ranks 16th," Oct. 2, 2003.
10. C.S. Lewis, "The Weight of Glory," *The Weight of Glory and Other Essays* (New York: Macmillan, 1980), 7.

Chapter 4

1. Mart De Haan, "Winning Big," http://www.christianitytoday.com/ss/ devotional/0072.html
2. Derek Ratcliffe, "Image and Reality: More Reflections on TV Natural History" in *ECOS,* a publication of the British Association of Natural Conservationalists, Vol. 21, NU, July 1, 2000, 5.

3. http://www.uefa.com/news/newsId=131979,printer.htmx
4. Andrew Curry, "Why We Work," *U.S. News and World Report.* Feb. 24, 2003.
5. James Shirley, "Death the Leveler," *The Oxford Book of English Verse* (Oxford: Clarendon, 1919).
6. William Lane Craig, *Reasonable Faith* (Wheaton, IL: Crossway Books, 1994), 58–59.
7. "Like Smoke and Cotton Candy" *Generation Magazine* 2, No. 2.
8. Clara T. Williams, "Satisfied," 1875.

Chapter 5
1. "Turn, Turn, Turn," written by Pete Seeger Copyright © 1962. Melody Trails Inc. BMI.
2. Dr. David Jeremiah, *A Bend in the Road* (Nashville: Word Publishing, 2000).
3. Rabbi Harold Kushner, *When Bad Things Happen to Good People.* New York:HarperCollins, 1982).
4. Donald Regan, *For the Record: From Wall Street to Washington.* (San Diego: Harcourt Brace Jovanovich Publishers, 1988), 232.
5. Robert J. Morgan, *From this Verse: 365 Inspiring Stories about the Power of God's Word* (Nashville: Thomas Nelson, 1998).
6. Thomas O.Chisholm & William Runyan, "Great is Thy Faithfulness" (Carol Stream, IL: Hope Publishing Co., 1951).

Chapter 6
1. "Philip Guston-exposing a futile existence," *Times Online,* Jan. 25, 2004.
2. William Shakespeare, *Macbeth.* Act 5, Scene 5
3. Brother Lawrence, *The Practice of the Presence of God* (Fleming H. Revell, 1999).
4. *In His Time,* words and music by Diane Ball. Copyright © 1978. Maranatha!Music, ASCAP.
5. Malcolm Muggeridge, *A Twentieth Century Testimony* (Nashville: Thomas Nelson, Inc., 1978), 18.
6. Allan C. Emery, *Turtle on a Fencepost* (Nashville: Thomas Nelson, 1980), 110–111).
7. Frederick W. Faber, *Jesus and Mary* (London: Richardson and Son, 1852).
8. Tommy Nelson, *The Problem of Life With God—Living with a Perfect God in an Imperfect World.* (Nashville: Broadman & Holman, 2002), 49.
9. C.S. Lewis, *Mere Christianity* (New York: Macmillan Publishing, 1952), 120.
10. Tom Bisset, *Good News About Prodigals* (Grand Rapids: Discovery House Publishers, 1997), 127–130.

Chapter 7
1. *"God Moves in a Mysterious Way,"* composed by William Cowper, 1774.

2. Jim McGuiggan, *The Irish Papers: Lessons from Life* (Fort Worth, TX: Star Bible & Tract Corporation, n.d.).
3. *Westminster Larger Catechism* (Phillipsburg, NJ: P & R Publishing, 2002).
4. Taken from "Ma Sunday Still Speaks: A transcription of the tape recording she made shortly before her death," published by Winona Lake Christian Assembly, Winona Lake, IN, 1957.

Chapter 8

1. Bob Woffinden, "Ear-print Landed Innocent Man in Jail for Murder," *The Guardian Unlimited,* Jan. 23, 2004.
2. Bureau of Justice Statistics, www.ojp.esdoj.gov/bjs, reported by *Associated Press,* May 28, 2004.
3. Paul Harvey Jr., ed., *Paul Harvey's For What It's Worth* (New York: Bantam Books, 1991), 129.
4. James Russell Lowell, "The Present Crisis," *Boston Courier,* Dec. 11, 1845.
5. William Wadsworth Longfellow, *Poems and Other Writings* (New York: Library of America, 2000).
6. Maurice S. Rawlings, *To Hell and Back* (Nashville: Thomas Nelson, 1993), 20.
7. "God Holds the Key of All Unknown," Words by J. Parker. Date unknown.

Chapter 9

1. Tommy Nelson, *The Problem of Life with God: Living with a Perfect God in an Imperfect World* (Nashville: Broadman & Holman Publishers, 2002), 59–60.
2. Mark Sidwell, *Free Indeed: Heroes of Black Christian History* (Greenville, SC: Bob Jones Univ. Press, 2001), 83.
3. "We'll Understand It Better By and By," written by Charles A. Tindley. Copyright © 1905, Tindley Music Company. BMI.
4. Robert J. Morgan, *Real Stories for the Soul* (Nashville, TN: Thomas Nelson, 2001), 20–22.
5. "Professional Jealousy Grips the Nation," posted on PersonnelToday.com: A Website for HR Professionals. Feb. 2, 2004.
6. Martha Irvine, "Young Adults Yearning for the Simple Life," *Salt Lake Tribune,* Jan. 26, 2004. Reprinted from Associated Press.

Chapter 10

1. T.S. Eliot, "The Cocktail Party," *Complete Poems and Play* (New York: Harcourt, Brace, & Co., 1952), 364.
2. Warren Wiersbe, *An Old Testament Study: Ecclesiastes: Be Satisfied—Looking for the Answer to the Meaning of Life* (Wheaton, IL: Victor Books, 1990), 58–59.
3. Steve Campbell, "The Ring is the Thing," *Houston Chronicle,* Jan. 28, 2004.

Chapter 11

1. Craig Brian Larson, ed., *750 Engaging Illustrations for Pastors, Teachers, and Writers* (Grand Rapids, MI: Baker Books, 2002), 51.
2. Julie Juola-Exline, "When God Disappoints: Difficulty in Forgiving God and Its Role in Negative Emotions," *Journal of Health Psychology* 3, No. 3, 1999.
3. Eva J. Alexander, "Rescuing Women," *Decision*, Oct., 1997, 4–5.

Chapter 12

1. Rev. John Rusk, *The Authentic Life of T. DeWitt Talmage* (L.G. Stahl, 1902), 371.
2. Robert Andrews, ed. *The Columbia Dictionary of Quotations* (Columbia University Press, 1993).

Chapter 13

1. "Hundreds of Coins Found in Patient's Belly," www.cnn.com, Feb. 20, 2004.
2. Quoted in Dough Rehberg, sermon "How to Die," www.hebrononlin.org/archives/01-12-03.pdf.
3. William MacDonald, *Changing the Wind* (Chicago: Moody Press, 1975), 47.
4. Peter Collier and David Horowitz, *The Rockefellers, an American Dynasty* (New York: Holt, Rinehart and Winston, 1976), 48.

Chapter 14

1. "Lottery Winner Dies in Accident Hours After Show," *Associated Press*, www.crm.com, Jan. 24, 2004.
2. Chuck Rasmussen, www.christianglobe.com/illustrations.
3. *Associated Press*, quoted at http://www.azcentral.com/news/articles/1224jackpot-winner24-ON.html
4. Jerry White, *The Power of Commitment* (Colorado Springs: NavPress, 1985), 46.
5. Warren Wiersbe, *An Old Testament Study: Ecclesiastes: "Be Satisfied—Looking for the Answer to the Meaning of Life* (Wheaton, IL: Victor Books, 1990, 74–75).
6. John Woodbridge, ed., *More Than Conquerors* (Chicago: Moody Press, 1992), 340–343.

Chapter 15

1. Barbara Davies, "'Depressed' Colly Books into Priory," Mirror.co.uk, May 3, 2004.
2. Marvin Lubenow, *Bones of Contention: A Creationist's Assessment of Human Fossils* (Grand Rapids: Baker Book House, 1992), 44.

3. Words and music by George A. Young, Copyright © 1903.
4. Robert J. Morgan, *Then Sings My Soul* 2 (Nashville: Thomas Nelson, 2004), 245.

Chapter 17

1. Warren Wiersbe, *An Old Testament Study: Ecclesiastes: "Be Satisfied—Looking for the Answer to the Meaning of Life* (Wheaton, IL: Victor Books, 1990), 84.
2. Bill Bright, *Slave by Choice: The Liberating Joy of Belonging to Jesus* (Santa Clarita, CA: New Life Publications, 2002).
3. Hudson Taylor, *To China with Love* (Grand Rapids, MI: Baker Books, 1972), 62–63.
4. *Our Daily Bread,* published by Radio Bible Class, date unknown.

Chapter 18

1. Conrad Hilton, *Be My Guest* (New York: Simon & Schuster, 1994) 76–77.
2. Gordon MacDonald, *Ordering Your Private World* (Nashville: Thomas Nelson, 1984) 115–116.
3. Moody Bible Institute Stewardship Department, *Today in the Word,* Nov. 9, 1995, 16.
4. J. Oswald Sanders, *Spiritual Leadership* (Chicago: Moody Press, 1967), 143.
5. Gordon MacDonald, *Restoring Your Spiritual Passion* (Nashville: Thomas Nelson, 1986), 192–193.

Chapter 19

1. Robert Frost, "Servant to Servant," *North of Boston* (New York: Henry Holt & Co., 1915).
2. Stephen Covey, *Seven Habits of Highly Effective People* (Free Press, 1989).
3. Andre Castelot, *Napoleon,* Guy Daniels, trans., (New York: Harper & Row, 1971), 231.
4. C.S. Lewis, *The Screwtape Letters* (New York: Macmillan Co., 1961), 56.
5. "O Child of God," words by Fanny Crosby, 1886. Music by Ira D. Sankey.

Chapter 20

1. W. Michael Cox and Richard Alm, "The Good Old Days Are Now," http://reason.com/9512/COXfeat.shtml
2. Arthur Bennett, "The Valley of Vision," Arthur Bennett, ed., *The Valley of Vision, A Collection of Puritan Prayers and Devotions* (Edinburgh: Banner of Truth Trust, 1975), xxiv.

Chapter 21

1. *Nelson's Complete Book of Stories, Illustrations, and Quotes* (Nashville: Thomas Nelson, 2000), 653–654.
2. "State of the World 2004: Richer, Fatter, and Not Much Happier," Worldwatch Institute, www.worldwatch.org, Jan. 8, 2004.

3. Warren Wiersbe, *An Old Testament Study: Ecclesiastes: Be Satisfied: Looking for the Answer to the Meaning of Life* (Wheaton, IL: Victor Books, 1990), 89–90.

Chapter 22

1. Ray Stedman, "Whoever Said Life Was Fair?" *Discovery Papers,* Oct. 31, 1982 (Palo Alto, CA: Peninsula Bible Church Discovery Publishing, 1982), 3.
2. Michael Guido, *The Michael Guido story* (Metter, GA: The Guido Evangelistic Association, Inc., 1990), 134.

Chapter 23

1. Rick Reilly, "Destiny Frowns on Kurt Warner," *Sports Illustrated,* Dec. 1, 2003.
2. Clark Clifford, *Counsel to the President* (New York: Random House, 1991), 140–141.
3. Constance E. Padwick, *Henry Martyn* (Chicago: Moody Press, 1980), 162.
4. Arthur W. Pink, *The Seven Sayings of the Savior on the Cross* (Grand Rapids: Baker Book House, 1958), 110.
5. Ruth Bell Graham, *Prodigals and Those Who Love Them* (Colorado Springs, CO: Focus on the Family Publishers, 1991).
6. Warren Wiersbe, *An Old Testament Study: Ecclesiastes: Be Satisfied: Looking for the Answer to the Meaning of Life* (Wheaton, IL: Victor Books, 1990), 100.
7. Ravi Zacharias, *Can Man Live Without God?* (Dallas: Word Publishing, 1994), 26.
8. Quoted in Wiersbe, *Be Satisfied,* 102.

Chapter 24

1. Warren Wiersbe, *An Old Testament Study: Ecclesiastes: Be Satisfied: Looking for the Answer to the Meaning of Life* (Wheaton, IL: Victor Books, 1990), 84.
2. J.C. Ryle, "A Common End," http://christianbeliefs.org/articles/death.html
3. Ray C. Stedman, "Ah, Sweet Mystery of Life," http://www.pbc.org/dp/stedman/eccles/pdf/3813.pdf
4. S.I. McMillen and David Stern, *None of These Diseases* (Grand Rapids: Fleming H. Revell, 2000), 227–228.
5. An ancient fable retold by W. Somerset Maugham in his play "Sheppey" in 1933.
6. From "Nightline" on ABC; transcript of Ted Koppel's interview with David Letterman.
7. Quoted in Mark Noll, *The Scandal of the Evangelical Mind* (Grand Rapids: MI: W.B. Eerdmans, 1994).

Chapter 25

1. "Thorpe qualifies for Athens," BBC SPORT; http://news.bbc.co.uk/sport2/hi/other_sports/3576529.stm
2. "Did They Have to Die?" *Christianity Today* 40, 1996, #10, 20.

3. Quoted in Raymond V. Edmon, *In Quietness and Confidence.* (Wheaton, IL: Scripture Press, 1953).

Chapter 26

1. Scott Bowles, "Hesitation Is a Fatal Mistake As California Firestorm Closes In," *USA Today,* Oct. 30, 2003.
2. Chuck Shepherd, "News of the Weird," *The Reader's Guide,* Jan. 16, 2004.
3. See www.spurgeon.org/sermons/0248.htm
4. Hannah Ward and Jennifer Wild, eds., *The Doubleday Christian Quotation Collection* (New York: Doubleday, 1998).
5. Craig Brian Larson, ed., *750 Engaging Illustrations for Pastors, Teachers, and Writers* (Grand Rapids, MI: Baker Books, 2002), 159.
7. Horatius Bonar, *God's Way of Holiness* (Presbyterian & Reformed Publishing Co., 1979).

Chapter 27

1. "The Quickest Way to Gardyloo Gully," news.telegraph.co.uk, Jan. 22, 2004.
2. Dwight Eisenhower, *At Ease: Stories I Tell to Friends* (New York: Doubleday, 1967).
3. Rudyard Kipling, *Rudyard Kipling Complete Verse* (New York: Anchor, 1989), 578.
4. Isobel Kuhn, *In the Arena* (Singapore:OMF International, 1995), 189–193.
5. Robert Greenleaf, *The Servant as Leader* (Indianapolis: Robert K. Greenleaf Center, 1982). See also http://www.greenleaf.org
6. Suzy Platt, ed., *Respectfully Quoted* (New York: Barnes and Noble Books, 1993), 193–194.
7. Peter F. Drucker, *The Effective Executive* (New York: Harper & Row Publishers, 1967), 1.
8. Pat Riley, *The Winner Within* (New York: Berkley Books, 1994), 36–37.
9. Quoted in J. Oswald Sanders, *Spiritual Leadership* (Chicago: Moody Press, 1967), 22.

Chapter 28

1. All of these examples came from a Web site devoted to "The Darwin Awards" for foolish behavior, found at http://www.ljayp.net/humor/dumb.htm
2. Dr. Robert Webber, "A Father's Influence," Gloria Gaither, ed., *What My Parents Did Right* (Nashville: Starsong Publishing Group, 1991), 207–208.
3. Zig Ziglar, *Top Performance* (Grand Rapids, MI: Revell, 2003).
4. Hymn by Benjamin Ramsey, 1919.

Notes

Chapter 29

1. Rosemary Smith, "Life is Proverbs to Eat Along the Way" http://www.news-journalonline.com/NewsJournalOnline/Opinion/Columnists/Close/03ColumnsCLOSE012204.htm
2. Paul Lee Tan, ed., *Encyclopedia of 7,700 Illustrations: Signs of the Times,* Electronic Edition, 1996).
3. As retold in "Tahtinen: We Will Prevail," www.admin.mut.edu/urel/breaking/2002/all.mem.html.
4. Hymn by Philip Doddridge, 1755.

Chapter 30

1. Dr. Benjamin Mays, "Life is Just a Minute."
2. Edward Caswall, trans., "When Morning Gilds the Skies," 1744.
3. See www.baseballamerica.com/today/features/040407leclair.html

Chapter 31

1. See http://justice.anglican.org/resources/bio/217.html.
2. Ruth Bell Graham, *Legacy of a Pack Rat* (Nashville: Thomas Nelson, 1989), 187.
3. See www.spurgeon.org/sermons/0015/htm.
4. C.S. Lewis, *The Great Divorce* (New York: Macmillan, 1946).

Conclusion

1. "Trust and Obey," by John H. Sammis, 1887.